The Myth of
Global Chaos

The Myth of Global Chaos

Yahya Sadowski

BROOKINGS INSTITUTION PRESS
Washington, D.C.

Copyright © 1998 by

THE BROOKINGS INSTITUTION
1775 Massachusetts Avenue, N.W.
Washington, D.C. 20036
www.brook.edu

Library of Congress Cataloging-in-Publication data

Sadowski, Yahya M.
    The myth of global chaos / by Yahya Sadowski.
    p.   cm.
    Includes bibliographical references and index.
    ISBN 0-8157-7664-0 (cloth)
    1. Ethnic relations.   2. Culture conflict.   3. International
relations and culture.   I. Title.
    GN496 .S33 1998
    305.8—ddc21   98-8943
                                                                  CIP

9 8 7 6 5 4 3 2 1

The paper used in this publication meets the minimum
requirements of the American National Standard for
Information Sciences—Permanence of Paper for Printed
Library Materials, ANSI Z39.48-1984

Typeset in Sabon

Composition by R. Lynn Rivenbark
Macon, Georgia

Printed by R. R. Donnelley and Sons
Harrisonburg, Virginia

₿ THE BROOKINGS INSTITUTION

The Brookings Institution is an independent organization devoted to nonpartisan research, education, and publication in economics, government, foreign policy, and the social sciences generally. Its principal purposes are to aid in the development of sound public policies and to promote public understanding of issues of national importance.

The Institution was founded on December 8, 1927, to merge the activities of the Institute for Government Research, founded in 1916, the Institute of Economics, founded in 1922, and the Robert Brookings Graduate School of Economics and Government, founded in 1924.

The Board of Trustees is responsible for the general administration of the Institution, while the immediate direction of the policies, program, and staff is vested in the President, assisted by an advisory committee of the officers and staff. The by-laws of the Institution state: "It is the function of the Trustees to make possible the conduct of scientific research, and publication, under the most favorable conditions, and to safeguard the independence of the research staff in pursuit of their studies and in the publication of the result of such studies. It is not a part of their function to determine, control, or influence the conduct of particular investigations or the conclusions reached."

The President bears final responsibility for the decision to publish a manuscript as a Brookings book. In reaching his judgment on the competence, accuracy, and objectivity of each study, the President is advised by the director of the appropriate research program and weighs the views of a panel of expert outside readers who report to him in confidence on the quality of the work. Publication of a work signifies that it is deemed a competent treatment worthy of public consideration but does not imply endorsement of conclusions or recommendations.

The Institution maintains its position of neutrality on issues of public policy in order to safeguard the intellectual freedom of the staff. Hence interpretations or conclusions in Brookings publications should be understood to be solely those of the authors and should not be attributed to the Institution, to its trustees, officers, or other staff members, or to the organizations that support its research.

Foreword

Since the end of the cold war policymakers have riveted attention on a set of trends that in the aggregate they describe as "globalization." One of these trends is the growing percolation of ideas and values across cultures, including McDonald's peddling of hamburgers in Beijing, American youths kickboxing like Jackie Chan, and nongovernmental organizations spreading the gospel of "universal" human rights into African villages. Another trend is the international movement of unprecedented flows of capital and the emergence of truly transnational manufacturing networks. The collapse of the newly industrialized economies in much of southeast Asia raises questions about how durable this trend might be—while reinforcing awareness of its potency. Still a third set of trends includes such global challenges as the diffusion of conventional and unconventional military power, terrorism, and drugs.

The political dimension of globalization has provoked the most intense policy debate. Some analysts insist that globalization presents an unprecedented opportunity for international cooperation and lays the foundation for a peaceful and prosperous new world order. Another influential group claims that globalization is fraught with potential peril. Culturally, globalization antagonizes traditional values. Economically, it dislocates people, driving them into cities where they are forced to live with strangers and aliens. Politically, it limits the power of governments, and, arguably, transforms the nature of sovereignty. It may also weaken the cohesion of nations, loosening the restraints once imposed on tribal or sectional hatreds.

Some thought that globalization was triggering a wave of internal conflicts, civil wars, and ethnic conflicts. Others thought it was fueling clashes between civilizations, mammoth struggles involving terrorism and weapons of mass destruction, with the future of the world hanging in the balance. Either way, the pessimists agreed that globalization was breeding a new wave of conflicts that would be more savage, more irrational, and more intractable than the cold war or its antecedents. The civil wars in Bosnia, Somalia, and Rwanda were harbingers of things to come.

The Myth of Global Chaos examines the claims of these pessimists in detail. It argues that those who anticipate a rapid descent into global chaos have mistaken scattered events for systematic trends. It presents evidence that the pessimists are wrong on three important points.

First, Yahya Sadowski maintains that, despite the attention that ethnic conflict, tribal secessions, fundamentalist terrorism, civilization clashes, and other culture wars have recently claimed, the world has not entered an epoch exploding with new conflicts. Most of the culture wars of the 1990s are not new: they are continuations of older conflicts, of battles that were already simmering during the cold war. The dissolution of the Soviet Union did momentarily increase the number of culture conflicts in the world, but by the mid-1990s most of these battles had sputtered out. In the 1990s internal conflict, within states, was no more common than it had been in the decades since World War II, and international conflict, between states, became rare indeed.

Second, although the culture wars of the 1990s are undeniably ugly affairs, they are not more savage or irrational than the other wars of the twentieth century. The genocides in Bosnia and even Rwanda are dwarfed by those unleashed by totalitarian ideologues in Germany, the Soviet Union, China, and Cambodia. Recent "ethnic conflicts" in Somalia, Kurdistan, and Chechnya are virtually identical to the "low-intensity conflicts" that attended the cold war in terms of their military organization, battlefield discipline, and percentage of civilian casualties. All the culture wars of the 1990s were triggered primarily by cold-blooded contests for the control of land, water, or power. None of them were just continuations of "ancient tribal hatreds."

Finally, globalization does not appear to have helped trigger recent culture wars. Many of the current culture wars first erupted during the wave of decolonization that followed World War II, and the vast majority were well under way long before the trend toward globalization accelerated during the 1980s. Moreover, culture wars are no more likely in countries that receive a great deal of foreign direct investment or foreign television broadcasts than they are in countries that are isolated from these trends.

Indeed, says the author, the research presented here highlights a striking fact: although culture wars can emerge anywhere, they are markedly less lethal in prosperous societies than in poor ones. It is easier for rival cultures to share power when they are not competing over basic resources. Economic growth has dampened ethnic violence in places like Quebec and Ireland—just as economic decline has aggravated it in countries like Indonesia and Yugoslavia. Thus, one of the most effective ways the United States and other powers can act to prevent new culture conflicts and to curb old ones is by promoting economic development. At least over the medium term, steady foreign investment may do more to curb ethnic conflict than armed foreign intervention.

The author wishes to thank Lila Abu-Lughod, the Academy of Arts and Sciences, Hamid Algar, Kanti Bajpai, Allison Berland, Annette Bourne, Bridget Butkevich, James Caporaso, Jeff Donnell, Maya Dragicevic, Magdi El-Shamma, Harvey Feigenbaum, Richard Haass, Owen Harries, Steven Heydemann, Erica Hoffmann, John Ikenberry, Andrew Janos, Robert Jervis, Sivim Kalyoncu, Devesh Kapur, Gail Kligman, Stacy Knobler, Susanne Lane, Terrence Lyons, Tom McNaugher, Fareed Mohammedi, Janne Nolan, Michael O'Hanlon, Soli Ozel, Agnieszka Paczynska, Elizabeth Pelletreau, Hanna Pitkin, Barry Posen, William Quandt, Stanley Reed, Wolfgang Reinicke, Sayres Rudy, Farid Senzai, Louise Skillings, Richard Sklar, the staff of the Montgomery County Public Library in Gaithersburg, Maryland, John Steinbruner, Mark Strauss, David Waldner, Lisa Wedeen, George Weigel, Joe White, and Susan Woodward.

In the Brookings Institution Press, Colleen McGuiness edited the manuscript, Joanne Lockard proofread it, and Susan Fels prepared the index.

The author is grateful to all of the above for helping to make this book substantially better and accepts responsibility for any remaining deficiencies. He wrote this book while a senior fellow in the Foreign Policy Studies program at Brookings. Currently, he is associate professor at the Paul H. Nitze School of Advanced International Studies of Johns Hopkins University.

The Brookings Institution gratefully acknowledges the financial support of the John D. and Catherine T. MacArthur Foundation.

The views expressed in this book are the author's alone and should not be ascribed to the people or organizations whose assistance is acknowledged above or to the trustees, officers, and other staff members of the Brookings Institution.

Michael H. Armacost
President

October 1998
Washington, D.C.

To Rick, Nadia, Suze, and Mary Scott

Contents

Figures

The Myth of
Global Chaos

CHAPTER ONE

Triumph and Despair

When the cold war ended in 1989, Americans were like a baby tasting its first mouthful of peanut butter: both delighted and confused. They felt triumphant about the rapid collapse of Soviet communism, but they could not quite swallow it. They could neither understand how it had happened so quickly nor figure out how to adjust to a world without the "red menace." For forty years, U.S. foreign policy had employed the Soviet threat as its centerpiece. When the Union of Soviet Socialist Republics (USSR) dissolved in 1991, Americans had to think about how they were going to deal with the world "from scratch."

Initially, the optimism of American society prevailed. The first vision of life after the cold war to capture the public imagination was the one articulated by Francis Fukuyama in his famous article "The End of History."[1] Fukuyama argued that the Soviet Union had been defeated not by the force of arms but by the universal allure of American values. Music videos, film noir, blue jeans, and other commodities had penetrated the iron curtain, carrying with them the romance of individualism, materialism, and liberty. The globalization of American values had convinced the Russians as well as the Poles and the Chinese and the Mozambicans of the superiority of the American way of life. Now the whole world was scrambling to emulate the democratic capitalism epitomized by the United States. And once done, capitalism would make the world more prosperous, and democracy would make it more peaceful.

But with the passage of time, the millennial hopes articulated by Fukuyama dimmed. The violent breakup of the USSR, the civil war in Somalia, the shocking genocide in Rwanda, all had a sobering effect. But the war in Bosnia in particular worked to reshape the national mood in America (and elsewhere) into one of pessimism. The Bosnian war was not only extremely violent, but it also appeared almost totally irrational.

The statistics regarding Bosnia were almost as chilling as any war photos: "Nearly 1 million Muslims have been trapped in besieged towns, subject to shelling, sniper fire, hunger, and disease." From a prewar population of 4.3 million, perhaps 2.7 million people were displaced or became refugees.[2] Most sources cite a death toll of 200,000.[3] The ways in which those 200,000 victims had been selected and butchered seemed to suggest that remarkable levels of hatred, bloodlust, and imagination were at work. The war's primary victims were noncombatants, especially women and children.

The combatants in Bosnia seemed particularly eager to target civilians. A Western journalist documented this in detail during the two-year-long siege of Sarajevo by Serb troops.

> Zjelko [a Serb sniper] claimed he never shot at civilians. . . . At a gun post farther back in the hills, I met a Serb, stoned on plum brandy, for whom this obviously wasn't the case. Reeling in the swivel seat of a mounted heavy-caliber machine gun, he fired round after round into downtown Sarajevo, declaring without affect: "It is just like killing rabbits. I feel nothing."

Even the sniper-with-scruples later declared:

> "I don't fight for nationalism—I sleep with girls of all nations," Zjelko said. "I don't fight for religion—God is no place." He trained his sniper scope on the downtown house that he'd fled three months before, fearing reprisals against Serbs. "I fight because I want to be back down there with my books and my CD player and Gitane cigarettes."[4]

If this kind of reportage slighted the genuinely patriotic motives of some Serbs, it accurately captured a type of drunken hooliganism that was all too common.

Not all of the horrors of this war could be attributed to "the fog of war" or the influence of slivovitsa [plum brandy]. Rape—a crime that accompanies most wars—was raised to a new level in Bosnia, where Serb separatists used it as an instrument of terror. An organized campaign was devised in which the victims were systematically transported to concentrated locations, held for weeks or months, and raped by men who had been "instructed" that this was a way of forcing Muslim women to bear Serb babies.[5] The exact numbers of Bosnian women assaulted are a matter of dispute, but in January 1993 the European Community produced a "mid-range" figure of twenty thousand.[6]

The war did not spare children either. According to UN International Children's Emergency Fund (UNICEF) estimates, by May 1993, when the siege of their city was barely a year old, 81 percent of the children of Sarajevo had been in situations where they could have been killed, 40 percent had been shot at by snipers, 48 percent had their homes occupied by someone else, 72 percent had their homes shelled or attacked, 51 percent had seen someone killed, 39 percent had a family member or members killed, 19 percent had witnessed massacres, and more than 50 percent had been turned into refugees.[7]

"Ethnic cleansing," the deliberate expulsion of one group to create living space for another, was practiced by all the major communities in Bosnia. The Serb separatists, however, cleansed areas with a systematic thoroughness unmatched by other groups, erecting a network of concentration camps at Omarska, Trnopolje, and a dozen other locations to hold the Muslim and Croat males who had been evicted from their homes. At one time these camps may have held as many as 130,000 people, many of whom were subjected to routine torture and murder.[8]

Concentration camps were not without precedent in modern European history—but that only made their revival more shocking. For two generations, Yugoslavian children had been taught about the atrocities of World War II and the horrors of fascism. The combatants in Bosnia knew all about the Holocaust, the Nuremburg trials, and the 1948 UN convention on genocide.[9] Yet none of this seemed to restrain them.

Many people—including many Bosnians—were shocked that war had broken out in Bosnia at all. This was not one of the poorest or most backward regions in Europe, or even in Yugoslavia. Bosnians had a reputation for being relatively cosmopolitan, urbane, secularized, even privileged by "socialist" standards. This was not Somalia, Cambodia, or Albania. "As Communism declined in the late 1980s, Yugoslavia was, in many ways, better placed than any other Communist state to make the transition to multi-party democracy, either as a single state, or as a group of successor states. There was a real chance for Yugoslavia to take its place in a new and, at that time, hopeful community of European nations."[10]

Many serious thinkers worried that what had happened to Bosnia seemed likely to spread elsewhere—and not just to neighboring Balkan states. The vicious hypernationalism that afflicted Bosnia was only one of several irrational ideologies that seemed to be sweeping the globe. Religious fundamentalism, ethnic bigotry, and plain old nihilism also seemed to be becoming more popular. The world seemed to be slipping over a precipice into an epoch of ethnic and cultural violence. It seemed less like the end of history than like the revenge of history. A real danger seemed to exist that the atrocities in Bosnia were a harbinger of worse things to come globally.

Meditating on this prospect, a group of American thinkers began to develop similar ideas. Gradually they converged toward the same three frightening conclusions:

1. The current trend for the political, economic, and cultural institutions of the West to be spread around the world—what is called "globalization"—is forcing more and more people to confront alien values, whether in the form of glitzy television commercials or through resettlement in industrial shantytowns where tribes of different religions are forced to live cheek-to-jowl.

2. When the basic values of a culture are threatened, violence becomes more common and more savage. For some, the decay of rationality means an easing of the restrictions against theft, murder, and rape. Others seek to resist the threat to traditional values through a fanatic, angry reassertion of fundamentalist tradition. Either way, apparently irrational violence increases.

3. As a result of globalization and the way it threatens traditional values, the world is witnessing an explosion of irrational violence, manifest in the drug wars of Latin America, the tribal massacres of Africa, fundamentalist revolts in the Middle East, and ethnic cleansing in the Balkans. Crime, warfare, and genocide all seem to be not only proliferating but also spinning out of control. Thus, the same process of globalization that Fukuyama thought had destroyed communism might be planting the seeds for an epoch of global chaos.

Thinkers who shared these three convictions never adopted a single common moniker, preferring instead to market their own individual epigrams: "the coming anarchy," "the clash of civilizations," "jihad vs. McWorld," and so on. In some newspapers, their ideas were collectively called "chaos theory," but this was unfortunate, because the same name had already been applied to a movement of physical scientists who applied new techniques of nonlinear mathematics.[11] Yet, because the central thesis of the new foreign policy pessimists was that globalization spawns political chaos, "global chaos theory" may be an accurate label for their ideas.[12]

The architects of global chaos theory include some of the sharpest political strategists working in America today. They have erected a complex school of thought that deals with urbanization, narcoterrorism, immigration, humanitarian disasters, debates over military intervention, rogue states, collapsed states, the profusion of transnational organizations, terrorist networks, fundamentalism, ethnic conflict, and so on. Their edifice is still growing and evolving and continues to exert influence on American policymakers.

But on close inspection, most of the major claims of global chaos theory turn out to be false. The great majority of the conflicts in the world today are not "clashes of civilizations" but fratricides that pit old neighbors, often from similar or identical cultures, against each other. Most ethnic conflicts are not the irrational result of "ageless tribal rivalries" but recent and rational quarrels over the distribution of resources. Societies in the throes of globalization are not any more likely to suffer anomic social violence, culture clashes, or ethnic conflict than countries that are not. The culture conflicts that worry global chaos theorists are not any more violent—or any more frequent—than the "brushfire wars" that plagued the third world during the long cold war.

In the final analysis, the end of the cold war may have changed the world less than either optimists or pessimists imagined.

CHAPTER TWO

Popularizing Chaos

In America, the idea that the world was sinking into an epoch of global chaos was popularized by two men, Robert D. Kaplan and Samuel P. Huntington.

Kaplan was a journalist who had spent many years covering trouble spots such as Afghanistan, Ethiopia, and the Middle East. Simultaneous with the April 1992 outbreak of the war in Bosnia, Kaplan's *Balkan Ghosts* was published, an account of his travels in Romania and the former Yugoslavia that was pregnant with his speculations about the region's post–Communist future. *Balkan Ghosts* was the only readable, up-to-date account of political life among the Serbs and Croats available when many Americans (including those who slept in the White House) were scrambling to understand the Bosnian tragedy.[1]

The analysis in *Balkan Ghosts* is rooted in Kaplan's conviction that values are the primary motors of human behavior. In the West, the values of "secular humanism" give society its own peculiar logic, but, in other parts of the world, most values still derive primarily from religion. This is particularly evident in the Balkans. Croats and Serbs do not differ from each other perceptibly in physical appearance, language, and so on.[2] The taproot of their violent assertion of distinct identities lies in religion.

Religion in this case is no mean thing. Because Catholicism arose in the West and Orthodoxy in the East, the difference between them is greater than that between, say, Catholicism and Protestantism, or even Catholicism and Judaism (which, on account of the Diaspora, also developed in the West). While Western religions emphasize

6

ideas and deeds, Eastern religions emphasize beauty and magic. The Eastern church service is almost a physical re-creation of heaven on earth. Even Catholicism, the most baroque of western religions, is, by the standards of Eastern Orthodoxy, austere and intellectual. Catholic monks (Franciscans, Jesuits, and so on) live industriously, participating in such worldly endeavors as teaching, writing, and community work. In contrast, Orthodox monks tend to be contemplatives, for whom work is almost a distraction, since it keeps them from the worship of heavenly beauty.[3]

Kaplan claims religious values impart to Serbs and Croats distinct outlooks, ethos, and patterns of behavior, despite their many other shared traits.

Differences in values make neighboring cultures not only distinct but also alien and sometimes outright disturbing to one another. Cultures do not mix well. At the very least, people from different cultures are prone to misunderstand one another. More often, their differences provoke fear and suspicion. Kaplan elaborates on this point while contemplating the architecture of a mosque in Macedonia: "My eyes became lost in the arabesque wall designs. The patterns went on and on, indecipherably, in a linear fashion. Like the contours of the desert, Islam is a world of abstraction, mathematical in severity, fearsome and alienating to the most mystical of Eastern Christians."[4] The mystical mindset of orthodox Christians and the mathematical perspective of Muslims, and other cultural differences, inevitably clash. Because each system of religious values claims to be revealed truth about the ultimate nature of the universe, the very existence of an alternative culture is a threat to the putative universality of each.

The more that different cultures have to deal with each other, the more their suspicions likely will provoke hostility and culminate in violence. Proximity breeds contempt.

Just as Croats felt their western Catholicism more intensely than did the Austrians or the Italians precisely because of their uneasy proximity to the Eastern Orthodox and Muslim worlds, so the Croats of Bosnia—because they shared the same mountains with both Orthodox Serbs and Muslims—felt their Croatianism much more intensely than did the Croats in Croatia proper, who enjoyed the psychological luxury of having only their ethnic compatriots as immediate neighbors.[5]

The tragedy of the Balkans is that they lie astride the fault lines where so many different cultures face off against each other. "Here . . . the battle between Communism and capitalism is merely one dimension of a struggle that pits Catholicism against Orthodoxy, Rome against Constantinople, the legacy of Habsburg Austria-Hungary against that of Ottoman Turkey—in other words, West against East, the ultimate historical and cultural conflict."[6] Pressing these contradictory cultures into the same peninsula is like leaving a bunch of oily rags in a hot garage; they are bound to burst into flame sooner or later.

Tragically, the drift and flow of recent history has had the effect of compressing these antagonistic peoples. For example, although differences of values have made Serbs and Croats potential enemies for centuries, in practice they were kept separate—and thus at peace—until relatively recently. Most Croats were ruled by the Austro-Hungarian Empire, while much of Serbia had been occupied by the Ottomans. The collapse of the Habsburg and Ottoman empires at the end of World War I led to a misconceived "predominantly oriental federation" called Yugoslavia that, for the first time, joined the Serbs and Croats together in a single state.[7] A similar process was repeated with the collapse of Communism in 1989. The limits that authoritarian rule had imposed on ethnic conflict within Yugoslavia were removed. Although Kaplan has few kind words for the Habsburgs, Ottomans, or Communists, he portrays them as having at least played a role in dampening public strife. Thus, he approvingly quotes his mentor, Rebecca West, who wrote, "I hate the corpses of empires, they stink as nothing else."[8]

Anything that draws alien peoples together invites conflict. As a result, Kaplan portrays migration as one of the leading causes of contemporary strife. In the Serbian province of Kosovo, for example, migration over the past century has steadily enlarged the Albanian component of the population. As the Albanian component of the population grew, the Serb component dwindled—dropping from 35 percent of the total in the 1950s to barely 10 percent by 1989.[9] Yet Kosovo had been the center of the medieval Serb kingdom and contained most of the key landmarks of Serb history. Clashes between the growing Albanian majority and the politically dominant Serbs grew increasingly violent through the 1980s. In one of many comparisons he makes between Yugoslavia and the Middle East, Kaplan calls Kosovo "the 'Judea and Samaria' of the Serbian national consciousness, the place where it all happened."[10]

Kaplan contends that this type of conflict, between alien cultures, has an unusual hallmark: It tends toward irrationality. The religious, other-worldly nature of the values in conflict makes the antagonists impervious to the usual rational restraints that limit the scope of violence.

The irrational urges that characterize these conflicts are evident in several traits. First, violence between alien cultures quickly and easily degenerates to an unusual level of savagery and brutality. Rape and massacre are more characteristic than encirclement and battle. Kaplan's *Balkan Ghosts* interviews are littered with visions of corpses, like his chat with an Albanian in a discotheque who says, "You don't know what it is like to kill with a hammer, with nails, clubs, do you?"

> Do you know why I don't like to drink plum brandy, why I drink beer always? Because the Chetniks [World War II Serbian partisans] used to do their killing after drinking plum brandy. Do you know what it is to throw a child in the air and catch it on a knife in front of its mother? To be tied to a burning log? To have your ass split with an axe so that you beg the Serbs, beg them, to shoot you in the head and they don't?[11]

(Kaplan's informant admitted that he himself had not seen these things done. Nor had anyone else that Kaplan talked to—at least that they would admit. But Kaplan's sundry chats clearly indicate that many people were thinking about, brooding upon, such atrocities. In that kind of atmosphere, it is hard to imagine someone not acting upon such fantasies sooner or later.)

Irrationality also appears in the fact that the urges that drive these conflicts cannot be easily assuaged. Rational processes of conflict resolution, bargaining, and compromise do not apply. The antagonists tend to be impervious to pain and punishment, so they cannot be deterred. Kaplan notes that Serb mosaics often feature the image of John the Baptist, who, because he "was too preoccupied with ideas to notice his physical suffering, he suffered not. This particularly oriental strength provides a starting point toward understanding why the Serbs have behaved as they have in this century."[12] Equally, the antagonists are typically impervious to bribes or incentives. Kaplan notes that both Yugoslav president Tito and the Israelis attempted to win over their ethnic enemies through economic inducements but failed.

Both assumed that, if you built things for people, they would stop hating you. On the West Bank, the Israelis built water, electrical, and health-care systems. This improved the quality of life and ignited a mass uprising, fueled by demographic pressure and higher expectations.[13]

The irrational insistence of the participants upon continuing their struggle, no matter what the cost, means such wars are not easily contained, much less terminated.

According to Kaplan, the most bizarre, yet most important, symptom of irrationality in these conflicts lies in the way the antagonists appear to be imprisoned by their own pasts, obsessed with ancient feuds and anachronistic grievances. Kaplan argues that in Southeastern Europe old insults are never forgiven and old wounds never forgotten. The Serbs feel they were deprived of their rightful place in history by the Ottoman invasion that destroyed their medieval state. This decisively colors their perception of the present. They do not see themselves as fighting the highly secularized Bosnians of twentieth-century Sarajevo; instead, they are still battling "the Turks." More ironic, the Croats also tend to see their modern battles with the Serbs as an extension of their medieval crusade against the Turks. "To the Catholic powers of Europe, and also to many Croats, it mattered not that Serbs and Croats were fellow Slavs. The Serbs were Eastern Orthodox and, therefore, as much a part of the hated East as the Muslim Turks."[14] Thus, even when a conflict appears to outsiders to be of recent provenance—such as the Serb versus Croat conflict, which has no real antecedents earlier than the formation of the modern state of Yugoslavia after World War I—to its participants it has the air of an "ancient tribal rivalry." Kaplan thus feels justified claiming that "Balkan violence is not a phenomenon of 'modern hate,' like that in Algeria and the West Bank, fed by rising economic expectations and demographic stress. Southeastern Europe is a caldron of history."[15]

The failure to heal old wounds is also part of why contemporary conflicts are so savage. Dame Rebecca writes: "The Turks ruined the Balkans, with a ruin so great that it has not yet been repaired. . . . There is a lot of emotion loose about the Balkans which has lost its legitimate employment now that the Turks have been expelled."

If like the Russian Nobel laureate Joseph Brodsky you view the Communist Empire as the twentieth-century equivalent of the Ottoman Turkish Empire, with the historical compass line of decrepit, Eastern despotism traveling north from Istanbul (formerly Constantinople) to Moscow—from the Sultan's Topkapi Palace to the Kremlin—then Dame Rebecca had already capsulized the situation in Serbia, in the rest of former Yugoslavia, and in the other Balkan states for the 1990s. Now that Communism has fallen and the Soviets have been expelled, *there is a lot of emotion loose about the Balkans which has lost its legitimate employment.*[16]

Modern Balkan battles often degenerate into savagery because they are fought not only to address contemporary problems but also to redress historical wrongs. And any psychologist or modern playwright can explain why this sort of situation is bound to ensure wounds will continue to fester. If the Serbs and Croats bash each other seeking vengeance for wrongs done by "the Turk," a ghost from the distant past, neither side will ever find satisfaction.

One of the stranger consequences of this, Kaplan insists, is that in the Balkans the distant past is often the best guide to current events. Kaplan claims this explains why Milovan Djilas, one of Tito's old cronies, became the most popular source for Western journalists in Yugoslavia.

After the first visits, our conversations became eerie affairs, because I realized that Djilas was always right. He was able to predict the future. His technique was a simple one for an East European, but a difficult one for an American: he seemed to ignore the daily newspapers and think purely historically. The present for him was merely a stage of the past moving quickly into the future. What appeared inconceivable to conventional analysts was always the natural outcome to him.[17]

To outsiders, the Serbs seem to be fighting the Bosnians, but in their own minds the Serbs are reenacting (and reversing) the historical drama of their 1389 conquest by the Turks. Their actions may appear perplexing as responses to current events, but they are explicable as roles in the medieval folk epics that obsess the Serbs. In the Balkans, people do not learn from history, they recycle it. In Kaplan's account, the memories of

Figure 2-1. *Has Bosnia Always Been Part of the Orient?*

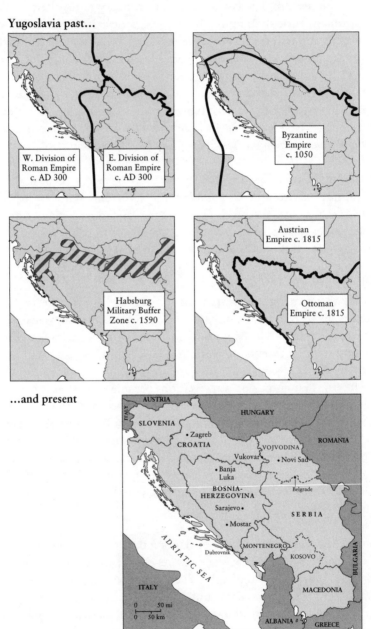

Source: "Bosnia: The Road to Ruin," *Economist*, May 24, 1993, p. 23.

ancient grievances, the "loose emotion," manifest themselves as the ghosts who haunt the Balkans.[18]

Kaplan's ideas about the Balkans meshed well with the suspicions of many Americans. As a result, his ideas gained currency in even the most influential circles. In one famous incident, President Bill Clinton invoked Kaplan to justify his veto of a plan to intervene militarily in Bosnia. Summoning Secretary of Defense Les Aspin and Joint Chiefs of Staff chairman Colin Powell to his office, Clinton announced

> he had been reading the book *Balkan Ghosts,* by Robert Kaplan, a haunting description of the Balkan people's historic propensity for war with each other. (Powell had read part of the book, and Mrs. Clinton had read it.) The book pointed out that these people had been killing each other in tribal and religious wars for centuries; the Serbs' National Day was a commemoration of the battle of Kosovo, in 1389 (which they lost to the Turks).[19]

Even though Kaplan himself disagreed with the president's decision, it both testified to and amplified his celebrity.

Kaplan's original ideas focused on the Balkans, but he came to believe they had global currency. Eventually he wrote an influential article, "The Coming Anarchy," that applied his insights to the entire international scene. This article summarized and augmented the work of scholars who had independently reached conclusions similar to Kaplan's.

The idea that East and West represent different systems of values that inevitably collide goes back to Herodotus.[20] In the earliest hours of the war in Bosnia, Europeans tended to view the conflict in these terms, as a legacy of the ancient battles of Islam and Christendom for control of the Balkans. Maps began to appear showing that Bosnia had always been on the frontlines of these battles—and usually part of the alien Orient (see figure 2-1).

Similar terms were invoked in discussions of whether to expand the North Atlantic Treaty Organization (NATO) or whether to aid economic reconstruction in Russia. Were the countries of Eastern Europe part of the Occident or a beachhead of the Orient? If they were Occidental, if they shared common values with the West, then aid and incorporation might be appropriate. If they were Oriental, then no amount of aid or good intentions could paper over their underlying conflict with the West. John Lukacs, an American historian of Hungarian origin, emerged as a leading

Figure 2-2. *Huntington's 'Velvet Curtain'*

Source: Samuel P. Huntington, "Clash of Civilizations?" *Foreign Affairs*, vol. 72, no. 3 (Summer 1993), p. 30.

proponent of the idea that Russia was part of the West and deserved support.[21] Zbigniew Brzezinski, an American political scientist of Polish origin, argued instead that, while Central Europe (Poland, Czechoslovakia, and Hungary) were part of the West, Russia was still Oriental.[22]

These arguments led to the development of new maps. Krzysztof Pomian, an analyst at the French National Scientific Research Center, published one showing Europe divided into East and West from the Barents Sea to the Mediterranean. This map, in turn, was described in an influential article by William Pfaff, one of the earliest and most subtle global chaos theorists.[23] However, the man who perfected this variant view of chaos was Samuel Huntington, whose thesis was epitomized in the title of his influential article, "The Clash of Civilizations?"[24]

Huntington, a political scientist at Harvard University, heartily concurred that the rash of conflicts in Eastern Europe were rooted in a clash of values between contending civilizations. His article reprinted a version of the Pomian map (see figure 2-2) with the following commentary:

The peoples to the east and south of this line are Orthodox or Muslim; they historically belonged to the Ottoman or Tsarist empires and were only lightly touched by the shaping events in the rest of Europe; they are generally less advanced economically; they seem much less likely to develop stable democratic political systems. The Velvet Curtain of culture has replaced the Iron Curtain of ideology as the most significant dividing line in Europe.[25]

However, he did not think that the East and the West were the only civilizations involved—or that Europe was the only continent being riven by such conflicts.

Huntington invoked another map, one that showed the world not divided between Occident and Orient but into nine discrete civilizations (see figure 2-3). The conflict in Bosnia involved three civilizations: the (Protestant and Catholic) West, the (Greek, Serbian, and Russian) Orthodox, and Islam. In other parts of the world, too, Huntington argued that new violence erupted primarily where alien civilizations abutted: where Islam and Orthodoxy clashed around the periphery of the former Soviet Union, where Islam and Hinduism shared turf in India, where Islam and "African civilization" eyed each other just south of the Sahara.

Figure 2-3. *Huntington's 'Clashing Civilizations?'*

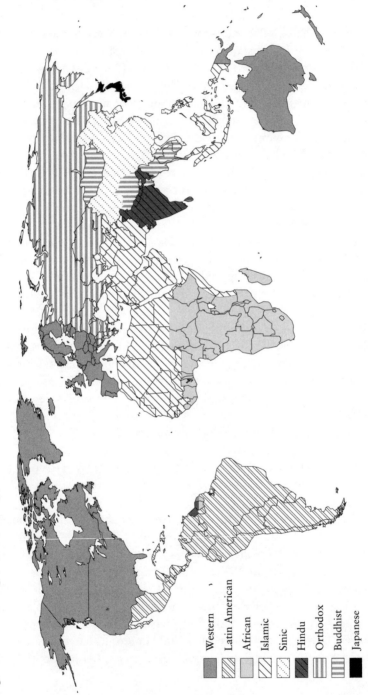

Western

Latin American

African

Islamic

Sinic

Hindu

Orthodox

Buddhist

Japanese

Source: Samuel P. Huntington, *The Clash of Civilizations and the Remaking of World Order* (New York: Touchstone, 1996), pp. 26–27.

From these maps, Huntington drew the conclusion that, in the post–cold war world, "the fundamental source of conflict" would

not be primarily ideological or primarily economic. The great divisions among humankind and the dominating source of conflict will be cultural. Nation states will remain the most powerful actors in world affairs, but the principal conflicts of global politics will occur between nations and groups of different civilizations. The clash of civilizations will dominate world politics. The fault lines between civilizations will be the battle lines of the future.[26]

Much as Kaplan had argued in *Balkan Ghosts,* Huntington thought that the globe would be increasingly afflicted by conflict and violence, rather than embraced by some benign "new world order." Both thought that the primary actors in this world would be cultural units, men and women bound together by a common loyalty to primordial values—particularly religious values. Both thought that conflicts would be most frequent and explosive where distinct cultures adjoined. Both claimed that at its heart the vicious war in Bosnia was a "clash of civilizations."

Kaplan later began to neglect this line of analysis to develop new ideas about ecological chaos, but Huntington continued to develop ever more systematic and nuanced ideas about civilizational conflicts. In the process, he gave a new twist to some of the common themes of global chaos theory. Instead of discussing globalization, for example, he insisted upon calling this process Westernization. He argued that the most obvious reason cultural conflicts were becoming more common was because they reflected a reaction against the tide of Westernization that inundated the world over the preceding two centuries. The West, through its overwhelming military power, if nothing else, had made itself the paramount culture and had tried to impose its institutions on the rest of the world. This breeds an understandable reaction, some kind of patriotism or nativism, that reasserts local values.

Western ideas of individualism, liberalism, constitutionalism, human rights, equality, liberty, the rule of law, democracy, free markets, the separation of church and state, often have little resonance in Islamic, Confucian, Japanese, Hindu, Buddhist or Orthodox cultures. Western efforts to propagate such ideas produce instead a reaction against "human rights imperialism" and a reaffirmation of indigenous values, as can be seen in the support for religious fundamentalism by the younger generation in non-Western cultures.[27]

Huntington even suggested that this sort of reaction had some justification: "The West in effect is using international institutions, military power and economic resources to run the world in ways that will maintain Western predominance, protect Western interests and promote Western political and economic values."[28]

Trends that Westerners blandly dubbed "globalization" were often, Huntington claimed, viewed as highly threatening and partisan actions. For example, many in the West lauded the global communications revolution, the growing network of satellite dishes, computer networks, and cellular phones that stitched an increasing number of societies together. They presumed that this would breed greater unity among cultures and economies. But Huntington stressed that a countertrend existed. As the world became "a smaller place,"

> The interactions between people of different civilizations are increasing; these increasing interactions intensify civilization consciousness and awareness of differences between civilizations and commonalities within civilizations. North African immigration to France generates hostility among Frenchmen and at the same time increased receptivity to immigration by "good" European Catholic Poles.[29]

Even when culture contact was not part of an obvious drive for Western superiority, even when it was prompted by benign efforts such as curiosity or trade, it could backfire. The worldwide explosion of audiences for the swimsuit–soap opera *Baywatch* could breed contempt, not affection, for Western culture.[30]

Huntington's ideas attracted an enormous amount of attention, provoking even more debate than Kaplan's. He circulated a draft of his thesis among his friends, so that in January 1993 U.S. senator Bill Bradley was able to outline Huntington's ideas at the annual meeting of world economic leaders at Davos.[31] In April they were summarized for an Australian audience by Owen Harries, the editor of a major American foreign policy journal (the *National Interest*), in an article that "elicited the most violent response of anything that I have ever published."[32] Huntington's own synopsis of his thesis first appeared in June as "The

Coming Clash of Civilizations: Or, the West against the Rest" on the editorial page of the *New York Times*.[33] The full text premiered in the prestigious journal *Foreign Affairs* a month later.[34] The article triggered a national debate and generated more sales for *Foreign Affairs* than any other issue since 1947, when it had run "The Sources of Soviet Conduct" by "X," the essay by George Kennan that defined the strategy the United States was to pursue during the cold war.[35]

CHAPTER THREE

Anomie and
Social Violence

Kaplan and Huntington are powerful writers, skilled at coining epigrams or weaving iconic images. But the popularity of their ideas in the early 1990s was not entirely a reflection of their prose skills. Both men had, in part, managed to articulate ideas or hunches that were already in circulation, that were part of the zeitgeist, the spirit of their times.

In 1992, as Kaplan was finishing *Balkan Ghosts,* he was not the only American who thought the world was going mad. For concerned Americans—that is, those who relied not only on television for their news but also surveyed one of the weekly digests such as *Time* or *Newsweek*— the year 1992 appeared as an almost uninterrupted sequence of wars, riots, massacres, firefights, combats, conflicts, and clashes. The data in table 3-1 detail the international news highlights that would have emerged from reading *Time* or *Newsweek* over the course of the year. And the acceleration of violence showed no signs of abating when the new year dawned. In 1993 the violence moved closer to home. In February a violent Islamist group, al-Jamᶜa al-Islamiyya, exploded a huge car bomb underneath the World Trade Center in New York City. The siege of the Branch Davidian cult in Waco, Texas, ended in April in a tragic firestorm that left seventy-five people (including twenty-five children) dead.[1] The thick March 15, 1993, issue of *Time* magazine was packed with gory pictures illustrating—and sometimes conflating—the threats of "Islamic fundamentalism," "right-wing militias," and "resurgent Balkan nationalism."

Not only did war appear to be becoming more common, but it also appeared to be more savage, more violent. The German writer Hans

Table 3-1. *International News Headlines from* Time *and* Newsweek, *1992*

Month	Headline
January	The first president of independent Georgia was ousted by armed militias
February	Russia endured the first domestic violence since the fall of communism, when communist-ultranationalist demonstrators clashed with police
March	In a plebiscite, a majority of Bosnians voted to follow Slovenia and Croatia out of Yugoslavia
April	The Rodney King riots blazed across Los Angeles; and the Mujahidin occupied Kabul, ending communism in Afghanistan but not ending the fighting
May	Government troops gunned down prodemocracy demonstrators in Thailand
June	The Danes voted down the Maastricht treaty, deflating the euphoria of European unification; and the Czech Republic and Slovakia agreed to separate
July	America was too preoccupied with the sex-drugs-love-and-attempted-murder trial of Amy Fischer to pay any attention to foreign affairs
August	The first photographs were published of starving prisoners behind the barbed wire of Bosnia's new concentration camps
September	Twenty-eight supporters of the African National Congress were massacred in Ciskei; and 150 incidents of violence occurred against immigrants in Germany
October	Forensic scientists exhumed sixty skeletons from the site of the 1981 El Mozote massacre in El Salvador
November	Pictures of starving children in Somalia provoked U.S. president George Bush to dispatch troops the following month
December	Hindu extremists with sledgehammers attacked and destroyed the historic Babri Masjid (mosque) at Ayodhya, triggering a wave of bloody communal rioting across India

Magnus Enzensberger devoted an entire (influential) book to the argument that "in today's civil wars, there is no longer any need to legitimize your actions. Violence has freed itself from ideology."[2] In *Civil Wars: From L.A. to Bosnia,* Enzensberger claimed that

> even the guerrillas and terrorists of the sixties and seventies thought it expedient to justify their actions. . . . Today's lot seem to find all that unnecessary. Their complete absence of conviction is striking.

The combatants in Latin America's civil wars don't think twice about slaughtering the farmers they claim to liberate. They are unembarrassed by, and feel no need to justify, their alliances with drug barons and the secret service. The Irish terrorist uses pensioners as living bombs and blows up cars full of children. The preferred victims of today's civil wars are women and children. The Chetniks aren't the only ones who boast of massacring all the patients in one hospital; it seems that everywhere the aim is to dispose of the defenceless. If you don't have a machine-gun you count as vermin.[3]

Lacking any real political purpose, warfare was becoming more nihilistic and less distinct from conventional crime and individual deviance.

Martin van Creveld, a brilliant Israeli military historian whose ideas were popular at the Pentagon, took this argument a step further.[4] *The Transformation of War,* van Creveld's literal tour de force, describes the historical processes by which modern, highly organized conventional warfare emerged from the sloppy, vicious conflicts that characterized Europe up through the Thirty Years' War (1618–48). However, in his concluding chapter, van Creveld argues that the era of conventional war is passing and the world is entering a new epoch of conflict. He notes that the spread of nuclear weapons has made conventional war much less viable and that, since the end of World War II, conventional armies have been consistently defeated by opponents who employed a strategy of "low-intensity conflict." Low-intensity conflicts do not rely on "the high-technology collective weapons that are the pride and joy of any modern armed force."[5] And because they do not deploy sophisticated technologies, they can be conducted by organizations that are both easier to erect and harder to defeat than the edifice of the modern state.

Van Creveld suspects that the world is already witnessing the first phases of a process of social evolution in which the modern state will lose its hard-won monopoly over the means of violence and will increasingly compete against alternative organizations that prove more adept at low-intensity warfare.

No more than Froissart could foresee the end of the feudal political system and its replacement by the modern one that is based on states, can we today foresee what kind of new order will arise after the latter's collapse. However, since none of perhaps two dozen armed conflicts now being fought all over the world involves a state on both sides we may offer an educated guess. In most of Africa the entities by which the wars in question are waged resemble tribes—indeed they are tribes, or whatever is left of them under the corrosive influence of modern civilization. In parts of Asia and Latin America the best analogy may be the robber barons who infested Europe during the early modern period, or else the vast feudal organizations that warred against each other in sixteenth-century Japan. In North America and Western Europe future warmaking entities will probably resemble the Assassins, the group which, motivated by religious [*sic*] and allegedly supporting itself on drugs, terrorized the medieval Middle East for two centuries.

In the future, war will not be waged by armies but by groups whom we today call terrorists, guerrillas, bandits, and robbers, but who will undoubtedly hit on more formal titles to describe themselves. Their organizations are likely to be constructed on charismatic lines rather than institutional ones, and to be motivated less by "professionalism" than by fanatical, ideologically-based, loyalties.[6]

One of the major effects of this shift in the organizational foundation of warfare will be to efface the traditional distinction between warfare and crime. Civilians would become increasingly legitimate targets. Terrorism will prove a more effective weapon. States, with their borders and taxes, would be replaced by "the occasional roadblock cropping up at unexpected places, manned by ruffians out to line their own pockets as well as those of their bosses."[7] Some readers found van Creveld's distopian description of the withering away of the modern state a bit far-fetched, as when he claimed that "America's current economic decline must be halted; or else one day the crime that is rampant in the streets of New York and Washington, D.C., may develop into low-intensity conflict by coalescing along racial, religious, social, and political lines, and run completely out of control."[8] But many thought his description of low-intensity war and its criminal propensities was chillingly accurate.

The criminal dimension of the new warfare, however, was not necessarily its most worrisome aspect. In the new wave of conflicts that swept the world around 1992, war often seemed to degenerate into something even stupider than hooliganism: It appeared self-destructive or even suicidal. In South Africa, the oppressed black majority seemed unable to unite in a struggle against apartheid; instead, the worst violence in the country's history grew from the fratricide that erupted between the

African National Congress and the Inkatha Freedom Party. The Hindutva radicals who destroyed the mosque at Ayodhya stood on its dome, hammering away, until it gave way underneath them and they fell to their deaths. The new state of Armenia rushed to liberate its conationals in Nagorno-Karabakh, devoting all its resources to a war with Azerbaijan, at a moment when its domestic economy was collapsing and famine was a real prospect. In many cases, the urge to kill seemed to have overwhelmed the instinct to survive.[9]

The putative irrationality of the Serbs was often invoked in arguments against American intervention in Bosnia. "It is imperative that the West understand the mythical power of Kosovo in the historical and national consciousness of the Serbian people. It should know why Serbs around the world will defend Serbia's right to protect its 'Jerusalem.'"[10] No less a luminary than Henry Kissinger, former U.S. secretary of state (1973–77), argued that U.S. troops should shy away from Bosnia because the conflict would prove too volatile and savage for Americans to stick to their mission:

> Ethnic conflicts are quit [*sic*] a different phenomenon from our historical experience. The Cold War encouraged some calculus of risks and rewards on which superpower policy could be based. Even in regions of intense passions such as the Middle East, the adversaries were clients of the superpowers and therefore to some extent restrained. By contrast, the hatred of ethnic conflicts transcends rational calculations. Each ethnic group hearkens back to some mythic Golden Age when it was dominant: the Muslims recall the Ottoman Empire; the Croats remember the Hapsburg preeminence; the Serbs are sustained by their endless wars of independence. The ideal ethnic map of each is incompatible with the ethnic maps of its rivals; each treats as anathema any arrangement dependent on the good faith of the other.[11]

The Serb separatists in Bosnia did their best to reinforce these arguments by loudly proclaiming that their passionate commitment to their cause insulated them against any blows that the United States, or NATO, or anyone else might launch against them. Radovan Karadžić, the leader of the Bosnian Serbs, repeatedly warned, "The United States sends in 2,000 Marines, then they have to send 10,000 more to save the 2,000. That is the best way to have another Vietnam."[12] Vojislav Seselj, who headed one of the most murderous Serbian militias that operated in Bosnia, was even more menacing: "If United States forces are used here, the war will be total. . . . We would have tens of thousands of volunteers, and we would score a glorious victory. The Americans would have to send thousands of body bags. It would be a new Vietnam."[13]

The Serbs were not the only group whose blind, suicidal fury made the world a more dangerous place. Serb militias fought drunk on plum brandy; Somali "technicals" (irregulars) battled while high on qat; Liberian militias went into combat after smoking dope.[14] These were not men who could be reasoned with. They, and the wars they fought, seemed to have stepped over the line into madness. Psychologists and philosophers might disagree over how best to define the concept of "irrationality," but none seemed to have any difficulty characterizing the new warfare as irrational—if not just plain nuts.[15] One influential Israeli analyst tried to dub the groups that prosecuted the new wave of wars as "high-intensity aggressive ideologies" and labeled their sponsors "crazy states."[16]

In the early 1990s growing numbers of people accepted the claim that the world was going crazy. A story that became popular during these years illustrated this stance. Originally, the story was told about the Middle East; later it was retold in a Balkan variant. But many Americans heard it for the first time in the movie *The Crying Game,* a story about sex and violence and confused identities set against the backdrop of Irish Republican Army terrorism. In that version, the tale goes like this: One day a scorpion, trudging across the desert, found itself blocked by a river. Because scorpions cannot swim, it turned and followed the riverbank, looking for a way across. Eventually it encountered a frog. Scorpions and frogs are hereditary enemies, so the frog kept its distance. But the scorpion called out, "Hey! I need your help crossing this river. Let me climb on your back and you can carry me across." The frog replied, "Do you think I'm crazy? If I let you get that close to me you'll kill me." The scorpion allayed his fears, explaining, "I wouldn't kill you; I need your help. Besides, if I stabbed you while we were in the water, I would drown, too." Persuaded, the frog let the scorpion climb on its back and began swimming into the stream. At they approached midstream, the scorpion became agitated and its tail began twitching. In a fit of uncontrollable passion, the scorpion thrust its stinger into the frog over and over again. As they both began to sink into the water, the frog turned to the scorpion in horror and asked, "But, why?" The scorpion answers: "Because it's my nature."[17]

Some people were content with stories of this kind that claimed irrationality was just a fact of life—albeit one that might be more common in the Balkans, the Middle East, and other "foreign parts." But many, including the global chaos theorists, looked for an explanation of why the world was suddenly going crazy. When a single individual goes insane, a huge variety of possible explanations exist: childhood trauma, drug abuse, double-bind social relationships, the phases of the moon, and so on. When large numbers of people start to act insane at the same time, however, fewer reasons are available. Mass hysteria is usually explained by reference to a handful of mechanisms, the most important of which was the concept of anomie.[18]

The idea of anomie was developed by the French sociologist Emile Durkheim at the beginning of the twentieth century as part of his study of suicide. Durkheim was trying to explain the apparent paradox that suicide rates seemed to rise as society got more prosperous. He argued that the shift from agrarian to industrial society, which made the increase of prosperity possible, involved the destruction of traditional moral values and their replacement by looser and more modern standards. During the transition between two forms of morality, certain individuals or classes might find themselves temporarily bereft of values, that is, in a condition of anomie (a Greek term originally meaning "lawless").[19]

Durkheim argued that during periods of anomie, violence—particularly self-destructive, suicidal violence—would increase for a number of reasons.

The scale [regulating needs] is upset; but a new scale cannot be improvised. . . . One no longer knows what is possible and what is not, what is just and what is unjust, which claims and expectations are legitimate and which are immoderate. As a result, there is no limit to men's aspirations. . . . Appetites, no longer restrained by a disoriented public opinion, no longer know where to stop. . . . [Moreover,] because prosperity has increased, desires are heightened. . . . But their very demands make it impossible to satisfy them. Overexcited ambitions always exceed the results obtained, whatever they may be; for they are not warned that they must go no further. Nothing, therefore, satisfied them and all this agitation is perpetually maintained without abatement. Above all, since this race toward an unattainable goal can afford no other pleasure than the race itself, if pleasure it is, once it is interrupted, one is left quite empty-handed. At the same time, the struggle grows more violent and painful, both because it is less regulated and because the competition is more keen. All classes are set against one another because there is no longer any established classification. Effort grows just when it becomes least productive. How, in these conditions, can the will to live not weaken?[20]

During periods of anomie, irrational violence will increase because social restraints on immorality decay at the same time that appetites and ambitions increase more rapidly than society's ability to satisfy them. As a result, large sections of society become possessed by something resembling a jealous rage.

Although Durkheim is not much read in America, his ideas have great currency. In the 1950s Robert Merton wrote an article that used the concept of anomie to analyze the problem of delinquency, which became the single most frequently cited work in the history of American sociology.[21] Merton showed that, long after the transition from agrarian to industrial society had been completed, other conditions could weaken values and thereby promote violence. Through Merton, Durkheim's ideas diffused into American discussions of crime and deviance.

The idea of anomie resurfaced (with great force) as part of the "culture wars" in the late 1980s and early 1990s.[22] Many Americans, left, right, and center, were concerned that rising divorce rates, increasingly vulgar television and movies, the slow decline of public schooling, and other social trends had combined to steadily undermine America's values. Conservative critics led by the sociologist Charles Murray went further, charging that the social policies and moral relativism of 1960s leftists had backfired disastrously, creating an urban underclass where family life had collapsed and where a culture of poverty, accompanied by addictions to drugs and violence, had taken root.[23] These anxieties all reflected the basic idea of anomie, which is that apparently senseless violence is a symptom of a collapse of values.[24] The concept of anomie has long been popular among conservatives because it provides a classic illustration of "perverse effects." Conservatives caution that good intentions can breed bad results, that change can inadvertently bring decay or chaos rather than progress.[25]

The right's leading spokesman in the culture wars, William J. Bennett, who had served as chairman of the National Endowment of the Humanities under President Ronald Reagan and as secretary of education for President George Bush, argued that since the 1960s the traditional values of the American people have come under steady fire, with the heavy artillery supplied by intellectuals. This all-out assault has taken its toll. In our time, too many Americans became either embarrassed, unwilling, or unable to explain with assurance to our children and to one another the difference between what is right and wrong, between what is helpful and what is destructive, what is ennobling and what is degrading. The fabric of support that the American people—families especially—could traditionally find in the culture at large became worn, torn, and unraveled.[26]

Bennett tried to provide an objective accounting of the damage that this subversion of values had inflicted on America. In 1993 he began to produce *The Index of Leading Cultural Indicators,* which tracked the increase of poverty, teenage pregnancy and suicide, and drug abuse and the decline of educational standards, church attendance, and the quality of popular culture in the United States.[27]

Republican House Speaker Newt Gingrich and his intellectual allies claimed that leftist subversion of American culture caused far more serious problems than just decadence and degeneracy; they were the major cause of rising crime rates. The right charged that the subversion of public morality and the family by the 1960s counterculture had fostered widespread "moral poverty," and that moral poverty in turn was the primary cause of crime.[28] "Moral poverty is the poverty of being without loving, capable, responsible adults who teach you right from wrong; the poverty of being without parents and other authorities who habituate you to feel joy at others' joy, pain at others' pain, satisfaction when you do right, remorse when you do wrong; the poverty of growing up in the virtual absence of people who teach morality by their own everyday example and who insist that you follow suit."[29]

Most Americans were convinced that crime rates had risen to unprecedented proportions. Moreover, a widespread belief existed that domestic crime was becoming more irrational. This trend was epitomized for many Americans by a series of incidents. On April 19, 1989, a woman jogging in New York's Central Park was dragged into the woods by a group of teenagers who beat her, raped and sodomized her, and left her for dead. In videotaped confessions, the youths stated that they had rendezvoused at the park to go "wilding": to seize whatever opportunities for violence presented themselves—not to enrich themselves or to make a political statement, but for the fun of it.[30] In September 1994 *Time* magazine ran a cover story about "Yummy" Sandifer, a eleven-year-old inhabitant of a Chicago public-housing project, who was murdered by other pre-teen gang members who were worried that he might squeal about their collective involvement in the killing of a fourteen-year-old.[31] In the same month Susan Smith, a young woman distraught, among other things, by the failure of her marriage and the rejection of her lover, grabbed unwanted national attention by drowning her two children.[32]

Not all criminologists agreed that crime was becoming more irrational or even more common. By the mid-1990s a clear statistical decline was evident in the rate of major violent crimes.[33] However, public fear of crime remained real and intense. The idea of moral poverty caught on and became an important force behind congressional efforts to dismantle welfare programs after 1994. And as these important political debates rose in rancor, the theme of anomie became more and more familiar to Americans. The idea of "moral poverty" was itself a direct descendent, a contemporary variation, on Durkheim's original concept of anomie. When values break down or are threatened, irrational or self-destructive violence results.

These ideas were so commonplace in domestic policy debates that they inevitably began to leach out into foreign policy. This was particularly evident in discussions of Africa. A discernable element of racism can be found in this. When many Americans hear about violence in Africa, they presume it is somehow similar to the violence that they think characterizes inner-city African Americans. Even a normally careful writer such as Robert Kaplan could not avoid exaggerating the comparison. In his article "The Coming Anarchy," Kaplan drew upon American discussions of family values to explain what he thought was a crime wave in West Africa.

> Most youths I met on the road in West Africa told me that they were from "extended" families, with a mother in one place and a father in another. Translated to an urban environment, loose family structures are largely responsible for the world's highest birth rates and the explosion of the HIV virus on the continent. . . . They provide a weak shield against the corrosive social effects of life in cities.[34]

In later analyses, Kaplan made the principle of anomie increasingly central: "In almost all poor countries, loyalty to the state is weakening and being replaced by loyalty to religious and ethnically based neighbor-hood groups. These groups often succeed at their primary task: keeping values and family structures from unraveling in a new and depersonal-izing environment."[35]

Other Americans were far less analytic when they drew comparisons between the decay of values in America and violence in Africa. During the U.S. intervention in Somalia, the press highlighted the similarity between the failures of the U.S. domestic welfare program (which some thought was inadvertently breeding a criminal underclass) and how an American humanitarian intervention had triggered a violent response. Editorial car-toonists illustrated the apparent irrationality of these policies by showing Somali children biting the hand that fed them or, employing a more sin-ister icon derived from domestic debates about welfare, depicting the Somalis as young black men with handguns threatening weaponless American troops, drawn as bemused, overweight white men. The *New Republic* even ran an article entitled "Welfare Warlords," claiming that welfare payments to Somali refugees in Canada were a major source of funding for the Somali militias that were fighting American troops.[36]

In this way, the idea of anomie slowly seeped into foreign policy debates.

CHAPTER FOUR

Globalization and
Culture Conflict

Until Kaplan and Huntington wrote their popular articles, the most influential single vision of the post–cold war world had been the one laid out by Francis Fukuyama in his widely read 1989 essay "The End of History."[1] Fukuyama had been as optimistic as the chaos theorists had been pessimistic. He argued that a single force—globalization—was revolutionizing international relations and laying the foundations for a more peaceful, more prosperous world. He outlined three distinct ways in which globalization was supposed to be bringing an end to traditional conflicts. First, the global spread of consumer culture, whether through commodities or electronic media, was supposed to be narrowing the differences of values between cultures. Second, the global spread of democracy was supposed to be making governments less warlike (it being a common—if controversial—maxim of international relations that democracies are unlikely to go to war with one another).[2] Third, the unification of the world into a single global economy made countries more interdependent, and the accompanying rise of living standards made them less belligerent.

Huntington, Kaplan, and most global chaos theorists were critical of Fukuyama. Many felt compelled to write systematically about the nature of the post–cold war world because they feared Fukuyama's delirious optimism had infected too many American policymakers.[3] Not surprisingly, many global chaos theorists developed three distinct critiques of Fukuyama—one for each of his claims about globalization.

Global chaos theorists suspected that the same collapse of values that seemed to afflict American society was also plaguing the world at large.

But if the 1960s counterculture had triggered this collapse within the United States, what force could be driving a similar decay internationally? Their critiques of Fukuyama led many to suspect the primary culprit was globalization. Although globalization entailed real benefits for many people, the chaos theorists suspected it also triggered a disastrous series of perverse reactions.

The Democracy Trap

A key, if not always popular, tenet of the reaction against Fukuyama was the claim that democratization itself might stimulate anomic violence. This was not an easy argument for any American to make; not because no evidence existed to this effect, but because most Americans felt that questioning the virtues of democracy was akin to blasphemy. Even men of great intellectual courage such as Samuel Huntington stopped short of suggesting democracy per se caused violence or other social problems. Huntington only claimed that too much democracy might lead to certain social ills. Among the global chaos theorists, however, some had the intellectual courage to challenge any orthodoxy.

One such person was Graham E. Fuller. When the cold war ended in 1989, Fuller was working at the CIA as the senior officer responsible for long-range national estimates. Shortly thereafter, he retired and took up a post at Fukuyama's alma mater, the Rand Corporation, where he began to sketch the worldview that Huntington would later make famous in "The Clash of Civilizations?" In *The Democracy Trap: The Perils of the Post–Cold War World,* Fuller outlined several distinct critiques of Fukuyama, including ripostes to his claims about globalizing trends in culture and the economy.[4] But his boldness in linking the problem of anomic violence and democracy remains almost unique.

Fuller argued that Fukuyama's claims about the benign effects of democratization were exaggerated and they ignored some major flaws in the democratic project. He warned that America was drifting into a "democracy trap"—"the possibility that democracy may not simply go on getting better, but may contain the seeds of its own decline, possibly spurring an eventual authoritarian response from within our own society" and triggering even nastier trends in less civilized societies.[5]

Fuller's description of the democracy trap drew heavily on the standard criticisms of American society that were being made by domestic conservatives in the 1980s. He noted that the democratic urge to expand freedom had led Americans down a slippery slope toward libertinism.

The ultimate challenge to democracy, of course, lies in our greater freedom of choice and the determination of our values. American values have moved decisively away from the "God-given" values that spring from the moral codes of the world's great religions such as Christianity, Judaism, Islam, and Hinduism. . . . Values and ethics have become highly negotiable and situation-oriented. Under such circumstances, American society has been naturally probing the limits of the licit, exploring the final extremes of public morality—and it is increasingly difficult to determine anymore what is morally "wrong."[6]

The consequences of this decay of values include the disruption of the family, the growth of the underclass, and the decline of social discipline.[7] The decay of values has also produced a national crisis of identity, an effect compounded by "rapid urbanization, the impersonalization and alienation that this modernization produces."[8] This identity crisis has two dangerous consequences. First, it encourages the rise of ethnic identities and racial factionalism, to replace the missing sense of community. Second, it increases the probability of anomic violence.

Fuller accepts the globalist premise that what happens in America holds up a mirror that shows the future of the entire world.

The pathology of American society today must therefore preoccupy the rest of the world as well, for the world will inevitably come to share many of America's problems. In fact, it already does. We can see this taking place as we read of the disastrous state of British mass education today, paralleling many of the worst features of American education, with more and more students seeming to know less and less. The same goes for crime and race relations. In Japan there are already signs that the vaunted sense of social discipline is beginning to slacken with newer generations that demand higher standards of living, greater social freedom, and a less rigid, hierarchic business culture. Pick up any popular magazine abroad today and recognize emerging social problems that we have long been dealing with here.[9]

And if American democracy, in a society with high living standards and a long history of civility, tends to aggravate the problems of anomie and ethnic conflict, how much worse must things be in the new democracies of Asia, Africa, and Eastern Europe? "Anomie—alienation and a sense of loss of self-identification—is a problem that affects the entire world, capitalist or socialist, advanced or underdeveloped. It is a disease of the modern condition. How do we define ourselves?"[10]

In newly liberated or developing countries,

> the collapse of totalitarian rule and new aspirations toward democracy will unleash profound forces of both neo-nationalist and radical religious movements that will destabilize large regions of the world. American values—such as the principle of national self-determination and our insistence on human rights—will serve to exacerbate these forces.[11]

The heightened expectation that they have a right to share in political power will lead many new groups to impose their demands on the state. The result will be the growth of what Fuller calls "neonationalism."

> Neonationalism includes separatist subnationalism, that is, the expression of communal/ethnic aspirations of groups *within* the nation-state that are unhappy about their lot: Shiites in Iraq, Sikhs in India, Uighur Turks in Chinese Turkestan. It involves strong new drives toward separatism and breakaway nationalism: Quebec in Canada, Biafra in Nigeria, the Moros in the Philippines, Georgians in the Soviet Union, Catholics in Northern Ireland, Hungarians in Rumania. Nationalist feelings and aspirations will acquire a new assertiveness that springs from international relaxation of tensions and from rising expectations of national and communal fulfillment.[12]

The association of democratization with the rise of neonationalism promises to turn Fukuyama's dream into a nightmare.

Fuller pointed to two additional reasons that he suspected would make "neonationalism" an especially grave problem in the new democracies. First was the temptation of demagoguery.

> The more alien the democratic tradition is to the state, the rawer the forms in which neotraditionalism will express itself. Newly liber-

ated Eastern Europe is rapidly rediscovering its old ethnic causes, which now threaten the very unity of states like Czechoslovakia and Yugoslavia.

Democracy exacerbates nationalist impulses because it enfranchises broad elements of society previously deprived of an active voice in national politics, making them more vulnerable to demagogic siren songs. . . . New leadership will prove highly responsive to the nationalist sensitivities of their constituents in the face of any seeming slights by great powers that dominate the international order.[13]

Thus, new democracies will not only be more prone to violent ethnic conflicts internally, but they will also be more likely to squabble with their neighbors and foreign powers.[14]

Fuller also argued that democratization in the former communist bloc would be particularly unsettling because it had lifted authoritarian restraints that had held old ethnic and national feuds in check. He noted that "the breakup of empire is always destabilizing, for it throws new hunks of real estate onto the international market, charts new boundaries, and establishes new relationships."[15] If the collapse of the Portuguese empire in 1975 threw Africa into a decade of turmoil, how much more destabilizing was the collapse of the Soviet Union likely to be?

Fuller was certainly not the only scholar making arguments of this kind; he was, after all, articulating a wider zeitgeist. In 1991 Thomas Hughes, then director of the Carnegie Endowment for Peace, made a related contribution to the birth of global chaos theory with the suggestion of an even broader mechanism of anomie than the decline of empire. He thought that the growth of irrational violence might be traced to the decline of the state per se.

In a curious way that we did not fully understand at the time, the world in recent decades has relied on the communist states in the East and on the more conventional nation-states elsewhere to curtail or override the lurking subsurface pluralism within their borders. In retrospect, this was another variation of the old tribute that vice pays to virtue, the nation-states' unacknowledged contribution to world order. Smoldering social unrest was a state problem whose eruption was stifled inside state borders, and managed or mismanaged by existing governments, rather than visited upon an unprepared world community.

With the collapse of communism and the erosion of the nation-state generally, these subnational tensions are reviving, sometimes in primitive forms. They threaten to splinter their erstwhile allegiances and spill across borders in disruptive, even menacing, ways. Neither neighboring countries nor rudimentary world institutions have seriously anticipated this phenomenon, let alone prepared themselves to come to grips with it. . . .

There is something primordial about all this world-wide provincialism, chauvinism, separatism, ethnicism and fundamentalism. People power has proved adept at leaping over governments, tumbling walls, collapsing political structures, punishing incumbents, and sending ideologies into the dustbin.[16]

The "people's power" movements of the 1980s, which had been viewed as engines of democratization and highly progressive, were seen in the 1990s as much more sinister and generally disruptive forces.[17]

Many chaos theorists began to suspect that any rapid political change held the potential for encouraging anomic violence. To explain a wave of racist attacks on immigrants in Germany, Stanley Kober, a scholar at the libertarian Cato Institute, quoted a youth services director who blamed the problem on national reunification.

The unification process has been compressed into too short a time. Kids feel disoriented and overwhelmed. They develop feelings of hatred. In moments of social crisis, people look for someone to blame. Foreigners are the most convenient target.[18]

Kober surveys a series of apparently promising political trends—democratization, the collapse of empires, the reunification of nations—and concludes: "It may be that, an initial calm notwithstanding, the shock of rapid and dramatic change has an inherent tendency to produce violence, and it is the absence of bloodshed in such conditions that should be regarded as remarkable."[19]

If anomie could be generated this easily, the likely course of world politics would be extremely violent. Kober's conclusions are stunningly pessimistic.

The next few years will severely test our sensibilities, as television images of unimaginable horror confront us night after night. The twentieth century has been one of breathtaking achievement, but it has also been, as Isaiah Berlin reminds us, "the worst century that Europe has ever had. . . . One can only hope that after the various peoples get exhausted from fighting, the bloody tide will subside." It is not much to hope for, admittedly, but it may have to do. "I have seen hate in my life," Elie Wiesel, a survivor of the Nazi death camps, has acknowledged, "but the hate that exists in Yugoslavia is incomparable." Incredible as it may seem, the worst part of the worst century in history might still be ahead of us.[20]

Most chaos theorists would accept the pessimism of Kober's conclusion—without necessarily endorsing the logic of his wider argument about politics. Many remained skittish about the claim that democratization or even political change itself always imperiled peace. But chaos theorists, like American pundits generally, reached rapid agreement that the collapse of the USSR and its hegemony in Eastern Europe created as many problems as it solved. Without blaming democracy for the rise of anomic violence, they admitted that it served as an inviting environment in which such violence could breed.

While global chaos theorists might display a certain ambivalence about faulting democratization, they had few qualms about blaming other aspects of globalization for the world's ills.

Cultural Anomie

The globalist claim that the spread of democracy would lead to world peace was always haunted by the apparent fragility of the new democracies. The much admired third wave of democratization was broad but thin, and many feared it could easily be reversed. No such doubts, however, tormented those who admired the global export of America's consumer culture. Despite the persistence of national cultures, American images, icons, and ideas continually flooded the globe. While the world was still a long way from a totally homogenous global culture, American show business, advertising, and (to a lesser extent) education clearly had established a common ground, a lingua franca, which intertwined all the world's major cultures.

But was this a good thing? The globalists had claimed that common ideas and cultural symbols, which fostered easier communications, would dampen nationalism and deter war. Chaos theorists suspected they would have the opposite effect.

After Fuller, one of the earlier global chaos theorists was Benjamin R. Barber, a political theorist at Rutgers University. In March 1992 an eloquent and provocative essay by Barber was published in the *Atlantic Monthly*; it was entitled "Jihad vs. McWorld." In this essay he argued that the revolution in international communications would not lead to universal peace and understanding; instead, it would fuel two distinct trends.

> The first is a retribalization of large swaths of humankind by war and bloodshed: a threatened Lebanonization of national states in which culture is pitted against culture, people against people, tribe against tribe—a Jihad in the name of a hundred narrowly conceived faiths against every kind of interdependence, every kind of artificial social cooperation and civic mutuality. The second is being borne in on us by the onrush of economic and ecological forces that demand integration and uniformity and that mesmerize the world with fast music, fast computers, and fast food—with MTV, Macintosh, and McDonald's pressing nations into one commercially homogenous global network: one McWorld tied together by technology, ecology, communications, and commerce. The planet is falling precipitantly apart and coming reluctantly together at the very same moment.[21]

Barber's primary concern, like Fuller's, was to refute the naive optimism of Fukuyama. Barber thought that the two great trends of the times were both bleak, neither democratic. No matter which prevailed, he was certain the world had not attained the end of history. "Neither McWorld nor Jihad is remotely democratic in impulse. Neither needs democracy; neither promotes democracy."[22] But Barber's argument did more than identify flaws in Fukuyama's encomium to the American way. Instead, he had provided the logic for a far darker and more pessimistic understanding of the impact of global communications.

The McWorld trend promoted a global culture, but one that hardly embodied the higher ideals of America and the West. Instead, its content was shallow and materialistic. In the course of tailoring ideas for export, they were not merely popularized but vulgarized.[23] For example, American television producers learned that to export successfully to the

European market they had to drop whole categories of products that lacked international appeal. Shows that were idiosyncratically American would not sell in Italy, much less in Ethiopia. Europeans showed little interest in many of the staples of American television, such as the formulaic romantic comedy where "boy meets girl, boy loses girl, boy gets girl." Instead, one producer described the proper formula for the 1990s as "car goes down the street, car makes wrong turn, car blows up." In the international market, four themes proved universal: lust, greed, sex, and power.[24]

This trend was beautifully illustrated in the countries that formerly comprised the Soviet Union. In 1991, immediately following the breakup of the USSR, Russian television had been dominated by "intense and highly detailed political discussions enlivened by writers and artists as well as politicians and lawyers, marathon debates in the legislatures, documentaries galore and old Hollywood movies."[25] But only a year later, the most popular TV show in Russia was an imported Mexican soap opera, "The Rich Also Cry."[26] The same trend was evident in the print media, where the most popular startup enterprise has been a profusion of sex magazines. Even in the mainstream papers, most stories focus on "pop culture, crime and sports."[27]

The steady vulgarization of the media was concurrent with an unpleasant change in sexual mores. A dramatic increase was seen in "promiscuity, prostitution, and related violence, a reflection of a push toward anarchy."[28] This decline of public morality provoked the same kind of reaction in Russia that it did in the United States. Russian newspapers began to publish calls for a defense of the traditional family, praising the sanctity of marriage and motherhood. Even Western reporters were struck by how rapidly a subculture in which alienation, sexual license, and organized crime commingled had established itself.[29]

Sex and violence tended to become the loudest voices in the chorus of international culture. And, at least in the view of chaos theorists, these seductive voices had the same corrosive effect on the morals of other societies that conservatives charged they had on American virtues. They were a threat to traditional morality, to the identity of more traditional societies. This homogenizing materialism of McWorld provoked the reassertion of local identities that Barber dubbed Jihad.[30]

Barber argued that the post–cold war world was being swept by "small-scale wars" whose aim is to redraw boundaries, to implode states and resecure parochial identities: to escape McWorld's dully insistent imperatives. The mood is that of Jihad: war not as an instrument of policy but as an emblem of identity, an expression of community, an end in itself. Even where there is no shooting war, there is fractiousness, secession, and the quest for ever smaller communities.[31]

Ethnic, nationalist, and fundamentalist movements provided their followers with a chance to reassert their identities and to defend old values.

Jihad delivers a different set of virtues: a vibrant local identity, a sense of community, solidarity among kinsmen, neighbors, and countrymen, narrowly conceived. But it also guarantees parochialism that is grounded in exclusion. Solidarity is secured through war against outsiders. And solidarity often means obedience to a hierarchy in governance, fanaticism in beliefs, and the obliteration of individual selves in the name of the group. Deference to leaders and intolerance toward outsiders (and toward "enemies within") are hallmarks of tribalism. . . . Where new democratic experiments have been conducted in retribalizing societies, in both Europe and the Third World, the result has often been anarchy, repression, persecution, and the coming of new, noncommunist forms of very old kinds of despotism.[32]

The success of this program required intense and apparently irrational violence. "The atmospherics of Jihad have resulted in a breakdown of civility in the name of identity, of comity in the name of community. International relations have sometimes taken on the aspect of gang war—cultural turf battles featuring tribal factions that were supposed to be sublimated as integral parts of large national, economic, post-colonial, and constitutional entities."[33]

Yet the glorification of sex and violence was not the only way in which the global information revolution promoted anomie, atavism, and alienation. Other analysts focused on alternative strains. For example, Charles Krauthammer contends that the global media have fueled anomic violence by broadcasting the importance of ethnic conflicts within the United States. He claimed, like many conservatives, that America's national unity "is now threatened by a process of relentless, deliberate Balkanization. The great engines of social life—the law, the schools, the arts—are systematically encouraging the division of America into racial, ethnic and gender separateness."[34] He warned, "Countries struggling to transcend their tribal separateness have long looked to America as their model. Now, however, America is going backward. . . . Without ever having thought it through, we are engaged in unmaking the American union and encouraging the very tribalism that is the bane of the modern world."[35]

Rather more systematically (and persuasively) Zbigniew Brzezinski argued that global media also promoted anomie by inflaming a particularly dangerous form of international envy. In his major proposal for a post–cold war American grand strategy, *Out of Control,* he warned that within the West itself moral decay has reached an advanced stage. He charged that the prevailing lifestyle in the West has become a "permissive cornucopia," warning that "the priority given to individual self-gratification, combined with the growing capacity of the human being to reshape itself through genetic and other forms of scientific self-alteration—with neither subject to moral restraint—tend to create a condition in which little self-control is exercised over the dynamics of the desire to consume and to tinker with the self."[36] And this libertine, materialistic image is then projected by the Western–dominated media, through satellite broadcasts and pirated compact disks, to the developing countries.

Brzezinski's concerns on this point are echoed in recent debates about China. The first scientific poll organized in China revealed the prevalence of an unapologetic materialism that eclipsed most other values. When asked about their "personal philosophy," 68 percent of Chinese neglected to mention Mao, Confucius, or Tiananmen Square and responded "work hard and get rich."[37] Western reporters suggested that "families are disintegrating, spawning a selfish 'me generation' of youths. Crime and corruption are at record levels."[38]

According to Brzezinski, although the decay of morality evident in China may have been typical of a wider global trend, in most countries the response would be different. China's rates of economic growth had been among the highest in the world through the 1980s; the average Chinese had some hope that he or she might satisfy the yearnings of the country's newfound materialism. But in most third world countries, even over the long term, the prospects for economic growth were much dimmer. Most of the world's poor had no real prospect of ever participating in the gluttonous amorality of the lifestyles they saw exalted in the global media. As a result, Brzezinski admonished,

> there is the risk in the current emphasis on cornucopian goals of a moral confusion that could become susceptible to a new wave of irrationality and escapism, driven by the sense of deprivation vis-á-vis the very visibly richer life-styles of the advanced Western countries—and also on the part of the poorer people toward the rich within the advanced countries themselves. The waning in the latter of deeper spiritual content means that their primary message to the poorer and more recently politically activated global masses is to stimulate their desire for material emulation—which, however, as a practical exercise—even with the most reasonable socioeconomic policies—is simply unattainable for most of the world's deprived. The message of material emulation thus unintentionally becomes the catalyst for frustrated but unstructured envy, which in turn could be easily manipulated by demagogic extremists.[39]

Brzezinski is arguing that envy of the unattainable material success of the West may help to fuel the same kind of anomic movements in the third world that Barber thought would arise from an identity crisis.[40]

> The danger on the eve of the twenty-first century . . . is that the politically activated masses outside of the rich, largely Western democracies are predominantly in the first phase of [political] awareness. Typically, that first stage is characterized by a narrowly defined political self-identity based to a high degree on ethnic exclusiveness. The public mood, therefore, still tends to be expressed through primitive ideas, susceptible to Manichaean appeals—both religious and political—and often escapist and self-righteous in their propounded solutions. The very notion of the complexity of the social condition is alien to that mode of thought, and so is the political practice of compromise. The old Leninist slogan, "Who is not with us is against us," can be appropriately redefined here as meaning "Who is not us is against us."[41]

Brzezinski anticipates the same explosion of anomic violence that Barber dubs Jihad. His focus on envy adds a mechanism by which the global media supposedly contribute to this crisis.[42]

The Economics of Political Chaos

On their own, the globalization neither of political liberalism nor of American consumer culture had sufficient momentum to transform the structure of world politics. The third wave of democratization appeared to have reached its climax and seemed to be receding. Benjamin Barber, the sharpest critic of cultural globalization, admitted that the spread of American consumer culture would not provoke anomie everywhere. Much of the time the result would be dull and nondemocratic—McWorld was not very violent or creative.

Despite the recent wave of interest in culturalism, many people still thought that economic forces were among the most consistently effective mechanisms of change. This conviction was widespread among students of anomie. The consensus among chaos theorists seemed to be that economic changes would provoke more instances of anomie, in more places, by more different means, than any other aspect of globalization.

The global spread of market capitalism was a notoriously disruptive force. Many different mechanisms exist by which economic globalization might erode values, foster anomie, and trigger spasms of irrational violence. A pair of early chaos theorists, the journalists Doyle McManus and Robin Wright, examined several of these mechanisms. But in their survey of the growing dangers of the post–cold war world, *Flashpoints,* they singled out one economic problem for special attention: the massive movement or dislocation of peoples that attended the growth of the global economy.[43]

Shrinking transport costs and growing communications facilities meant that not only goods but people also had an easier time moving from one country to another. In search of employment, business opportunities, or even recreation, growing numbers trampled traditional borders. In 1994 tourists took an estimated 528.4 million trips abroad, spending $321 billion in the quest for exotic cultures or cheap thrills.[44] In 1992 a record eighty-three million people emigrated, resettling permanently in another country. Of these, about twenty million were fleeing political violence or natural disasters. The rest, sixty-three million people, were moving largely for economic reasons—seeking either to escape poverty or at least to move to regions of economic opportunity.[45]

Perhaps the most massive movement of peoples, however, eluded these statistics. This was the dislocation of peoples within their native countries, which was also largely driven by economics. Families left the countryside as peasant agriculture grew uncompetitive. They moved from relatively backward regions to centers of industrial growth. And, in overwhelming numbers, they packed into the burgeoning "megacities" of the third world.

In *Flashpoints,* McManus and Wright noted that this contemporary wave of urbanization was different in its causes and effects from the nineteenth century urbanizing episode that accompanied the birth of capitalist industry. They quoted a World Bank strategist who noted that

> at the close of the twentieth century, the historic role of cities is now being compromised. On the one hand, they still offer the main means for upward mobility and modernization. But, simultaneously, they now include all the negative aspects of excessive overcrowding and violence. The problem is that cities are becoming massive ghettos of people confined in small spaces with very little interaction with the rest of the city except through violence or illegal activities.[46]

In 1950, seven of the ten largest cities in the world were in industrialized countries. According to the UN population fund, by the end of the 1990s, eight of the ten largest will be in developing countries.[47] Where historically the role of cities had been to promote "civilization and cosmopolitanism" (words derived, respectively, from the Latin and Greek words for city), the new megacities—and even many smaller ones—no longer served this function.

The reason is partly that the megacities grew so rapidly that little planning was done for adequate facilities. Recent arrivals from the countryside could no longer be integrated into the structure of the city. They lived in barrios or bidonvilles, slums that were only villages in an urban setting. The numbers of migrants overwhelmed the employment opportunities available in the industrial sector, forcing most to eke out a living in the "informal sector" as street pedlars, casual laborers, or providers of technically illegal services.

> The volume of informal sectors in several countries, however, has converted them into de facto states-within-states, each illegal or unrecognized, but most so powerful that they rival the state for local authority and control. Excluded from the formal empowerment process, the informals are increasingly empowering themselves.

Long term, they represent a challenge to the Modern age's emphasis on order—in organizing the form of human settlements, in reg-
ulating norms and conduct of human life, in providing standards
for commerce, education, development or political intercourse.[48]

The problem is not just that the power structure of the new cities is
multipolar, with diverse and competing authorities. The concentration of
diverse and dissimilar groups in close proximity to each other is an invitation to violence.

The increasing imbalance in development also threatens to heighten
social tensions within the new megacities and hypercities. By 1990,
many squatters' camps and "built-by-night" suburbs worldwide
were riddled with drug traffic, crime and prostitution. . . . An even
greater danger, however, is that, left on the fringe, the informal's
alienation and isolation will turn to open hostility—and conflict.
"Urbanization usually means housing problems, job problems,
overcrowding, disease, social conflict," commented Dr. Simon
Baynham of Pretoria's Africa Institute. "As more and more impoverished people come in from the rural areas, they come into areas
that are already limited in terms of the amount of land available. So
you've got fighting over land, fighting over housing, fighting over
influence in these areas." And the cleavage has been further accen-
tuated by the fact that informals often come from racial or ethnic
lower classes—such as blacks in South Africa or mestizos and
Indians in Peru.[49]

Urbanization, by concentrating people with dissimilar values and contrasting cultures in a single congested location, had been the circumstance
that had prompted Emile Durkheim to coin the idea of anomie.

The idea that rapid urbanization might breed crime and violence was
not new. In the United States, it had been a standard hypothesis in discussions of the origin of the underclass.[50] But in the developing countries,
the problem had long appeared to be particularly acute. In 1978 a book
entitled *Sons of the Soil: Migration and Ethnic Conflict in India* by
Myron Weiner (who had coauthored several books with Sam Huntington) was published.[51] This study, about the political effects of population
movements in India, showed that (contrary to the implications of the then
dominant modernization theory) urbanization often promoted the

growth of ethnic ties. He argued that many ethnic identities seem to have originated as instrumental solidarities in the contest for influence between long-settled "locals" and more recent migrants. This rapid development and juxtaposition of ethnic identities provided a mechanism by which migration and urbanization triggered anomic violence—by pitting Eriksonian "in-groups" against "out-groups."

The largest and most disruptive population movements in the 1990s were occurring within the less developed countries. Probably the largest component of this movement (although precise numbers are unavailable) took the form of urbanization. In the early 1990s, 125 cities in the developing countries had populations of one million or more. By the year 2000, there would be more than 300. Smaller—but still impressive—numbers of people moved across international borders in search of jobs.[52] In 1993 estimates suggested there were thirty-five million such economic migrants in sub–Saharan Africa, fifteen million in Western Europe, fifteen million in North America, and another fifteen million in Asia and the Middle East: eighty million people in all.[53]

Within the industrial countries, urbanization had already peaked. A smaller, but significant, volume of economic migration to the industrial countries was still occurring. In 1992 there were perhaps fifteen million economic migrants in Western Europe and another fifteen million in North America.[54] The United States was the most popular target of economic migration. As of 1990 the United States was absorbing two million legal and illegal immigrants each year.[55] In comparison, in 1992 the total immigrant population in Germany was 4.4 million; in France, 2.4 million.[56]

In the developed countries, economic migration was, objectively, a much smaller problem than it was in the less developed countries. The volume of immigration to industrial countries was nowhere large enough that it threatened to create megacities or to overburden and collapse municipal services. Virtually all studies agreed that legal migration—as opposed to the absorption of refugees and, to a lesser extent, illegal immigrants—was economically advantageous for the host societies.[57] But chaos theorists argued that the economic balance sheet would not be the decisive factor in the way such migrants were received.[58]

After all, economic globalization had made national borders more porous. This meant that immigrants could flow more quickly across boundaries, as could the ills that nativists feared accompanied immigration. Two of the standard charges that nativists leveled against immigrants were that they were carriers of disease and crime.[59] European unions fueled fears that the Italian Mafia would break out of Sicily and Calabria to infect the continent.[60] A small library could have been filled with the literature that developed about the growth of organized crime in Russia and its potential for penetrating other societies—including the United States.[61] And, in the age of acquired immune deficiency syndrome (AIDS), the fear of immigrants or even tourists from any vaguely tropical country reached panic proportions. In the United States, best-selling books such as *The Hot Zone* and movies such as *Outbreak* led to widespread alarm about Ebola, an exceptionally lethal microorganism that killed its victims in a particularly grotesque fashion and that might be communicable through the air.

A hot virus from the rain forest lives within a twenty-four-hour plane flight from every city on earth. All of the earth's cities are connected by a web of airline routes. The web is a network. Once a virus hits the net, it can shoot anywhere in a day—Paris, Tokyo, New York, Los Angeles, wherever planes fly.[62]

This threat led some security experts and environmentalists to argue that the United States needed to develop a new profession, "microsecurity," to study and prepare to repel the viral threat.[63]

Some chaos theorists—Kaplan in particular—included disease, crime, and ecological decay among the ills they ascribed to globalization.[64] And nativists around the world found that the combination of job loss, crime, and disease provided an emotionally explosive—if not always accurate— political cocktail. Joel Kotkin, an immigration policy expert affiliated with a number of Los Angeles think tanks, argued that this combination was fueling a groundswell of reaction against immigration that was building up in California and around the United States. Hostility to immigration was evident in Pat Buchanan's presidential campaign, and even centrists such as Michael Lind, the editor of the *New Republic,* were tilting toward nativism.[65] Kotkin thought this was part of a global trend that included Turk–bashing skinheads in Germany, Le Pen's National Front in France, the neofascist Social Movement in Italy, and Zhirinovsky's appeals to racism in Russia. Unless Western elites worked to allay the fears of their citizens by curbing migration, opposing bilingualism, and otherwise assuaging the fears of the nativists, Kotkin thought that fascism would soon be "back in fashion."[66]

Kotkin was something of an authority on the linkages between economic forces, migration, and ethnic identity. In his major book *Tribes: How Race, Religion, and Identity Determine Success in the New Global Economy,* he argued that economic globalization was breeding a new wave of ethnic awareness—through a novel and previously unrecognized mechanism. As the world's economy grew larger and more dynamic, Kotkin thought that specific ethnic minorities were unusually well positioned to seize the opportunities for profit. Jews, British, Japanese, Chinese, and Indian minorities shared three key characteristics:

1. A strong ethnic identity and sense of mutual dependence that helps the group adjust to changes in the global economic and political order without losing essential unity.

2. A global network based on mutual trust that allows the tribe to function collectively beyond the confines of national or regional borders.

3. A passion for technical and other knowledge from all possible sources, combined with an essential open-mindedness that fosters rapid cultural and scientific development critical for success in the late-twentieth century world economy.[67]

In *Tribes,* Kotkin worked hard to accentuate the positive and focus upon how the "great revival" of ethnic identity might promote prosperity for some groups.[68] But he admitted, "For many in enlightened society this trend represents a throwback to the basest kind of clannishness. Usually identified with the excesses of Islamic fundamentalism, irredentist chaos within the former Soviet bloc, or racial strife in American cities such as Los Angeles, increased emphasis on religion and ethnic culture often suggests the prospect of a humanity breaking itself into narrow, exclusive and often hostile groups."[69]

Another business guru made an argument about economic globalization that had similar implications to Kotkin's. In *Global Paradox,* John Naisbitt claimed that the emerging world economy was increasingly characterized by "diseconomies of scale."

Big companies and "economies of scale" succeeded in the comparatively slow-moving world of the four decades to the mid-1980s. But now, only small and medium-sized companies—or big companies that have restyled themselves as networks of entrepreneurs—will survive to be viable when we turn the corner of the next century. Already 50 percent of U.S. exports are created by companies with 19 or fewer employees; the same is true of Germany.[70]

Like Kotkin, Naisbitt thought that this economic change would encourage the growth of a "new tribalism," a "belief in fidelity to one's own kind."[71] Just as economic globalization gave companies incentives to decentralize into networks of entrepreneurs, it gave countries incentives to reorganize themselves as regions or city states.[72] Naisbitt was confident that the world was therefore

moving toward a world of 1,000 countries because:
—Many people of the new tribalism want self-rule and every day they see others getting self-rule, or moving toward it.
—The nation-state is dead. Not because nation-states were subsumed by super-states, but because they are breaking up to smaller, more efficient parts—just like big companies.
—The revolution in telecommunications not only informs this tremendous move to democratic self-rule but monitors and makes transparent the character and nature of the process. Modern telecommunications also allow and encourage extraordinary cooperation among people, companies, and countries.[73]

For Naisbitt, dividing the world into one thousand countries was an exhilarating prospect, a move that would not only promote economic efficiency but also create new opportunities for democratization and national self-expression. Not everyone viewed this trend with such glee, however. Examining Naisbitt's thesis, the *Wall Street Journal* followed its implications to their logical conclusion: a global wave of secessionism. Secessionist tendencies seemed to be reviving among Quebecois Canadians, Flemish Belgian, Tamil Indians, and myriad other ethnicities who understood that "now even tiny groups of people can contemplate breaking away from the central state and plugging into the world economy on their own."[74] Some scholars argued that secessionism or separatism would form the most common single challenge to the conduct of U.S. foreign policy.[75] There were clear examples of this. The shared sense that they might do better economically if they were independent politically was one of the major factors that impelled Slovenes to press for secession from Yugoslavia—and that led directly to the massacres that followed in Bosnia.

> Some had hoped that the onset of economic interdependence might bring world harmony, as every country saw its interests intertwine with others'. The result was quite the contrary. Increased trade and financial flows made countries more interdependent, but that new intimacy provoked political and cultural backlashes that were the seeds of serious conflict.[76]

If the chaos theorists were correct, Bosnia might be only the first of many countries that would be destroyed by globalization.

CHAPTER FIVE

The Varieties of Global Chaos Theory

Intellectual movements in foreign policy, like oatmeal, can have different consistencies. Some are dry and firm; others are loose and watery. Some consist of people who share one common objective but are otherwise diverse and without apparent solidarity. The isolationist movement of the 1930s was loose, uniting corporations that owned plantations in Latin America, principled pacifists, right-wing Americans of German ancestry, and disparate other groups around a program that was itself subject to radically different interpretations.[1] Other movements are inspired by a single teacher, or guided by a single text, or their members share tight organizational links through a formal association or informal network. The neoconservative movement of the 1980s was relatively tight.[2] Movements that become too loose dissipate into incoherence, such as the antiwar movement in the mid-1970s. Movements that become too tight run the danger of degenerating into cults, such as the followers of Lyndon Larouche or economics professors addicted to neoclassical orthodoxy.

The movement to which Kaplan and Huntington lent their voices clearly lay at the loose end of the spectrum. Its constituents (they cannot be called members or followers, because there was no organization to join and no mentor to follow) came from many walks of life and often did not know one another personally. Kaplan was not the only journalist in the group; the type of ideas he purveyed were also promoted by William Pfaff, who wrote for the *New Yorker* and the *International Herald Tribune,* and Robin Wright, who wrote for the *Los Angeles Times.* Huntington was not the only academic; his arguments were mirrored by those of Benjamin Barber, who taught at Rutgers University, and Walker

Connor, who directed the National Humanities Center. Some broadcast their ideas via television, such as Michael Ignatieff, who produced a documentary series about nationalism (*Blood and Belonging*), and Martin Marty and R. Scott Appleby, who made a similar series about fundamentalism (*The Glory and the Power*).[3] The movement even included at least one prominent politician: Democratic senator Daniel Patrick Moynihan of New York.

Still, its members shared no common political identity. They were not even all Americans. Mathew Horsman and Andrew Marshall represented the school in Great Britain, Conor Cruise O'Brien in Ireland, and Hans Magnus Enzenberger in Germany.[4] A few thought of themselves as being on the left (Benjamin Barber), others worked entirely on the right (Alvin and Heidi Toffler), and many saw themselves as "centrists" (Samuel Huntington had often voted Democratic but endorsed the Republican candidate in the 1996 election).[5] Sometimes these political divisions prevented them from seeing that they shared the same views, much less acting as allies. Barber reacted with angry denials when an article in the *New Yorker* lumped his work and Kaplan's together.[6] Members rarely shared the same platform. The only time the two most prominent advocates of the movement, Robert Kaplan and Samuel Huntington, appear to have collaborated was when the U.S. Institute of Peace invited them to act as keynote speakers at its 1994 conference on the theme of "Managing Chaos."[7]

Not surprisingly, then, each global chaos theorist developed his own special perspective. While they all invoked the ideas of globalization, anomie, and chaos, they often developed individual twists or emphases. At least three major subtraditions can be discerned within the wider current of global chaos theory.

The subschool of global chaos theory that attracted the most international attention was the perspective that Kaplan subscribed to when he wrote *Balkan Ghosts* and that Huntington made even more famous. It stressed the clash of Occident with Orient, or the collision of cultures worldwide. But two other visions probably had even larger followings among global chaos theorists.

A distinct subschool of chaos theory stressed the importance of ecological pressures as triggers of chaos. Extreme population pressure (such as that in Rwanda and Burundi), for example, sometimes drove crowds of soccer fans to go mad with violence.[8] Drought and deforestation can force estranged peoples into hostile contact. Devastating new diseases commonly lead to suspicion of immigrants and even neighbors and might trigger worse forms of mass hysteria.

Robert Kaplan, evolving beyond the views he had expressed in *Balkan Ghosts,* eventually emerged as a major spokesman for this ecological variant of global chaos theory. It formed the centerpiece not only of his influential article "The Coming Anarchy," but also of his tour de horizon of the world's trouble spots, *The Ends of the Earth.* However, a dozen other thinkers had already pioneered this approach. Thomas F. Homer-Dixon, author of "On the Threshold: Environmental Changes as Causes of Acute Conflict," had introduced Kaplan to this perspective and had developed a well-placed following of his own: Vice-President Al Gore feted him in Washington.[9] Norman Myers and George Moffett developed similar ideas.[10] Perhaps the most influential proponent of this view, however, was Jessica Mathews. As senior fellow at the Council on Foreign Relations and a regular columnist for the *Washington Post* who eventually became the director of the Carnegie Endowment for International Peace, she used her access to high-profile publications to argue that "except for Bosnia and North Korea, the major conflicts that have owned the front pages for the past two years—Somalia, Rwanda, Haiti and the Middle East—are all rooted in a varying mix of too many people, environmental shortages and acute poverty." These conflicts, she warned, were "capable of dismembering nations as thoroughly as any external attack and of metastasizing to neighboring states through ethnic tensions and floods of refugees."[11]

One trait that followed from this ecological perspective was a common emphasis on the idea that the threat of chaos was a global one. It might manifest itself first in poor regions of the world, but it would quickly become a worldwide concern. Killer viruses and atmospheric warming showed no respect for borders. Those who shared a fear of ecological chaos thought that the distinction between a country's internal and international affairs had effectively collapsed. Thus, someone such as Kaplan could urge Americans to pay close attention to income distribution within China— hardly a traditional foreign policy concern. But, Kaplan argued, "the loss of agricultural land, combined with an increasing concentration of wealth in the coastal cities, has puts tens of millions of Chinese on the move. Since the 1980s, China has been experiencing the urbanization that Iran experienced from the 1950s to the 1970s."[12] And if China experienced the kind of turmoil that followed the Iranian revolution of 1979, the repercussions would be global. It would be not just chaos, but "super-chaos."[13]

Those who heralded an era of ecological chaos, although they grew chic in some circles, never formed one of the larger subschools of global chaos theory. The largest such subtradition claimed that the greatest threat to world peace came from a renaissance of radical nationalist, fundamentalist, and xenophobic ethnic movements. Sometimes these three phenomena were lumped together and called "ethnonationalism" or "religious nationalism."

During the early 1990s the wars in Bosnia, Somalia, Rwanda, Chechnya, and elsewhere fueled a great expansion of interest in the diverse forms of ethnic conflict. The majority of people who shared this interest were not proponents of global chaos theory. America's two foremost experts on ethnic conflict, Ted Robert Gurr and Donald Horowitz, had been studying the phenomenon so long they were suspicious about claims that it was closely tied to any recent tendency such as globalization.[14] Yet within the vast community of people who developed an interest in ethnic conflict, several advocates of global chaos theory emerged as unusually important and articulate figures.

One such eminence was Conor Cruise O'Brien, a leading Irish intellectual who also wrote regularly for the *Atlantic Monthly*. In books such as *On the Eve of the Millennium,* he argued that, although ethnicity derived its power from ancient, "primordial" bonds, recent events had unleashed its irrational power in ways never before seen.[15] Moynihan, echoing the same arguments, described the destination of global trends in the title of his book about ethnic war, *Pandaemonium*. Mark Juergensmeyer, an authority on the religions of India, claimed that a worldwide confrontation between secularists and Christian, Muslim, and Hindu revivalists—with their special penchant for cosmic violence—might soon trigger *The New Cold War*.[16] Unlike other students of ethnicity, all these men emphasized the role of irrationality, anomie, and a new level of violence or *Mass Hate*.[17] On problems such as Bosnia, they echoed (and Moynihan quoted) the *Economist*'s editorialist who wrote:

Yugoslavia's may well be the war of the future: one waged between different tribes, harbouring centuries-old grudges about language, religion, and territory, and provoking bitterness for generations to come. In their details, conflicts like these vary from place to place. The tribes may want to dominate each other, to escape each other's clutches or merely to kill each other. But the main ingredient is the same: visceral hatred of the neighbours.[18]

The West against the Rest

Yet, precisely because they gave different emphases or "spins" to the same basic ideas, the global chaos theorists had some difficulty agreeing about what the overall implications of their vision were for U.S. foreign policy. Both the experts on ecological calamities and on ethnic conflict tended to focus on the need for global action, rather than urging specific programs on Washington. The most famous attempt to translate global chaos theory into a grand strategy for America came from Sam Huntington, who had been a strategist long before he became a chaos theorist.[19]

Huntington's "The Clash of Civilizations?" article was almost unique among works of global chaos theory because it focused more on prescription, on outlining the desirable policy response to the new wave of culture conflicts, than it did etiology, on explaining its causes or dynamics. Huntington understood that, to be translated into a plausible "grand strategy," global chaos theory would have to do three things.[20] First, it would have to provide a description of U.S. foreign policy interests and establish a rough order of priority among them. Huntington had already devoted several articles to this. In a 1991 piece, "America's Changing Strategic Interests," he supplied a succinct outline of the country's vital national interests:

> (i) to maintain the United States as the premier global power, which in the coming decade means countering the Japanese economic challenge;
> (ii) to prevent the emergence of a political-military hegemonic power in Eurasia; and
> (iii) to protect concrete American interests in the Third World, which are primarily in the Persian Gulf and Middle America.[21]

He provided elaborate detail about what operational objectives would be necessary to secure these strategic goals, including pressuring Japan to open its economy, limiting German power in the new Europe, and maintaining access to Arabian oil.

Second, a credible grand strategy would have to identify the salient threats to American interests. Global chaos theory excelled in this area. Its description of America's perils was the most persuasive since Mikhail S. Gorbachev began to show how much steam had leaked out of the "red menace." Huntington was, again, unusually lucid and explicit. In his analysis, war and conflict were most likely where civilizations abutted, along the "fault lines" that included the famous velvet curtain that divided eastern from western Europe. While this was the hottest zone in the early 1990s, Huntington predicted that other civilizational fault lines would also soon become active, including those that separated Islamic civilization from its African neighbors in the southwest and from Slavic-Orthodox civilization to the northwest (see figure 2-3).

Third, a viable grand strategy would have to specify remedies, concrete ideas about how America's interests could best be protected from the burgeoning threats. Huntington perhaps made his most original contribution here. His analysis of civilizations seemed to offer the possibility of a general theory of alliances that could help America and the West ensure their victory. The same map that showed where the threats were could be used to locate new opportunities.

When the cold war ended in 1989, the neorealist scholars who were the leading students of alliance theory in the United States argued that a certain pattern of change would likely follow.[22] The collapse of the Soviet Union meant that the bipolar alliance pattern, in which smaller states grouped themselves under the umbrella of one of the two competing superpowers, was dead. For a short while, a unipolar system in which the United States was free to throw its weight around was possible. But soon and inevitably, Europe and Japan, freed of the need to "bandwagon" with the Americans, and perhaps now joined by a renascent Russia, would begin to assert their independence from Washington. The result would be a multipolar system in which the industrial powers would probably be neither enemies nor allies, just competitors.[23]

Huntington's map of world civilizations bore some resemblance to the multipolar model. Yet it differed in some subtle but critical ways. Most important, it suggested that Europe and America, although they might compete economically, shared a foundation of values and interests that assured their long-term cooperation. Together, they formed "Western civilization." Both the strength of the historical traditions they shared and the common hostility of non-Westerners to their power would pressure them to coordinate their actions and made them natural allies. (A revealing continuity can be found here: Huntington, and most global chaos theorists, had been strong proponents of the Atlantic alliance during the cold war. Chaos theory seems to represent the latest evolution of the Atlanticist-internationalist tradition in U.S. foreign policy.)[24]

Such an association certainly would not happen spontaneously; the unification of the West would have to be worked at. But cooperation among Western states was the most logical and potentially the most effective means to bolster America's own power. "In the short term, it is clearly in the interest of the West to promote greater cooperation and unity in its own civilization, particularly between its European and North American components; to incorporate into the West those societies in Eastern Europe and Latin America whose cultures are close to those of the West."[25]

However, on Huntington's map of world civilizations, Japan is not part of the West. During the years just before writing "The Clash of Civilizations?" Huntington had often argued that Japan loomed as the most immediate threat to America's economic interests. He warned that "Japanese strategy, behavior, and declarations all posit the existence of an economic cold war between Japan and the United States" and urged that Washington reply in kind.[26] Once he developed his civilizational perspective, the economic cold war appeared even more threatening:

> Here cultural difference exacerbates economic conflict. People on each side allege racism on the other, but at least on the American side the antipathies are not racial but cultural. The basic values, attitudes, behavioral patterns of the two societies could hardly be more different. The economic issues between the United States and Europe are no less serious than those between the United States and Japan, but they do not have the same political salience and emotional intensity because the differences between American culture and European culture are so much less than those between American civilization and Japanese civilization.[27]

Huntington stops short of predicting an inevitable clash between Japan and America. But he clearly thinks that "peaceful coexistence" rather than outright alliance is a more realistic model for relations between Washington and Tokyo.

However, he does think that some as-yet-not-Western societies might be brought into the Western alliance. "Torn countries," he suggests, "have a fair degree of cultural homogeneity but are divided over whether their society belongs to one civilization or another."[28] Three of these are particularly important because they are potentially powerful, occupy strategic locations, and yet are torn between attachments to the West and some other civilization: Turkey, Mexico, and Russia. The West has a stake in, if not promoting Westernization, at least preventing these states from joining the anti–Western coalitions.

Over the longer term, Huntington argues that preventing coalitions or alliances among non–Western states may be nearly as important as fostering cooperation among Western states. He is particularly worried about the growth of linkages between two traditionally anti–Western civilizations. Both Islamic and Confucian civilizations remain resentful of the West, which displaced them from their medieval positions of glory, and continue to harbor ambitions of displacing the West. If they ever learned to pool their resources, to cooperate against the West, they would pose a serious threat. Huntington discerned a trend of this sort in the growing cooperation between China and Iran and between North Korea and Syria, particularly on weapons development. He warned policymakers in Washington that neutralizing this "Confucian-Islamic connection" was nearly as important as promoting the unity of the West.[29]

Civilization versus Chaos

Huntington's elaborate theses about the dynamics of alliances within and between civilizations offered a general and logical vision of global chaos theory's strategic implications, and other global chaos theorists cited his work admiringly, often invoking phrases or metaphors he had coined. Yet the grand strategy Huntington offered won few if any converts.[30] Many who shared his broad perspective thought he had put exaggerated emphasis on the power of religion and simple xenophobia.

A more widely accepted vision of global chaos theory's strategic consequences had already been spelled out by an author who received much less government attention: William Pfaff. In the aftermath of the Vietnam War, Pfaff emerged as one of the most consistent and insightful critics of American military intervention in the less developed countries. He argued that the results were too often disastrous for both the United States and for its local interlocutors and that a succession of American presidencies had been crippled in the process: Lyndon B. Johnson in Vietnam, Jimmy Carter in Iran, and Ronald Reagan in Lebanon.[31] The consistent theme in these disasters, he thought, was that the United States projected onto the third world values, aspirations, and fears that had no basis in local reality.

We are in an odd situation. At one level of intelligence, or conscious-ness, Americans—conservatives, liberals, the rest—know that their political language is false and that their ideas are sentimental and self-aggrandizing. People recognize perfectly well that the Lebanese, Iranians, Nicaraguans, Salvadorans, Filipinos, Africans—not to speak of the Europeans, Japanese, and Chinese—all lead lives more or less remote from the American national experience, with different perceptions and national ambitions, motivated by different values. This is evident to those who make American policy; it is the main obstacle to the success of that policy. There would be no problem in the Middle East or Central America—or in any of the other places where the United States finds itself in collision with local feelings—if it were really true that American values were universally admired and sought, or would be if these were properly explained. That we are the norm of the world is simply an ancient and self-serving theme of American political rhetoric, of interest, these days, only to ourselves.[32]

Because of this problem of psychological projection, Americans tended to pursue unrealistic objectives, intervene where they were not wanted, and fatally misunderstand the real history of the countries they dealt with. They saw "events as manifestations of good and evil, and policies in terms of crusades."[33]

Pfaff devoted much of his books and articles to trying to explain to Americans the complex realities of politics in the third world. A highly learned man, he could quote medieval Arabic poetry and Manchu histor-ical texts. For example, in a 1991 article in which he cautioned his coun-trymen against rushing to intervene in the conflict between Kuwait and Iraq, he provided a detailed history of the development of nationalism in the Middle East, the role of European empires in demarcating the region's borders, and an elaborate warning about "the resentment and sense of powerlessness engendered within Islam by its domination by the West."[34]

Pfaff (like other global chaos theorists) thought that this cultural con-frontation was the real taproot of violence in the Persian Gulf, but he fur-ther argued that military action, no matter how decisive, was unlikely to resolve it.

What has happened in Iraq, and happened before that in Iran, and the terrible traumas that have been produced by the struggle between Palestinians and the Israelis all arise from the provisional defeat of a people and a religion by a rival, yet related, civilization. This is what the crisis in the Middle East is fundamentally about. The grievances (and grief) of modern Islam, its paranoia and defiance come from that. It follows that the present conflict cannot settle anything worth settling, except who controls certain oil sources and who rules a given country. These may be matters that require settling, but they should be understood as the relatively small matters they are, and such settlements as they produce should be understood as assuredly insecure ones, productive of further chains of consequence which are very likely to leave all those involved worse off than they are now.[35]

At first this sounds very much like Huntington, right down to a paragraph where Pfaff details the historical clashes of Islam and the West from Tours to the second siege of Vienna. But despite their similarities, the two authors had different recommendations for grand strategy. Unlike Huntington, Pfaff understood that most of the fury and anger within Islam was focused internally, channeled between competing local factions, rather than into the clash of civilizations. The West became a target for that rage chiefly when it intervened, intruding on local disputes.

Pfaff argued that the political struggles of the less developed countries revolved around the quest for stable nationhood.

The number of nations that are fully mature is quite small. One may speak of historical maturity as a more or less homogenous society's possession of a fixed place, with fixed and acknowledged borders; a recognized history and distinctive national culture; and an absence of what in the political vocabulary are called revindications—claims on others' territories, claims on populations held elsewhere, claims to be satisfied only at the expense of others. A primary characteristic of a mature nation is that it is a satisfied nation, an achieved nation.[36]

While this was the goal they aspired to, most of the third world was still ages from seeing its fruition. In South America, where nationalist movements had been operating since the beginning of the nineteenth century, something like stable secure borders had been achieved. Japan and China, too, had ancient national identities. But for much of the rest of the world (even, until recently, in such apparently modern countries as Germany), nationalism remains a force of disruption rather than order. In parts of Central America, in most of Africa, and particularly in the Arab world, society "remains today, largely unready for the forms of national existence characteristic of Western Europe and North America."[37]

When the United States interfered in the political battles that accompanied the development of nations, it was begging for trouble.

> The achievement of nationhood is a product of time as well as circumstance, and time is the one thing the makers of American foreign policy do not conceive of having at their disposal. It is all but useless to preach detachment, or patience with history, to an American government committed to action and problem-solving. Nonetheless, one would think a record of four disrupted American Presidencies a considerable lesson in the futility of interventions meant to dominate or check long-term historical forces of the kind recently at work in Vietnam and Iran and now evident amidst the uproar of the Middle East. A great power has the resources to influence such things, and to survive them, but it is unable to stop history. Throwing American military power against forces of this sort, at work within turbulently unachieved nations, has done nothing except damage the United States.[38]

Long before Fukuyama wrote about the end of history, Pfaff was cautioning Americans against the millennial fantasies implicit in the idea of the "American century."

When Pfaff used the term "civilization," unlike Huntington, he was not referring to a series of discrete units that divided the surface of the globe and occasionally collided like tectonic plates. Instead, he was referring to a level of attainment, to a pattern of peace, stability, and civility, that many different nations and cultures might strive for. Civilization was not a type of power bloc; it was a category comprising those cultures that had made peace with themselves. The rest of the world, those countries where nationhood had not matured and violence was still endemic, belonged to a different category. The traditional antonym to civilization was "barbarism."[39]

For Pfaff, the common denominator between Europe and America was not "Western civilization" but just civilization. This fundamentally reshaped the way that he understood the fault lines that divided cultures and societies. Pfaff thought that the divide between Western and Eastern Europe had little to do with different religious values and much to do with the divergent levels of political order.

> No sizable place in Western Europe, outside of Scandinavia, can claim to be ethnically "pure." . . . The differences between the Irish and English, or Scottish and English, or between Catalans and Castillians, or between Catalans, Basques, or Bretons and the Gaulish and Germanic French, are not trivial. However, they are certainly nonlethal—"folkloric," as the French say—and manageable within the framework of mature nation states.
>
> This is not the case with differences in the east of Europe, where modern nations were established in the nineteenth and early twentieth centuries with the disintegration of the Ottoman and Hapsburg Empires. Since the Soviet Union's retreat from the region, and the collapse of central power in the Soviet Union itself, ethnic conflict has reemerged as a powerful force.[40]

For Pfaff, the basis of the clash between Serbia and Croatia lies not in the opposition of Latin and Greek Christianity, but in that both countries have not yet attained the pattern of stable nationhood, of civilization, that is common among the Catholic and Protestant countries of Western Europe.

Sometimes the fault line that divided the likelihood of civilization from barbarism ran right through the middle of regions that Huntington would have lumped together because of their common culture. Pfaff thought that "the instability of the Middle East occurs at a fault line dividing two histories, two pasts. Trouble arises along this line where real nations abut a zone of historical non-nationhood." Most of the Arabian Peninsula, Syria, and Jordan formed a region with no history of stable nationhood in which political development was likely to be slow and painful. Egypt, Israel, Lebanon, Turkey, Iran, Yemen, and Iraq were countries with ancient histories of nationhood and would probably advance to a European level of stability and civility more rapidly.[41]

Important to note, then, is that the boundaries between civilization and barbarism were fluid, not fixed. Over time, nations could congeal, peace could take root, and cultures transit into the glories of civilization. But it was not a process that could be hurried. Like other global chaos theorists, Pfaff thought the West's attempts to export its values and institutions generally backfired.

Pfaff's view of the world divided into two spheres, one violent and one peaceful—not Huntington's idea of a dozen competing civilizations—articulated the vision of a majority of global chaos theorists. Some acquired this vision from Pfaff, many seem to have developed it independently. Pfaff's terminology, the contrast of civilization and barbarism, did not catch on—in the hands of all but the most masterful authors it would quickly degenerate into ethnocentrism.

However, as dualist visions similar to Pfaff's became popular, alternative vocabularies emerged. One of the most popular was proffered by Max Singer (former head of the Hudson Institute) and Aaron Wildavsky (a prestigious political scientist at the University of California) in their book *The Real World Order,* which opened as follows:

> The key to understanding the real world order is to separate the world into two parts. One part is zones of peace, wealth, and democracy. The other part is zones of turmoil, war, and development. . . . The zones of peace and democracy include Western Europe, the United States and Canada, Japan, and the Antipodes, which together have about 15 percent of the world's population. The rest of the world, including Eastern and Southeastern Europe, the territory of the former Soviet Union, and most of Africa, Asia, and Latin America, is composed, for now, of zones of turmoil and development.

The idea of contrasting a zone, or zones, of peace with a zone of turmoil percolated into policy discussions.[42] The "Defense Planning Guidance" for 1992, the official presentation of Pentagon strategy, argued that the "less visible" part of America's cold war victory was "the integration of Germany and Japan into a U.S.-led system of collective security and the creation of a democratic 'zone of peace.'"[43]

One proponent of this dualist image of the world was Robert Kaplan. His arguments for intervention in Bosnia had always emphasized the idea that Bosnia was part of the West, that things could be done there that would not succeed in darker regions of the globe.

> a military intervention in the Balkans has meaning because there is a societal status quo ante to return to: The problems may be political, ethnic and historical, but they are not, as in Africa, social. For example, Rwanda is one of the most densely populated and over-tilled regions of

Africa. The average woman in Rwanda gives birth to eight children over her lifetime. The average woman in Bosnia gives birth to less than two. . . . If you can fix the political problems in Bosnia, there is a fair chance that the society won't decompose again after the foreign troops leave.[44]

In his major 1994 article, "The Coming Anarchy," Kaplan emphasized the growing difference between his own ideas and Huntington's "clash of civilizations" thesis—although the latter was similar to the argument Kaplan had earlier laid out in *Balkan Ghosts*. Not only was he becoming interested in ecological issues, but Kaplan had also begun to see the world in terms similar to Pfaff or Wildavsky and Singer.

We are entering a bifurcated world. Part of the globe is inhabited by Hegel's and Fukuyama's Last Man, healthy, well fed, and pampered by technology. The other, larger, part is inhabited by Hobbes's First Man, condemned to a life that is "poor, nasty, brutish, and short." Although both parts will be threatened by environmental stress, the Last Man will be able to master it; the First Man will not.[45]

In another passage, he supplied an even darker metaphor for this bifurcation.

While a minority of the human population will be, as Francis Fukuyama would put it, sufficiently sheltered so as to enter a "post-historical" realm, living in cities and suburbs in which the environment has been mastered and ethnic animosities have been quelled by bourgeois prosperity, an increasingly large number of people will be stuck in history, living in shantytowns where attempts to rise above poverty, cultural dysfunction, and ethnic strife will be doomed by a lack of water to drink, soil to till, and space to survive in. In the developing world environmental stress will present people with a choice that is increasingly among totalitarianism (as in Iraq), fascist-tending mini-states (as in Serb-held Bosnia), and road-warrior cultures (as in Somalia).[46]

The global chaos theorists did not think Fukuyama's "end of history" was at hand, but, despite their general pessimism, they foresaw one or two reasons to remain hopeful. If much of the world was going to hell, other parts looked well positioned to enter a period of peace and prosperity. Within the zone of peace, the pattern of international collaboration and respect for law that American idealists had been urging since Woodrow Wilson seemed poised to flourish.

Pfaff, among others, argued that once their nationhood matures and democracy takes root, states such as America, Japan, and particularly the members of the European Union can do an enormous amount of effective collaboration with each other. He cites

> the Council of Europe, the organization for Economic Cooperation and Development (which originated as the agency directing the use of Marshall Plan aid), the European Community itself, the European Free Trade Association, the European Bank for Reconstruction and Development, the Group of Seven finance ministers' meetings and the annual economic "summits," NATO, the North Atlantic Council, the Western European Union, the Conference on Security and Cooperation in Europe. In addition there are thousands, possibly hundreds of thousands, of semi-public or private institutions of cooperation acting across the frontiers of the democracies and beyond them, from multinational corporations to academic seminars and journals, some self-interested, some devoted to the public interest, but all together providing a dialogue of unprecedented intensity, complexity, and breadth.

Taken together, Pfaff suggests this already amounts to "an unacknowledged commonwealth of the democratic states."[47] It may fall short of realizing "the end of history," but it means that realist fears of renewed combat among the industrialized nations are probably misplaced.

CHAPTER SIX

The Policy Implications
of Global Chaos

Global chaos theory caught widespread attention in America in 1993. During that single year, three major works of global chaos theory appeared: Sam Huntington's "The Clash of Civilizations?" article, Daniel Patrick Moynihan's *Pandaemonium: Ethnicity in International Politics*, and William Pfaff's *The Wrath of Nations: Civilization and the Furies of Militant Nationalism*.[1] Even scholars and pundits who did not fully align themselves with global chaos theory wrote works that captured the same zeitgeist and reinforced the same themes. This was true of both Zbigniew Brzezinski's *Out of Control: Global Turmoil on the Eve of the Twenty-First Century* and Paul Kennedy's *Preparing for the Twenty-First Century*.[2] Inevitably, these works and the discussions they provoked had an impact upon policymakers in Washington.

Yet, despite the hopes, lobbying, and prominent access enjoyed by its proponents, global chaos theory never came close to being adopted as America's grand strategy for the post–cold war world. Huntington's broad program was rejected (explicitly, by National Security Advisor Anthony Lake) and Pfaff's was largely ignored.[3] Instead, global chaos theory penetrated Washington discourse not as an integrated system of analysis, as a grand strategy, but as a piecemeal assemblage of epigrams. The metaphors and icons that the chaos theorists invented—such as the slogan "the West against the rest" and the image of nations locked in the fanatic death-grip of jihad—gained greatest currency.[4]

In part, this fragmented reception of global chaos theory reflects the fractious nature of the movement itself. The individuals who developed chaos theory were diverse, accustomed to working independently, and differed from each other over how to interpret the significance of their work. Moreover, the great majority of chaos theorists did not attempt to devise anything like a grand strategy, instead contenting themselves with disparate and ad hoc policy recommendations.

But other forces worked against wholesale adoption of the global chaos theory program as well. In particular, the prevailing pattern of discourse "inside the beltway," in Washington itself, seemed prejudiced against any such reception. In the 1990s rhetoric in Washington was rooted in the quest for successful "soundbites"—brief phrases that were easy to remember, emotionally evocative, and politically pointed. Large, complex theories were difficult to communicate over television.[5] But soundbites communicated easily, grabbed attention, and created audiences or even constituencies.[6] Not everyone in Washington approved of this trend, but scholarly research confirmed that it was an almost inexorable reality.[7]

Some of the architects of global chaos theory had a real gift for coining colorful images. Phrases such as "the new tribalism" or "virulent nationalism" lent themselves to use in soundbites.[8] Naturally, these phrases—rather than the movement's more ponderous thinking about grand strategy—percolated into discussions and writings in Washington.

Thus, when Bill Clinton cited *Balkan Ghosts* to justify his policies in Bosnia, he was not endorsing (much less embracing) Robert Kaplan's vision of the world. Rather, he was lifting a few evocative images that supported a conclusion he had arrived at independently. His decision not to commit America to supporting the Bosnians seemed more palatable after one heard the soundbite that this war was just another example of the "age-old tribal rivalries" that had led people in the Balkans to kill each other for centuries.

This opportunism helps to explain how Clinton and Kaplan could have arrived at diametrically opposed readings of *Balkan Ghosts*. When Kaplan heard how Clinton had invoked his work, he protested that it should not be read as a justification for a "hands off" policy toward Bosnia. Personally, Kaplan tended to favor military intervention.

It is frustrating to find *Balkan Ghosts* cast as an anti-intervention tract: I myself have been an outspoken hawk. Since the first half of 1993, I have publicly advocated "lift-and-strike," even raising the possibility of involving U.S. ground troops, on CNN [Cable News Network] and C-SPAN [Cable Satellite Public Affairs Network], in the *Washington Post* Outlook section, and in other forums. For several years at Fort Leavenworth and Carlisle Barracks, I have made the case for intervention to the U.S. Army.[9]

Moreover, Kaplan claims that his advocacy of intervention is consistent with the arguments he made in *Balkan Ghosts*. He notes that his book is silent on the subject of U.S. policy toward Bosnia because the war had not started when he was writing it. And he insists that anyone who cited *Balkan Ghosts* in support of an anti-interventionist policy must have misread—and perhaps misrepresented—his work:

> I suspect, *Balkan Ghosts* supplies handy ammunition whenever inaction is the policy. Back in 1993, Clinton had so little resolve that he was casting around for any excuse not to act.[10]

Although Clinton took what he wanted from *Balkan Ghosts* and left the rest, he did not do much violence to the spirit of the work. Many, probably a majority, of global chaos theorists read Kaplan and the meaning of the Bosnian war in the same way. If the Serbs really were irrational, if the conflict in Bosnia reflected an anomic collapse of rational values, how could American intervention succeed?

Some of the most hard-headed members of the global chaos movement, such as Benjamin Schwartz, not only warned against intervention but also argued that America was going to have to live with the war in Bosnia and many others like it. "Lamentably," he wrote, "the most stable and lasting solution to ethnic and nationalist conflicts has been ethnic cleansing and partition," citing the stability that Poland and Czechoslovakia achieved after World War II by deporting their German minorities.[11] He urged Americans to embrace the brutal implications of this logic:

> Although the Pentagon, the State Department, and the Carnegie Endowment have spent enormous energy of late generating ideas and strategies for how America can prevent, tame, or end ENS [ethnic, nationalist, secessionist] conflicts, the United States really has only two options in these situations. Adopting a passive role once violence has erupted in a failed state, Washington can await the time when mutual exhaustion or the triumph of one group over another will create an opening for intervention in a purely peacekeeping capacity. Alternatively, the United States can effectively intervene,

not by building civil societies or pacifying such conflicts but by helping one side impose its will on the other, as Turkey did in Cyprus.[12]

The phrase "ENS conflict" indicates the growing influence of global chaos theory at the Pentagon. Various elements within the Department of Defense borrowed elements of chaos theory. The profusion of ethnic conflicts predicted by global chaos theorists helped to justify America's continually massive defense budgets. The director of the Defense Intelligence Agency told an alarmed Congress that

> the abrupt end of the Cold War, the rapid spread of western values, ideals and institutions, and the dramatic personal, societal, and global changes underway as a result of the global village phenomenon and broad technology proliferation, are changing fundamental concepts, beliefs, and allegiances in many areas of the world. Those peoples, groups, and governments who are unable to cope with or unwilling to embrace these changes frequently resent the dominant role played by the United States in the international security environment, and attempt to undermine US and Western influence and interests.[13]

In the new world disorder, crises might erupt anywhere, anytime—and Washington needed a large, flexible, modern military to deal with them.

Although dealing with the backlash against the West might form a major mission for the U.S. military, not all officers were enthusiastic about confronting it. The commandant of the Marine Corps noted:

> We have a whole new world coming. If we go to war it's not going to be linear and symmetric. . . . It's going to be chaos. . . . Picture someone with the cunning and tenacity of a Chechnyan rebel, who is armed with a weapon that if it can sense you, it can kill you.[14]

When most of the world's conflicts involved opponents who were suicidally savage, the United States should think twice about becoming involved. Many Defense Department officials quoted global chaos theory in support of the "Powell doctrine"—fostered by Gen. Colin L. Powell, Jr., who served as chairman of the Joint Chiefs of Staff from 1989 to 1993—that the military should not be committed to any conflict unless "Congress supports it and total victory is the almost certain outcome."[15]

Even deploying overwhelming force could not guarantee victory in an ethnic conflict. In an influential article, Maj. Ralph Peters, an unorthodox military intellectual and a devoted fan of Huntington, argued that the new wave of ethnic conflicts was being fought not by "soldiers" but by "warriors—erratic primitives of shifting allegiance, habituated to violence, with no stake in civil order."[16] He warned that

> we need to ask ourselves some difficult questions. Do we have the strength of will, as a military and as a nation, to defeat an enemy who has nothing to lose? When we face warriors, we will often face men who have acquired a taste for killing, who do not behave rationally according to our definition of rationality, who are capable of atrocities that challenge the descriptive powers of language, and who will sacrifice their own kind in order to survive. We will face opponents for whom treachery is routine, and they will not be impressed by tepid shows of force with restrictive rules of engagement. Are we able to engage in and sustain the level of sheer violence it can take to eradicate this kind of threat? To date, the Somalia experience says "No."[17]

Torn between the allure of ethnic conflicts as a justification for defense budgets and the perceived hopelessness of participating in them, the Department of Defense split the difference. Its reports increasingly invoked ethnic wars, transnational threats, and humanitarian emergencies—but when confronted with practical decisions about whether to become involved in Rwanda or Bosnia, the military routinely voted no.[18]

The military was not the only Washington bureaucracy that adopted elements of global chaos theory. The CIA, which was trying to invent a new mission for itself once the Soviet Union collapsed, also paid close attention to "transnational threats." In congressional testimony, Clinton's first director of central intelligence, R. James Woolsey, warned, "Yes, we have slain a large dragon. But we live now in a jungle filled with a bewildering variety of poisonous snakes. And in many ways, the dragon was easier to keep track of."[19] The agency began to pay closer attention to the threats that globalization had made more salient: smuggling of narcotics and weapons, proliferation of sophisticated military technologies and weapons of mass destruction, the spread of disease, refugees, and related humanitarian emergencies. Woolsey warned that the United States should pay particular attention to new organized crime groups (particularly the

Russian "mafia") because the end of the cold war inaugurated what he called "the Era of Anarchic Proliferation."[20]

Other government agencies also cannibalized ideas from global chaos theory. The ecological version of global chaos theory put down roots at the State Department. In interagency debates over drafting a new national security strategy for the United States, the State Department in 1994 pressed for putting primary emphasis upon "'transnational threats' such as climate change, drug smuggling, AIDS and the decline of biological diversity."[21] Partly under pressure from the State Department, both the Defense Intelligence Agency and the Central Intelligence Agency began to devote assets to the study of "famine, soil erosion, rapid population growth, the expansion of deserts—that they believe will produce many of the world crises of tomorrow."[22] By the end of Clinton's first term, his secretary of state, Warren Christopher, had become a fervent convert to the environmental perspective: "I kept running into political or security problems that had a very large environmental content. . . . Haiti stuck out in my mind, with the overpopulation and the deforestation of the country. And in Eastern Europe, those new democracies are struggling with a legacy of environmental abuse and are never going to recover."[23]

In February 1994, a year after the publication of *Balkan Ghosts,* Kaplan wrote an even more influential article entitled "The Coming Anarchy." This article, although again cast in the form of a travelogue, was an intellectual survey that laid out and elaborated on the ideas of three thinkers whom Kaplan viewed as kindred spirits: Martin van Creveld, Samuel Huntington, and Thomas Fraser Homer-Dixon. Brian Atwood, appointed by Clinton as director of the Agency for International Development (USAID), which supervises all U.S. economic assistance to foreign countries, endorsed "The Coming Anarchy" in several speeches and in a widely read *Washington Post* editorial that explained the new mission of his department.[24] One observer of AID politics noted

Kaplan's "Coming Anarchy" had an enormous effect. If I had a nickel for every time someone in USAID or State asked me if I'd read the article I'd be living on the beach in Belize eating lobsters today. . . . In USAID Africa Kaplan is used as the justification for budgets—giving Africans American corn can no longer be used to contain communism, to promote markets for American exports doesn't work . . . so the argument is "give aid to Africa or else they will go crazy and start another Rwanda."[25]

Not coincidentally, U.S. assistance to Africa declined dramatically under the Clinton administration.

The influence of "The Coming Anarchy" was felt far beyond the State Department. Clinton cited it in his speeches, and "Vice-President Gore ordered the CIA to consult with a team of regional, environmental, and security experts and undertake a large study of around seventy 'countries at risk.' And high officials in the United Nations Secretariat—already completely overwhelmed by the plethora of Somalias and Rwandas that were landing on their laps—convened meetings to consider the further, gloomier implications of what Kaplan was saying."[26]

Clinton not only continued to cite Kaplan, but he also began to deploy phrases that might have been lifted from Huntington.[27] He warned graduates of the U.S. Naval Academy that, because of the cold war's end, America faced "a new world threatened with instability, even abject chaos, rooted in the economic dislocations that are inherent in the change from communist to market economics, rooted in religious and ethnic battles long covered over by authoritarian regimes now gone, rooted in tribal slaughters, aggravated by environmental disaster, by abject hunger by mass migrations."[28] He advised the French parliament that the West had to unite to confront a global rise of "militant nationalism" that was "transforming the healthy pride of nations, tribes, religious and ethnic groups into cancerous prejudice, eating away at states and leaving their people addicted to the political pain-killers of violence and demagoguery."[29] Clinton also endorsed Benjamin Barber's "Jihad vs. McWorld" at a breakfast gathering of religious leaders that was broadcast by C-SPAN.[30] The propositions of global chaos theory echoed well outside of the Clinton administration as well, finding disciples in the Republican-controlled Congress. House Speaker Newt Gingrich publicly proselytized on behalf of the writings of Alvin Toffler (the man who popularized the concept of "culture shock," a key form of anomie) and privately viewed himself as "the arouser of those who form civilization," the defender of Western values against their foreign and domestic enemies.[31]

Global chaos theory also gained important followings overseas. At the United Nations, the high commissioner for refugees warned of "an alarming upsurge of hostile and xenophobic attitudes."[32] Huntington's article was widely interpreted abroad as a statement of official (if perhaps undeclared) U.S. policy. In Japan and Malaysia, prominent conservatives argued that Washington had concluded that a "clash of civilizations" with the emerging economic powers of East Asia was inevitable and that these countries should start making their own counterpreparations.[33] Both Russians and Arabs argued over how the looming clash of civilizations might affect their societies.[34] On the day that Germany decided to end its "critical dialogue" with Iran, Samuel Huntington was lecturing to the German parliament in Bonn.[35]

If the global chaos theorists were trying to replicate the success of Kennan's "X" telegram, to translate their work into the foundations of American strategy for the new epoch, they failed. But it is not as if anyone else succeeded. Fukuyama's ideas, which attracted even greater attention, were also rejected. The problem may have been that the United States was not ready for a new grand strategy. Its citizens had always been sharply divided over foreign policy issues. A huge gap always existed between the isolationist preferences and Wilsonian enthusiasms of the American in the street and the internationalist convictions and realpolitic skepticism that prevailed among the foreign policy elite. These internal divisions had been submerged or held in abeyance during the cold war because a pressing external threat compelled national unity. But the united spirit of that epoch had not emerged spontaneously. Men such as John Foster Dulles and Dean Rusk had worked hard to build a bipartisan consensus on foreign policy that made common adoption and sustained pursuit of the containment strategy possible.[36]

In the 1990s no clear external threat arose, no bipartisan consensus emerged, and no great national interest in building one was evident. The great political debates of the period focused on domestic, not foreign, policy. Instead, U.S. foreign policy was being made in a national environment that resembled conditions before World War II. The foreign policy elite was divided internally into diverse factions. Foreign policy decisions tended to be made ad hoc, pastiched together by political coalitions that formed to deal with a single event. And, lacking a strong public mandate, executive action tended to be cautious, reactive rather than proactive, or outright waffling.

The global chaos theorists had attained about as much policy influence as was possible in this kind of environment. Their vision had not imposed itself on Washington, but their soundbites were popular in all the major branches of government. Their recommendations were not being systematically, deliberately pursued; but their epigrams had a slow, steady influence on the way many people thought and acted. In the context of the 1990s, that had to be counted as, if not total victory, at least an impressive success.

The motto of one prestigious Washington think tank is that "ideas matter." This may still be true, but in the 1990s the pithiest ideas, the ones that fit most easily inside a fortune cookie, tended to matter most. The elements of global chaos theory that seeped into American public consciousness passed this test. What counted in Washington was the soundbite, the bumper sticker, the photo op, and the vivid image—and global chaos theory supplied many of these. In the 1960s, when Robert S. McNamara's "wiz kids" were applying systems theory to the Pentagon, chaos theory might have been appropriated wholesale. But in the 1990s foreign policy wonks were no longer "mandarins"; they had become courtiers.[37] Discussions among policymakers in America increasingly resembled repartee and innuendo that earned admiration at the eighteenth century French court: The bon mot had the last word.

CHAPTER SEVEN

The Age
of Fratricide

Global chaos theory is an intellectually elegant construct, built on well-established traditions. It offered Americans a sense of direction, when the end of the cold war had sowed confusion and division. Much can be said in its favor. Unfortunately, chaos theory is seriously flawed as an understanding of what is going on in the world.

All global chaos theorists believe, like Huntington, that values are important—that the disruption of values, the destruction of cultural restraints is provoking the new wave of savage violence that they see engulfing the world. But Huntington had given this concept a distinctive twist. He claimed that values were divided into natural families, that is, civilizations. Bosniaks and Turks and Saudis and Iranians did have slightly different values, but, in a more basic and fundamental sense, they all shared in the same civilization: Islam.[1] While they might conflict with each other, they were likely to rally together whenever they were confronted by a threat from a non–Muslim civilization.[2]

Civilizations derived their common values from a shared history, economic and political linkages, and, most important, a common religion. According to Huntington, religion was the ultimate foundation of a society's values. He thought that the import of religion had been generally underestimated by social scientists. In his studies of democratization, for example, he concluded that the advance of liberty had consistently been preceded by certain changes in the religious sphere. The first global wave of democratization had been concentrated in Protestant countries. More recently, a wave of democratization had been pioneered by Portugal in 1974 then spread throughout Latin America and to other Catholic countries. Recent changes in Catholic doctrine had finally made these countries amenable to freedom. Other cultures, meanwhile, remained resistant. Huntington warned that "'Confucian democracy' is clearly a contradiction in terms."[3]

This idea about the fundamental importance of religion was not original to Huntington. He appears to have picked it up in the same place that he acquired the phrase "clash of civilizations"—from the writings of Bernard Lewis, a highly respected historian of the Middle East at Princeton University.[4]

Lewis was one of the last great defenders of the central dogma of Orientalism—the claim that Islam had always been and still remained the primary source of values and thus the chief determinant of social behavior, political identity, artistic practices, and just about every other facet of civilization in the Muslim world.

> For most of the last fourteen centuries, the determinant of identity and loyalty in the Middle East has been religion—not country, not language, not ethnic origin, but membership of the religio-political community of Islam. The attempt during the last hundred years to introduce new political loyalties based on such themes as patriotism and nationalism was due very largely to the working of foreign, chiefly European, ideas, which are now denounced and rejected as such by those who seek a return to what they regard as Islamic values.[5]

For an Orientalist, then, even today the best way to get to the heart of Middle Eastern society is by studying the language and analyzing the texts of the Islamic classics and showing how they structure the Muslim's world view.[6]

One natural corollary of this dogma is that Muslim societies not only exhibit a great number of traits in common, but also form a largely cohesive unit, a civilization.

> Islam has not yet undergone the differentiation which has overtaken Christianity in the last few centuries. Islam, not only chronologically, is in its fourteenth not its twentieth century; it has still to experience the processes of reform and secularization which have transformed

and divided the once-united Christian world. In modern times, Islamic identity has been reinforced by a new shared experience—the penetration, domination, and (in most areas) the departure of European colonialists.[7]

Much of Lewis's work in recent years has focused upon demonstrating that, because Islamic society was so homogenous, so comprehensive, the shock of its domination by the West over the last century was unusually traumatic.[8]

This trauma formed the theme of Lewis's most influential article (if only because Huntington relied upon it), "The Roots of Muslim Rage."[9] This was an expanded version of a speech Lewis wrote when he was invited to give the 1990 Jefferson Lecture, "the highest honor accorded by the U.S. government to a scholar for achievement in the humanities."[10] In it, Lewis asked why Muslims focused their anger on the United States, a country that had not participated in the nineteenth century colonization of Muslim societies by the West. His explanation was that Muslim ire was not a response to imperialism or to support for Israel or to CIA meddling. Instead, it was a reaction to the threat Western values posed to the traditional Islamic way of life.

For a long time now there has been a rising tide of rebellion against this Western paramountcy, and a desire to reassert Muslim values and restore Muslim greatness. The Muslim has suffered successive stages of defeat. The first was his loss of domination in the world, to the advancing power of Russia and the West. The second was the undermining of his authority in his own country, through an invasion of foreign ideas and laws and ways of life and sometimes even foreign rulers or settlers, and the enfranchisement of native non-Muslim elements. The third—the last straw—was the challenge to his mastery in his own house, from emancipated women and rebellious children. It was too much to endure, and the outbreak of rage against these alien, infidel, and incomprehensible forces that had subverted his dominance, disrupted his society, and finally violated the sanctuary of his home was inevitable.[11]

And, although the United States might not have participated much in the imperialist movement of the nineteenth century, it was at the forefront of the crusade to propagate Western values. Thus, "since the United States is the legitimate heir of European civilization and the recognized and unchallenged leader of the West, the United States has inherited the resulting grievances and become the focus for the pent-up hate and anger."[12]

Lewis appears to have been one of the key sources that persuaded Huntington that civilizations acted as units, got angry when their values were challenged, and collided with one another in spasms of unusually fanatic violence.[13] Certainly his "The Clash of Civilizations?" focused upon the long conflict of Islam with the West as the key metaphor, the icon that illustrated how and why civilizations challenged each other. He recounted for readers a long series of apocalyptic confrontations between Islam and the West: the battle of Tours (732), the retaking of Jerusalem by the First Crusade (1099), the fall of Constantinople (1453), and the two Ottoman sieges of Vienna (1556 and 1689). He even portrays Operation Desert Storm in 1991 as just the latest in this long series of clashes. Huntington suggests that most of the warfare along the velvet curtain of culture that divides central Europe has been with Islam.[14]

Unfortunately for Huntington, the idea that civilizations form discrete units that compete with one another is not generally popular. Particularly in Middle East studies, it has been challenged and, for many, discredited. While the Orientalists contributed a great deal to Western understanding of Islam, their claim that Islamic societies cling together as a homogenous civilization has not withstood close scrutiny.

The central tenets of Orientalism were already under attack in the 1960s.[15] Perhaps the worst assault they suffered came, almost inadvertently, from an anthropologist at Princeton. In 1968 Clifford Geertz's *Islam Observed: Religious Development in Morocco and Indonesia* was published. Geertz's avowed purpose in this monograph was to "both lay out a general framework for the comparative analysis of religion and to apply it to a study of the development of a supposedly single creed, Islam, in two quite contrasting civilizations, the Indonesian and the Moroccan."[16] For students of the Middle East, however, the comparison of two distinctive Muslim societies, not the general framework, was most memorable. Geertz showed that, despite sharing a common religion and certain symbols associated with it, Indonesia and Morocco were parts of radically different civilizations. One was a densely populated island in the tropics, where people lived in peasant villages and practiced an Islam that has been "adaptive, absorbent, pragmatic, and gradualistic." The other was a desert expanse inhabited by tribal population that evolved a version of Islam characterized by "aggressive fundamentalism, an active attempt to impress a seamless orthodoxy on the entire population."[17]

Cultural conditions in the two societies contrasted so sharply that Islam itself, as practiced in the two, was almost two different religions.

> In short, to say that Morocco and Indonesia are both Islamic societies, in the sense that most everyone in them (well over nine-tenths of the population in either case) professes to be a Muslim, is as much to point up their differences as it is to locate their similarities. Religious faith, even when it is fed from a common source, is as much a particularizing force as a generalizing one, and indeed whatever universality a given religious tradition manages to attain arises from its ability to engage a widening set of individual, even idiosyncratic, conceptions of life and yet somehow sustain and elaborate them all.[18]

Since *Islam Observed* was published, several generations of Middle East scholars who reject the assumptions of Orientalism have been trained and increasingly dominate the field.[19]

Huntington's Orientalist assumption that the cultural values that distinguish civilizations ultimately derive from religion is not only a problem for his analysis of Islam, but also for other regions. Detailed studies, based on special surveys, of how values differ within and between countries is reshaping ideas about where the fault lines between civilizations fall. They reveal, for example, that within the so-called West profound differences exist between the attitudes of Catholic Europe (France, Austria, Italy, and so on) and those of northern Europe (comprising Britain, Germany, and Scandinavia). Even more surprising, the values of northern Europeans may be more similar to those of Confucian cultures such as China, Japan, and South Korea than they are to those of Eastern Europe (Russia, Czechoslovakia, and so on).[20]

The practical implications of this change for Huntington and his "The Clash of Civilizations?" thesis were brought home by Fouad Ajami, a leading student of modern Arab politics, when he was invited to write a response to Huntington for the succeeding issue of *Foreign Affairs*. Where Huntington had seen a growing solidarity of Muslims against the West, Ajami recognized a more painful truth: The vast majority of battles in which Muslims participated pitted them against other Muslims. Sometimes, as in Operation Desert Storm, one Muslim state (Iraq) lined up against others (Saudi Arabia, Kuwait, Egypt, and Syria). In other cases, the battle took the form of civil war, such as those bleeding Algeria, Egypt, Afghanistan, Turkey, and dozens of other Islamic states.

Ajami was not writing from a perspective that was completely alien to Huntington's. He, too, was an opponent of "new world order" utopianism. He, too, thought that the great battles of the current time are ones where adherents of opposing value systems face each other. But he had insights into the dynamics of how Islam became politicized that Lewis and Huntington lacked.

We have been hearing from the traditionalists, but we should not exaggerate their power, for traditions are often most insistent and loud when they rupture, when people no longer really believe and when age-old customs lose their ability to keep men and women at home. The phenomenon we have dubbed as Islamic fundamentalism is less a sign of resurgence than of panic and bewilderment and guilt.[21]

Neither Lewis nor Huntington understood that the primary target of the traditionalists was not the West, but the champions of modernity and secularism within Islamic societies. They consistently underestimated the power and durability of these champions. In Algeria, Egypt, and Turkey, "caught between a regime they despised and a reign of virtue they feared, the professionals and the women and the modernists of the middle class threw their support to the forces of 'order.'"[22] Despite their weaknesses, secular states regularly prevailed against those who revolted in the name of Islamic civilization.

Ajami's wider claim that "civilizations do not control states, states control civilizations" was supported by evidence from outside the Muslim world as well. In India, too, the "vast middle class" would defend the tradition of secularism. He even challenged the idea that the war in Bosnia had anything to do with clashing civilizations.

"An outsider who travels the highway between Zagreb and Belgrade is struck not by the decisive historical fault line which falls across the lush Slavonian plain but by its opposite. Serbs and Croats speak the same language, give or take a few hundred words, have shared the same village way of life for centuries." The cruel genius of Slobodan Milošević and Franjo Tudjman, men on horseback familiar in lands and situations of distress, was to make their bids for power into grand civilizational undertakings—the ramparts of the Enlightenment defended against Islam or, in Tudjman's case, against the heirs of the Slavic-Orthodox faith. Differences had to be magnified.[23]

The battles in Bosnia did not much resemble Tours or Lepanto. Instead of pitting the contrasting forces of cross and crescent, they involved men who looked the same, spoke the same, and had often known each other intimately for their entire lives.

No physical differences existed among Bosnian Muslims, Serbs, and Croats, all of whom are descended from the same Slavic stock. And despite strident assertions by all sides, no consistent linguistic differences are apparent among these groups either. Although Serbs insist upon writing with Cyrillic characters and Croats with Roman, each of the major dialects of Serbo-Croat is spoken by large numbers of both groups—and Muslims, Serbs, and Croats speak the same dialect in Bosnia.[24] This absence of physical or linguistic distinctions has led some observers—including Kaplan and Huntington—to emphasize the religious dimension of the conflict.

The three contending Bosnian populations all manifest microcultural differences to some extent, but, except for the religious factors, these are relatively so slight that it is hard to imagine that they could be the source for so much intense mutual animosity among them. But as we have already noted, each differs from the others in its elemental form of religion. The religious differences among Catholic Croats, Orthodox Serbs, and Muslims in Bosnia run much deeper than mere matters of dogma or the name of a single God in whom they all believe. The differences go to the root of all the belligerents' innate sense of universal human reality and their own unique place within it. Each sees the others as posing a threat to its belief in the "way things are" and "must be."[25]

However, a major problem exists with this resort to religion as the explanation of the conflict: Few, if any, of the participants claim to be motivated by religion or show any real interest in religion on or off the battlefield.[26]

A thirty-year-old survey conducted in a Bosnian peasant village suggested that, within its Muslim community, 55 percent described themselves as "traditional believers," 7 percent as "vacillating believers," and 1 percent as "theologically convinced believers." Thirty-six-and-one-half percent of the Muslims described themselves as atheists, which meant that 63.5 percent—the first three groups—were in some sense "believers" in Islam. Looked at another way, however, only 1 percent of the population practiced the kind of Islam that prevailed in the Middle East. The Serbs in the district were even less religious than the local Muslims; only 42.1 percent were believers of any sort.[27]

Most evidence indicates that over the succeeding decades the level of religiosity declined further. For one thing, the urban population was always less religious than its country cousins; and urbanization had progressed steadily. This particularly affected the Muslims, who made up a disproportionate share of the urban population. By the time Yugoslavia dissolved, Bosnia's Muslim community was among the most highly secularized in the world. A nationwide poll conducted in 1985 suggested that only 17 percent of Bosnia's Muslims thought of themselves as believers in Islam.[28] (One estimate suggests only 3 percent of the population attended mosques.)[29] "Muslim" identity tended to be a strictly cultural classification defined not by common convictions but by common customs, including

> Muslim names, circumcision, baklava and the celebration of Ramazan Bajram [the feast that marks the end of the fasting month of Ramadan], getting a godparent to cut a one-year-old child's hair, a preference for tiny coffee cups without handles, a sympathy for spiders and various other traditional practices, the origins of which are frequently unknown to those who practice them.[30]

The extent of secularization was especially evident in the ease with which Bosnian Muslims intermarried with non-Muslims. Already in

1981, 15.8 percent of Bosnian children were the products of mixed marriages.[31] In Sarajevo the figure was even higher—45 percent of families
were mixed, and members were often not even certain to which community their spouses belonged.[32] Bosnian Muslims have never been linguisti-
cally or physiologically distinguishable from their Serb and Croat neighbors; by the 1980s at least the urban branches of these three communities
had also come to share similar values.[33]

During the war, religion was invoked most often to explain the motives
of one's opponents rather than the objectives of one's own community.
Thus, the propaganda of the Serb separatists regularly emphasized the
idea that the Muslim Bosniaks were "fundamentalists" who sought to
create an Iranian-style Islamic republic in Bosnia by means of a jihad or
holy war.[34] However, most of the Bosniaks—and the many Serbs and
Croats who fought for the Bosnian government—hoped their country
would keep alive the cosmopolitan, multiconfessional identity that they
had admired in the old Yugoslavia. Even after years of war and ethnic
cleansing had produced a backlash within the Bosniak community, it bred
not a religious revival but a Muslim nationalism that strikingly resembled
its Croat and Serb counterparts.[35]

Bosnia's Muslims did not have much in common with their Middle
Eastern cousins. Until recently, they thought of themselves primarily as
Yugoslavs, and all still think of themselves as Europeans. They prefer to
wear berets, not fezzes. Many like a drink of wine or beer once in a while.
And the war in Bosnia was not a "clash of civilizations" that pitted
Occidentals against Orientals. It was a fratricide among people who
spoke the same language, shared the same love of phyllo dough and plum
brandy, and had traded and intermarried for centuries. The Bosniaks still
have much more in common even with the Serbs and the Croats than
they ever will with the Iranians or the Saudis.

Few global chaos theorists had Ajami's level of understanding about
the roots of the conflict in Bosnia. But many had noticed the wider point
that he was making. The wave of conflicts that seemed to sweep the
world did not cluster along civilizational fault lines. In many cases it
focused not only on neighboring societies but also on neighborhoods. A
high percentage of the new conflicts were, as Enzensberger had noted,
civil wars.

The information in table 7-1 helps to illustrate this point. All wars that
were active between 1980 and 1993, and thus might be considered part

Table 7-1. Active Wars between 1980 and 1995

Country	Dates	Number of deaths			Civilian deaths as a percent of total	Clashing civilizations
		Civilian	Military	Total		
Guatemalan government versus Indians	1966–95	100,000	40,000	140,000	71	No
Philippine government versus Communists	1972–94	20,000	20,000	40,000	50	No
Philippine government versus Muslims	1972–95	20,000	15,000	35,000	57	Yes
Eritrean revolt against Ethiopia	1974–92	500,000	75,000	575,000	87	No
Indonesia invades East Timor	1975–82	100,000	50,000	150,000	67	No
Morocco versus Sahrawi insurrection	1976–87	3,000	13,000	16,000	19	No
Angolan civil war	1975–95	n.a.	n.a.	750,000	n.a.	No
Ethiopia versus Somalia	1976–83	15,000	24,000	39,000	38	No
Cambodia versus Vietnam	1978–89	14,000	51,000	65,000	22	No
Iranian civil strife	1978–89	70,000	18,000	88,000	80	No
Afghan civil war and USSR	1978–92	1,000,000	500,000	1,500,000	67	Yes
El Salvador rebels versus government	1979–91	50,000	25,000	75,000	67	No
Jamaican election violence	1980	1,000	0	1,000	100	No
South Korean government against students	1980	1,000	0	1,000	100	No
Brazilian right versus left	1980	n.a.	n.a.	1,000	n.a.	No
Burma: Communists versus government	1980	n.a.	n.a.	5,000	n.a.	No
Nigeria: Islamists versus government	1980–81	n.a.	n.a.	5,000	n.a.	No
Chadian civil war	1980–87	2,000	5,000	7,000	29	Yes
Iran versus Iraq	1980–88	50,000	450,000	500,000	10	No
Peru: Shining Path versus government	1980–95	25,000	10,000	35,000	71	No
Ghana: Konkomba versus Nanumba	1981	n.a.	n.a.	1,000	n.a.	No
Ugandan army versus civilians	1981–87	300,000	8,000	308,000	97	No
Nicaraguan contras versus Sandinistas	1981–88	15,000	15,000	30,000	50	No
Mozambique civil war	1981–94	1,000,000	50,000	1,050,000	95	No
Syrian government versus Islamists	1982	20,000	0	20,000	100	No

Conflict	Years					
Argentina versus UK	1982	0	1,000	1,000	0	Yes
Lebanon versus Israel	1982–90	41,000	22,000	63,000	65	Yes
Zimbabwe political violence	1983–84	2,000	0	2,000	100	No
Chinese government executions	1983–84	5,000	0	5,000	100	No
South African ethnopolitical violence	1983–94	16,000	0	16,000	100	Yes
Ethnic violence in India	1983–95	n.a.	n.a.	37,000	0	Yes
Nigeria: Islamists versus government	1984	n.a.	n.a.	1,000	n.a.	No
Tamils versus Sinhala in Sri Lanka	1984–95	23,000	27,000	50,000	46	Yes
Sudanese civil war	1984–95	1,460,000	40,000	1,500,000	97	Yes
Turkish government versus Kurds	1984–95	4,000	14,000	18,000	22	No
Reprisals for Liberian coup attempt	1985–88	5,000	0	5,000	100	No
Burma: rebels versus government	1985–95	n.a.	n.a.	8,000	n.a.	No
South Yemeni civil war	1986–87	7,000	4,000	11,000	64	No
Colombian government versus civilians	1986–95	36,000	9,000	45,000	80	No
Chilean government versus miners	1987	3,000	0	3,000	100	No
China versus Vietnam	1987	0	1,000	1,000	0	No
Iraqi government versus Kurds	1988	9,000	1,000	10,000	90	No
Burundi Tutsi massacre Hutu	1988–95	170,000	0	170,000	100	No
Somali civil war	1988–95	350,000	5,000	355,000	99	No
Romanian government versus demonstrators	1989	1,000	0	1,000	100	No
Chinese government versus students	1989	1,000	0	1,000	100	No
Panama versus United States	1989	1,000	0	1,000	100	Yes
Armenia versus Azerbaijan	1989–95	n.a.	n.a.	20,000	n.a.	Yes
Kuwait and United States versus Iraq	1990–91	100,000	100,000	200,000	50	Yes
Chad: government versus southern rebellion	1990–94	n.a.	n.a.	6,000	n.a.	No
Liberian civil war	1990–95	n.a.	n.a.	150,000	n.a.	No
Shi'a and Kurds revolt in Iraq	1991–92	n.a.	n.a.	30,000	n.a.	No
Ethnic violence in Nigeria	1991–92	5,000	0	5,000	100	No
Haiti: political coup and U.S. intervention	1991–94	n.a.	n.a.	3,000	n.a.	No

(continued)

Table 7-1. Active Wars between 1980 and 1995 (Continued)

Country	Dates	Number of deaths			Civilian deaths as a percent of total	Clashing civilizations
		Civilian	Military	Total		
Sierra Leonean civil war	1991–95	n.a.	n.a.	30,000	n.a.	No
Ethnic violence in Kenya	1991–95	n.a.	n.a.	1,500	n.a.	No
Afghan factions vie for government	1991–95	n.a.	n.a.	50,000	n.a.	No
Croatia: Serbs versus Croats	1992	n.a.	n.a.	25,000	n.a.	Yes
Moldova: Russians versus Rumanians	1992	n.a.	n.a.	1,000	n.a.	No
Rwandan Tutsi versus Hutu	1992	2,000	0	2,000	100	No
Georgia versus Ossetians	1992–95	n.a.	n.a.	3,000	n.a.	No
Bosnia: Serbs versus Muslims versus Croats	1992–95	n.a.	n.a.	263,000	n.a.	Yes
Algerian government versus Islamists	1992–95	n.a.	n.a.	50,000	n.a.	No
Tajikistan: Communists versus Muslims	1992–95	n.a.	n.a.	50,000	n.a.	No
Georgia versus Abkhazians	1992–95	n.a.	n.a.	3,000	n.a.	Yes
Congo: ethnic violence	1993	n.a.	n.a.	2,000	n.a.	No
Ghana: ethnic violence	1994	n.a.	n.a.	1,000	n.a.	No
Yemen: government versus secessionists	1994	n.a.	n.a.	7,000	n.a.	No
Pakistan: ethnic, religious killings	1994–95	2,000	0	2,000	100	No
Russia versus Chechens	1994–95	24,000	6,000	30,000	80	Yes
Iraqi Kurds	1994–95	n.a.	n.a.	2,000	n.a.	No
Rwanda: ethnic massacres	1994–95	n.a.	n.a.	500,000	n.a.	No

Source: Ruth Leger Sivard, *World Military and Social Expenditures 1996* (Washington: World Priorities, 1996), pp. 18–19.
n.a. Not available.

of the new wave of violence, are listed. Only a handful (sixteen out of seventy-two) could plausibly be considered clashes of civilization. And some of these—such as the battle of Armenia and Azerbaijan—fit uncomfortably in that category. (Iran, for example, tended to back Christian Armenia against Muslim Azerbaijan.) In contrast, forty-three out of seventy-two (60 percent) were internal wars pitting government troops against rebels or secessionists.

Far from witnessing a clash of civilizations, most analysts—including a majority of global chaos theorists—thought the world was in an age of fratricide (see box on the long-term changes in the pattern of warfare). They thought this was one of the traits that most clearly distinguished "the new world disorder" from the cold war epoch, when warfare was prompted mostly by nationalisms and ideologies. The putative ravages of

Long-Term Changes in the Pattern of Warfare

Until the end of World War II, Europe was the most warlike region of the world. The classic study of the subject, Lewis Richardson's *Statistics of Deadly Quarrels*, showed that from 1820 until 1945, the countries most often involved in wars were (in descending order) Great Britain, France, Russia, Turkey, China, Spain, Germany or Prussia, Italy or Piedmont, and Austria.[41] For most of modern times, wars were caused by major (overwhelmingly European) powers attacking one another or weaker, non-European states.

After World War II, however, the pattern began to change. Although the United States and the USSR occasionally sent their own troops into combat in countries such as Korea or Hungary, increasingly they relied upon proxies to do the fighting for them. The whole locale of battle shifted away from Europe and into what was dubbed "the third world." And the organization of battle increasingly moved from what World War II had defined as "conventional warfare" toward increasing use of irregular troops, guerrilla tactics, and what eventually was dubbed "low-intensity conflict."

(continued)

Long-Term Changes in the Pattern of Warfare
(Continued)

The experts still do not agree about what wrought this change. Many claim that it was a direct result of the invention of nuclear weapons. Because both the United States and the USSR recognized that they possessed the ability to annihilate each other entirely, they chose to confine their struggle instead to the safer form of proxy; third world, low-intensity conflicts.[42] Others suggest that it reflects a deeper and more profound change—a transformation of values in industrial (especially democratic) societies that makes them less reluctant to engage in aggression, or perhaps just more fearful of military casualties of any sort.[43]

Whatever the truth of such claims, conventional wars clearly are now rarer than low-intensity conflicts. For that matter, even among third world countries, international conflicts are much rarer than civil strife. Beginning around 1970, the number of internal wars as a percentage of all wars began to steadily increase.[44] In 1994 and 1995 all of the world's major armed conflicts were internal.[45]

Internal wars can result from the clash of distinct cultures. But they tend to be cultures that are familiar with each other and often closely related to one another. The preponderance of internal war in today's world confirms that it is passing through an age of fratricide.

anomie and the fight over values usually exhibited themselves in battles among members of the same community. They increasingly appeared to take the form of "ethnic conflicts" (see box on ethnic conflicts).

As of 1996 all of the "hot" or active wars around the globe were civil wars. The clear predominance of fratricide among contemporary wars poses major problems for Huntington's analysis—but it also raises some questions about global chaos theory as a whole. In civil wars, the parties confronting each other are usually not wildly alien or unfamiliar to each other. Often they share large numbers of social traits and are distin-

What Makes a Conflict Ethnic?

As the fratricidal nature of warfare in the 1990s became evident, references to such battles as "ethnic conflicts" became more popular. The choice of phrase was unfortunate, because only a minority of these battles were ethnic conflicts.

The term "ethnic" had evolved radically over the years. It came from a Greek root and originally meant an alien or unbeliever. During the 1950s the prominent anthropologist Ashley Montagu popularized it as a preferred alternative to the older and less scientific concept of "race." Most people thought that race referred to a common pool of genetic characteristics. Montagu showed that commonly used racial categories were cultural constructs that bore little or no resemblance to the realities of gene pools. The huge group that Westerners call "blacks" contains incredible genetic diversity. Several genetic groups that are labeled "black" are more closely related to Caucasians than they are to other blacks.[46]

As a result, the term "ethnic" was applied to a group of people sharing common cultural characteristics. By the 1960s, with the debate generated by the civil rights movement in the United States, it had come to refer to groups that shared the same political system but were culturally distinct.[47] Usage of the term was always sloppy: Americans tended to think that blacks and Irish were ethnic groups, but not Protestants and Catholics—yet they would speak of Hindu and Muslim Indians or Sunni and Shiᶜa Iraqis as if they were ethnic groups.[48]

The same sloppiness is evident now that the term has been increasingly applied to international affairs. Consider the war in Bosnia. Serbs and Croat elites had developed a sense of national consciousness before World War I. That consciousness developed further when the two groups were united into Yugoslavia during the interwar period and erupted with great violence during World War II. Their battles during that war, and again after 1991, were similar to those between Czechs and Germans over Bohemia. Was World

(continued)

> ## What Makes a Conflict Ethnic? *(Continued)*
>
> War II therefore an "ethnic conflict"? Few would claim so, because the concept of "ethnic conflict" has come to carry a connotation of pettiness, atavism, and irrationality that is incompatible with ideas about the great struggle against fascism.[49]
>
> An oft-cited 1993 article in the *New York Times* counted forty-eight major ethnic conflicts in the world.[50] Of these, seven were clearly nationalist battles, albeit ones involving minorities trapped outside their kin state: Bosnia, Croatia, Northern Ireland, Romania, Moldova, Azerbaijan, and Bhutan. Another eleven were national conflicts involving insurgencies by groups seeking to secede and form independent states: Spain, Russia, Georgia, Turkey, Iraq, Israel, India, Sri Lanka, China, Indonesia, and Papua New Guinea. Six were civil wars where the battle was not over ethnic issues: Algeria, Egypt, Somalia, Tajikstan, Cambodia, and Colombia. That left only twenty-four conflicts that could be labeled "ethnic" with confidence: Germany, Sudan, Mauritania, Mali, Chad, Senegal, Liberia, Togo, Nigeria, Uganda, Rwanda, Burundi, Kenya, Zaire, Angola, South Africa, Afghanistan, Pakistan, Bangladesh, Myanmar, Fiji, Guatemala, Peru, and Brazil. Thus, only half as many ethnic conflicts may have occurred as a cursory reading of the article implied.[51]

guished by only a handful of others. In Bosnia, the similarities between Muslims (Bosniaks), Serbs, and Croats were so strong that to determine the ethnicity of prisoners they were sometimes ordered to drop their pants—to reveal who had been circumcised. Hutu and Tutsi speak the same language and follow the same faiths; experts claim that efforts by Rwandans to categorize one or the other on the basis of physical characteristics fail half of the time.[36]

Many civil wars and ethnic conflicts involve what Freud called "the tyranny of small differences": an apparent obsession with tiny distinctions that are almost invisible to outsiders. If xenophobia plays any role in producing such obsessions, it works in conjunction with a much more obvious and powerful force—the stresses and strains of living together, of having to share the same resources, of working within the same political system to see "who gets what when."[37] Frustrations and feelings of injustice are most likely to be expressed in the tyranny of small differences among groups that are intermingled, that share much in common.

This is, some scholars have noted, what makes internal wars more difficult to end than international conflicts. In international wars, the combatants have only to agree to a common border and some indemnities that permit them to coexist at arm's length. When a civil war ends, both sides must not only stop fighting but also agree about how they are going to work together to build a common government—often one that has to survive the stresses of old disagreements.[38]

Put this way, intercultural cooperation or ethnic coexistence seemingly would not stand a chance. Building any government is hard, much less one that heals old wounds. How can a state survive when every decision about the distribution of resources might be interpreted as an ethnic slight? Yet, remarkably, it happens all the time. In every society, the politics of distributing scarce resources entails the risk that different groups—whether their identity is defined by ethnicity, region, or class—will feel aggrieved and try to either withdraw from the system or dominate it. One of the central purposes of politics is to find ways to distribute things without fatally antagonizing people.

Most societies, in all periods of history, have been multicultural and multiethnic. The idea that a country might be made ethnically pure is a modern one that only became popular in the late nineteenth century.[39] It is almost as if a counterforce existed to xenophobia, something that held people together despite their differences. A whole school of psychology has grown up, which claims that life among diversity is natural to people as well as appealing.[40] To put it bluntly, the exotic is erotic.

Whatever the exact psychological or sociological explanation may be, cultural coexistence is commonplace. As near as scholars can tell, multiethnic societies do not seem to be any more likely than homogenous societies to become involved in domestic or international wars (see table 7-2).

With a will, and some skill, people can find ways to live together. And great benefits derive from doing so. It sure beats ethnic cleansing.

Table 7-2. *Ethnic Homogeneity and Culture Conflict*

Country	Rank	Ethnic homogeneity index	Culture war	Culture strife
Tanzania	135	7		
Uganda	134	10		✔
Zaire	133	10	✔	
Cameroon	132	11		
India	131	11	✔	
South Africa	130	12	✔	
Nigeria	129	13		✔
Ivory Coast	128	14		
Kenya	127	17		✔
Chad	126	17	✔	
Liberia	125	17	✔	
Zambia	124	18		
Mali	123	22		
Angola	122	22		
Sierra Leone	121	23	✔	
Iran	120	24		✔
Indonesia	119	24		✔
Yugoslavia	118	25		✔
Guinea	117	25		
Canada	116	25		✔
Philippines	115	26		✔
Gambia	114	27		
Sudan	113	27	✔	
Niger	112	27		
Senegal	111	28		
Malaysia	110	28		
Togo	109	29		
Ghana	108	29		
Nepal	107	30		
Gabon	106	31		
Ethiopia	105	31	✔	
Central African Republic	104	31		✔
Burkina Faso	103	32		
Bolivia	102	32		
Soviet Union	101	33	✔	
Thailand	100	34		
Congo	99	34		✔
Afghanistan	98	34	✔	
Mozambique	97	35		
Pakistan	96	36		✔
Guatemala	95	36	✔	
Malawi	94	38		
Colombia	94	24		✔
Benin	93	38		
Laos	92	40		

(continued)

Table 7-2. *Ethnic Homogeneity and Culture Conflict (Continued)*

Country	Rank	Ethnic homogeneity index	Culture war	Culture strife
Peru	91	41	✔	
Mauritius	90	42		
Guyana	89	42		
Trinidad and Tobago	88	44		
Belgium	87	45		
Zimbabwe	86	46		
Morocco	85	47		✔
Ecuador	84	47		
Botswana	83	49		
United States	82	50		✔
Switzerland	81	50		
Czechoslovakia	80	51		
Sri Lanka	79	53	✔	
Union of Myanmar	78	53		✔
Spain	77	56		✔
Algeria	76	57	✔	
Taiwan	75	58		
Singapore	74	58		
Papua New Guinea	73	58		
Mongolia	72	62		
New Zealand	71	63		
Iraq	70	64	✔	
Cyprus	69	65		✔
Mauritania	68	67		✔
Australia	67	68		
United Kingdom	66	68		✔
Argentina	65	69		
Mexico	64	70		✔
Cambodia	63	70		✔
Panama	62	72		✔
France	61	74		✔
Turkey	60	75	✔	
Romania	59	75		
Libya	58	77		✔
Syria	57	78	✔	
Lesotho	56	78		
Bulgaria	55	78		✔
Uruguay	53	80		
Israel	52	80		✔
Vietnam	51	81		
Kuwait	49	82		✔
Nicaragua	48	82		✔
El Salvador	47	83		
Tunisia	46	84		
Honduras	45	84		

(continued)

Table 7-2. *Ethnic Homogeneity and Culture Conflict (Continued)*

Country	Rank	Ethnic homogeneity index	Culture war	Culture strife
Finland	44	84		
Rwanda	42	86	✔	
Paraguay	41	86		
Chile	40	86		
Lebanon	39	87	✔	
Austria	38	87		
China	37	88		✔
Venezuela	36	89		
Netherlands	35	90		
Hungary	34	90		
Greece	33	90		
Albania	32	91		✔
Sweden	31	92		
Somalia	30	92	✔	
Costa Rica	28	93		
Brazil	27	93		✔
Saudi Arabia	26	94		✔
Madagascar	25	94		
Jordan	23	95		
Jamaica	22	95		
Denmark	20	95		
Norway	19	96		
Italy	18	96		
Ireland	17	95		
Dominican Republic	16	96		
Cuba	15	96		
Burundi	14	96	✔	
Egypt	13	96		✔
Poland	11	97		
Germany	9 and 10	97.5		✔
Yemen	3 and 12	97.5		
Hong Kong	8	98		
Puerto Rico	7	98		
Haiti	6	99		
Japan	5	99		
Portugal	4	99		
South Korea	2	100		
North Korea	1	100		

Source: For ethnic homogeneity index, George Thomas Kurian, *The New Book of World Rankings* (New York: Facts on File, 1991), pp. 47–49.

Note: Germany and Yemen received two rankings because, at the time the ethnic homogeneity index was constructed, each was subdivided into two countries: West Germany and East Germany and North Yemen and South Yemen, respectively.

CHAPTER EIGHT

Globaloney

The chaos theorists outline three distinct mechanisms by which, they claim, globalization triggers violence. First, the linking together of cultural mediums in diverse societies and their infusion by a common low-tech vision breeds violent reaction. Second, economic globalization forces movements of peoples that foster a growth of xenophobia. Third, the wave of democratization in the 1970s and 1980s swept away many of the restraints that authoritarian regimes had previously imposed on atavism.

The chaos theorists have generally been content to make these claims on the basis of slim evidence.[1] In *The Ends of the Earth*, Robert Kaplan traveled to a series of countries where he said global integration was fueling xenophobic violence. But, as Paul Kennedy pointed out, Kaplan's book suffered from a bad case of selection bias. If he had chosen a different travel itinerary—one that took him from Costa Rica's stable democracy to Chile's expanding economy and then to the prosperity of Botswana or the high-tech industry of Bangalore, concluding with the newly industrialized might of Singapore or Taiwan—a different and more sanguine picture of the developing countries would have emerged.[2]

A slightly more systematic test of the claims of the global chaos theorists is possible. The existing data are perhaps not reliable enough to justify doing a full-scale, rigorous statistical analysis with formal correlation coefficients and regressions. However, they will sustain a series of "back-of-the-envelope" sketches, revealing something about the crude plausibility of these claims (see appendix).

One note about terminology may be helpful before introducing the tests. Given the diversity of their outlooks, the global chaos theorists, not surprisingly, never agreed upon a common nomenclature to identify the conflicts they were talking about. What Huntington called "clashes of civilization," Moynihan called "ethnic conflicts" and Enzensberger dubbed "civil wars." The Pentagon, with its inimitable gift for acronyms, called these battles "ENS conflicts," meaning "ethnic, nationalist, separatist conflicts."

All the global chaos theorists agree, however, that what sets these battles apart from conventional contests between ideologies or states is that they arise from the clash of different systems of values, different cultures. Thus, such contests will be called "culture conflicts" or "culture clashes" here. These clashes are further distinguished on the basis of their intensity. The most violent ones, involving organized military units, are dubbed "culture wars." The less violent ones, sometimes involving no more than skirmishes or riots, are called "culture strife."

The Globalization of Culture

Chaos theorists worry that those forces that, with increasing ardor, purvey a low-brow, materialistic, and superficially universalist variant of Western values to the rest of the world will breed a violent reaction. The array of such forces is impressive in its diversity. Any form of contact between the West and the rest of the world may find the former explicitly or implicitly pressing its values on the latter. When a McDonald's opens in Moscow or Beijing, it does more than sell french fries; its mere presence conveys a vision of consumerism as a lifestyle that may be an affront to local values. When tourists—528.4 million of them in 1994—move between cultures, the exchange of values might appear to work both ways.[3] But in practice, Western values usually prevail. To draw hard-currency tourists, Egyptian tombs and Balinese temples have to be surrounded by four-star hotels, Occidental-style restaurants, and multilingual cab stands that do much more to Westernize local society than the mute ruins can do to Orientalize the tourists.[4]

Among the varied vehicles by which Western values are broadcast to the rest of the world, however, information media deserve pride of place. Transmitting words and images is easier and cheaper than goods and people. Books and newspapers make a contribution, albeit one that may be limited by the low literacy rates in many developing countries. Radio and boom boxes also participate, although the diversity of world languages mitigates some of their impact. ("May contain explicit lyrics" warnings are not required when kids in south China listen to Guns 'n Roses cassettes.) Thus, the most potent means for implanting Western values in non–Western societies are the visual media: films, videocassettes, and—arguably more than anything else—television. When globalists argued that the information revolution was making the world safe for universal democracy, they portrayed television as its heavy artillery. And when chaos theorists fret over the growth of the culture clashes, they, too, depict television as the Lord of the Battlefield.[5]

Television and other audio-visual media are supposed to encourage culture conflict through at least three distinct mechanisms. First, they erode traditional values and moral restraints by portraying "the world according to Hollywood," full of glitz and glamour, where morals are loose and action is fast. Second, particularly in developing countries, they inflame the passions by holding out visions of wealth and power, of throbbing sportscars and recumbent women—temptations as alluring as they are (for most viewers) unobtainable. Third, in many societies governments or parties systematically employ the audio-visual media to foster nationalism or less respectable forms of xenophobia.[6] Television performs these tasks with particular effectiveness not only because television programming is rooted in the art of stringing together emotionally powerful icons, but also because the medium itself combines the appeal of "high tech and low culture."[7]

The power of television, rooted in its combination of the sophistication of the most up-to-date microprocessors with the flagrant merchandizing it inherited as the latest embodiment of the world's oldest profession, is so potent that worries about its effects are not confined to non–Western or even developing countries. Even in the United States, a country most chaos theorists think is relatively immune to the downside of globalization, a major debate continues about whether television fosters violence. In Washington, journalists whine about whether their coverage of terrorist incidents provides free advertising for violent minorities, while, in Wausau, mothers worry about the ideas their kids may pick up watching Power Rangers.[8]

Despite (or perhaps because of) the energy and commitment of its participants, the debate over the relationship between television and violence has not produced any policy consensus. "Researchers have been trying to work out the truth for more than 30 years, producing over a thousand studies in America and dozens in Europe. Does screen violence stimulate aggressive behavior, particularly in children? If so, to what extent? . . .

The broad answers seem respectively to be yes, and not a lot."[9] Even those who place primary blame on television for the decay of civility in America admit that it has promoted violence largely through diffuse and indirect mechanisms. For example, Robert Putnam, a political scientist at Harvard University who has often made headlines by stressing the power of culture, claims that television—rather than rising divorce rates, women's liberation, or the expansion of the welfare state—was the overarching cause of the decline of trust and sociability that he says afflicted America after the 1950s. His surveys suggest that, irrespective of their level of education or income, as Americans watched more hours of television they spent less time participating in community activities and voluntary associations.[10] A social atmosphere may have resulted in which Americans were less trusting and more suspicious of one another, and this may have permitted a rise of violence. But the linkage from television to violence is highly indirect and mediated by many other variables. In Japan, cartoons contain much more violence and outright pornography than in America, yet levels of social violence are much lower.

Chaos theorists, however, are concerned about a different issue. They are not interested in whether people emulate the violence they see on television, but in whether viewing any television programming that displays alien values breeds culture conflicts and anomic violence. In this vision, letting children in Côte d'Ivoire watch *Masterpiece Theater* may be as dangerous as allowing them to see *Miami Vice*. This is a much stronger—and less obvious—claim than the idea that people may emulate screen violence.

No systematic studies of this question have been made. Chaos theorists tend to rely upon anecdotal evidence. And on this issue, they tend to resort to vague allusions rather than concrete anecdotes. So to determine the strength of their case, crude, "back-of-the-envelope" studies must be relied upon.

Does any evidence exist that countries that watch more television are more likely to suffer violent culture conflicts? Statistics on how many hours people spend watching the tube are only broadly available for industrialized countries. But, based on countries for which data are available, generally speaking, as people spend more time watching television they buy more television sets. Sales figures for television sets can be collected for a broad array of countries. Table 8-1 relates how many televisions were available for every one thousand people in an array of developed and less developed countries in the late 1980s. (It also tries to

Table 8-1. *The News Media and Culture Conflict*

Country	Number of TV sets	Number of radio sets	Newspapers in circulation	Culture strife	Culture war
Bhutan	n.a.	15	n.a.	xxx	
Rwanda	n.a.	54	n.a.		xxx
Singapore	n.a.	n.a.	357		
Malawi	n.a.	197	2		
Somalia	0	38	n.a.		xxx
Burundi	0	56	n.a.		xxx
Mali	0	37	n.a.		
Mauritania	1	139	n.a.	xxx	
Union of Myanmar	1	79	7	xxx	
Tanzania	1	16	4		
Nepal	1	31	n.a.		
Mozambique	1	36	6		
Zaire	1	98	n.a.		xxx
Chad	1	237	n.a.		xxx
Guinea	2	33	2		
Central African Republic	2	60	n.a.	xxx	
Laos	2	123	n.a.		
Papua New Guinea	2	64	12		
Ethiopia	2	193	1		xxx
Niger	3	163	1		
Bangladesh	3	40	n.a.	xxx	
Congo	3	120	n.a.	xxx	
Benin	4	75	n.a.		
Haiti	4	41	n.a.		
Burkina Faso	5	24	n.a.		
Angola	5	49	11		xxx
Ivory Coast	5	131	8		
Togo	5	178	n.a.		
Madagascar	6	193	6		
Nigeria	6	163	n.a.	xxx	
Kenya	6	90	13	xxx	
Uganda	6	96	2	xxx	
Lesotho	7	68	29		
Botswana	7	130	16		
India	7	77	28		xxx
Afghanistan	8	102	n.a.		xxx
North Yemen	8	34	n.a.		
Sierra Leone	9	216	3		xxx
Namibia	11	123	13		
Cameroon	12	125	3		
North Korea	12	110	n.a.		
Ghana	13	293	n.a.		
Pakistan	14	86	n.a.	xxx	
Fiji	14	573	96	xxx	
Zambia	15	73	14		

(continued)

Table 8-1. *The News Media and Culture Conflict (Continued)*

Country	Number of TV sets	Number of radio sets	Newspapers in circulation	Culture strife	Culture war
		Per 1,000 population			
Guyana	15	303	80		
China	17	184	n.a.	xxx	
Liberia	18	224	n.a.		xxx
Zimbabwe	22	85	24		
Gabon	23	119	15		
Paraguay	24	165	n.a.		
Sri Lanka	31	187	n.a.		xxx
Mongolia	31	128	90		
Senegal	32	103	8		
Vietnam	34	99	n.a.		
Philippines	36	135	n.a.	xxx	
Guatemala	37	65	n.a.		xxx
Indonesia	40	145	16	xxx	
Sudan	52	229	n.a.		xxx
Iran	53	236	n.a.	xxx	
Morocco	56	206	n.a.	xxx	
Syria	58	231	31		xxx
Nicaragua	60	237	n.a.	xxx	
Libya	63	221	n.a.	xxx	
Iraq	64	199	n.a.		xxx
Honduras	67	376	65		
Tunisia	68	171	n.a.		
Jordan	69	237	42		
Algeria	70	227	36		xxx
Bolivia	77	527	n.a.		
Dominican Republic	79	164	42		
Costa Rica	79	258	n.a.		
Ecuador	81	292	n.a.		
El Salvador	82	401	n.a.		
Egypt	83	310	50	xxx	
Albania	83	167	45	xxx	
Peru	84	241	n.a.		xxx
United Arab Emirates	92	319	n.a.		
South Africa	97	319	45		xxx
Thailand	103	174	15		
Colombia	108	167	n.a.	xxx	
Jamaica	108	400	n.a.		
Mexico	120	241	127	xxx	
Cyprus	132	250	124	xxx	
Malaysia	140	436	n.a.		
Venezuela	142	395	n.a.		
Portugal	159	212	47		
Chile	163	335	n.a.		
Panama	163	220	n.a.	xxx	
Romania	166	288	159		

(continued)

Table 8-1. *The News Media and Culture Conflict (Continued)*

| | Per 1,000 population | | | | |
Country	Number of TV sets	Number of radio sets	Newspapers in circulation	Culture strife	Culture war
Turkey	172	160	n.a.		xxx
Uruguay	173	594	n.a.		
Greece	175	411	n.a.		
Yugoslavia	175	n.a.	108	xxx	
Mauritius	188	263	71		
Bulgaria	189	221	316	xxx	
Brazil	191	368	48	xxx	
Cuba	193	334	107		
South Korea	194	986	n.a.		
Argentina	217	659	n.a.		
Ireland	228	580	181		
Hong Kong	241	633	n.a.		
Puerto Rico	247	675	171		
Italy	257	786	99		
Kuwait	261	327	n.a.	xxx	
Poland	263	n.a.	200		
Israel	264	470	n.a.	xxx	
Saudi Arabia	268	272	n.a.	xxx	
Czechoslovakia	285	256	332		
Trinidad and Tobago	290	457	146		
Lebanon	302	772	n.a.		xxx
USSR	314	685	442		xxx
Belgium	320	465	221		
France	333	893	193	xxx	
Norway	348	790	530		
Spain	368	295	75	xxx	
New Zealand	369	923	328		
Finland	374	991	543		
West Germany	385	954	344	xxx	
Denmark	386	879	367		
Sweden	395	875	534		
Bahrain	399	518	43	xxx	
Hungary	402	586	262		
Switzerland	405	400	500		
United Kingdom	434	1,145	421	xxx	
Netherlands	469	908			
Austria	480	358	358		
Australia	483	1,270	264		
Canada	577	953	225	xxx	
Japan	587	863	566		
Oman	739	649	40		
United States	811	2,119	259	xxx	

Source: *The Economist Book of Vital World Statistics* (Time Books, 1990), pp. 126–27.
n.a. Not available.

broaden the sense of how linked these countries are to the global communications revolution by indicating the availability of other major consumer goods: radios, telephones, and automobiles.)

Those countries that experienced culture conflicts in the years since 1980 are indicated in the right-hand columns. These are the cases where culture conflicts might have been triggered or at least aggravated by the intrusion of alien values via television during the preceding decade. In this case, the data are not comprehensive or precise enough to justify doing elaborate statistical analysis, but they are adequate to indicate a general trend. Only a handful of culture wars occurred in countries where television sets were commonplace. The former Yugoslavia was the most prominent such case, combining wars of third world intensity with the same availability of television enjoyed by Denmark. In other TV-intensive societies, what culture clashes existed—Turk-bashing in Germany, Shiᶜite riots in Bahrain, or the secessionist struggles in the Basque lands and northern Ireland—tended to involve either low levels of violence or old struggles that originated long before the "boob tube." The trend becomes even clearer if the countries in the sample are divided into five evenly sized subgroups (quintiles). The results are depicted in table 8-2. Culture conflicts were less common (7–8 percent) among the countries in the two quintiles with the most television sets per capita than among the remaining three quintiles (30+ percent).

The frequency and intensity of violent cultural conflict seems to increase as television sets become scarcer. Mexico, where 8.4 people have to share each television set, seems to mark some sort of threshold: As the ratio of persons per TV rises, violence becomes increasingly common. In Rwanda and Burundi, scenes of some of the worst ethnic violence in recent times, the persons per TV ratio rises to dizzying proportions— imagine 4,860 Burundians clustered around a single black-and-white Sony TV, and you can almost feel the tension and frustration rising among the crowd.

An inverse correlation between the availability of television and the frequency of cultural conflict does not mean any direct causal linkage exists between the two. Correlation does not prove causation. Perhaps both the availability of television and the frequency of cultural violence are themselves symptoms of some third cause? How many people own televisions and other consumer goods rises directly in proportion to the wealth of a country. Burundi is a poor country, which is why it has so few

Table 8-2. *Relationship between Countries with Televisions and Culture Clashes*

	Rank in number of television sets per capita				
	First	Second	Third	Fourth	Fifth
Number of countries	26	25	26	25	26
Number of countries with culture strife	9	7	9	5	6
Number of countries with culture war	2	1	7	5	6
Percent of countries with culture strife	35	28	35	20	23
Percent of countries with culture war	8	4	27	20	23

Source: *The Economist Book of Vital World Statistics*, pp. 126–27.

television sets. And poverty, rather than television, might plausibly be the trigger for conflict in Bujumbura.

A sophisticated global chaos theorist might object that not just the number of television sets determines how disruptive the infusion of alien cultural values will be. The content of television programming makes a difference. When more hours are devoted to broadcasting *Dynasty* or *Love Connection,* television may be more likely to promote conflict than when it confines itself to native films and local news. For that matter, the absolute number of television sets available may be less important than how rapidly television consumption is growing. Most theorists of anomie suggest that the first exposure to alien values is the most shocking. So perhaps in countries where television ownership is rare, but television audiences are just beginning to establish themselves and to grow rapidly, its effects will be most disruptive.

Unfortunately, no studies have done a decent job of measuring local versus imported program content. Figures are available, however, that show how rapidly television markets have been growing. The increased availability of television sets during the 1980s is depicted in figure 8-1. Once again, discerning any pattern that would support the idea that exposure to alien cultural values breeds violence is difficult.

In Somalia and Zaire, where television was introduced during the 1980s, levels of cultural violence were high. But during the same period, television spread through Tanzania, Botswana, Vietnam, and a half dozen other countries where cultural conflict was rare or nonexistent. Similarly, among the countries that showed the most rapid increase in the availability of television, India was plagued by several savage cultural conflicts. In Yemen, too, a dramatic increase in the availability of

Figure 8-1. *Growing Access to TV Sets, 1980–89*

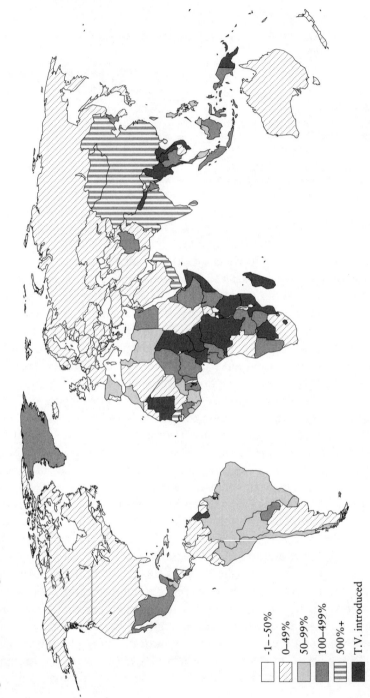

-1--50%

0-49%

50-99%

100-499%

500%+

T.V. introduced

Source: United Nations Department of Economic and Social Information and Policy Analysis, Statistical Division, *Statistical Yearbook, 1990–91* (New York: United Nations, 1993).

television coincided with a short civil war. But in the other countries where the number of television sets grew by 500 percent or more—Mongolia, Oman, and Senegal—no acute cultural conflicts occurred. In the former Yugoslavia the number of television sets per capita increased during the 1980s from 300 to 309. This increase hardly seems likely to have been a major source of conflict. If any connection exists between the increase of television watching and cultural violence, it is a subtle one.

Although crude, this evidence does seem to confound the assertion of the chaos theorists that the global communications revolution produces a xenophobic reaction that fuels cultural violence. Although television watching is becoming widespread, television sets are still a relatively expensive consumer good and simple economics has slowed their spread within the less developed countries. Dish antennas of the type required to receive satellite broadcasts are even more expensive. The real impact of CNN and other supposedly "global" television broadcasts has been confined to serving as an "office intercom for the elite."[11]

Radio, which is both cheaper to obtain and to broadcast, still reaches a dramatically larger share of the world population than television.[12] Yet radio programs tend to be much less culturally intrusive. Broadcasts are much more likely to be in a local language, and there is no such thing as a "hit" international radio program. No radio equivalent of *Baywatch* is being eagerly consumed by unsuspecting non–Western cultures.[13]

Radio programming highlights a contradiction implicit in the claims of the chaos theorists about the impact of electronic communications. On the one hand, they assert that the program content of electronic media will embody Western values that will provoke local envy or anomie. On the other hand, they argue that local governments and parties will take control of the electronic media and use them to reassert local values and traditions. Concrete examples can easily be found of both. In Turkey, renascent Islamic movements are using television to combat the established culture of secular Kemalism.[14] In Iran, Islamic revolutionaries rush to combat the infiltration of American rock videos via MTV that they claim is undermining traditional values.[15] Both trends dampen the likelihood that a single global culture, the homogenization of values that was supposed to lead to the new world order, will evolve soon. Yet these two trends also tend to counterbalance each other, lessening the chance that a clash of cultures will lead to violence. Electronic media can be used to erode local cultures or to defend their values.[16] (Some cultural analysts contend that Western pop culture, far from undermining conservative values, often implicitly defends them with sappy homilies about the importance of family and harmony.)[17] And so long as both processes are occurring, a collapse of local culture into anomie remains unlikely.

The lack of any evidence that increased access to electronic media correlates with increased incidence of cultural violence does not mean that no relationship exists between the two phenomena. In the months before the 1994 massacres in Rwanda, radio stations controlled by the Hutu-dominated government systematically stirred up fears that Tutsi rebels were preparing to murder their Hutu neighbors. As a result, when the mass exterminations of Tutsis began, many Hutus genuinely thought they were acting in self-defense.[18] But this was not a case of the media juxtaposing values and triggering anomie. It was an old-fashioned, albeit unusually deadly, exercise of political propaganda. Adolf Hitler was one of the great modern masters in the use of radio and film propaganda, but this hardly means these media "caused" the Holocaust. A potential relationship exists between the media and cultural violence—but it is one in which the media can be used by political agents to incite and organize conflict, not in which the media spontaneously trigger conflict by themselves.

The Global Wave of Democratization

Chaos theorists also point to a second dimension of globalization that they claim is promoting anomie: democratization. Exactly what qualities of a political system qualify it as a democracy remains a matter of debate—and probably always will.[19] Even so, there is enough concurrence about global trends to allow for some "back-of-the-envelope" calculations. And even these crude calculations again suggest that chaos theorists have greatly exaggerated the force with which democratization might be contributing to global anomie.

Since the early 1970s, Freedom House, a mildly right-of-center nonprofit organization based in New York, has been tracking the growth and retreat of liberties around the world. In the past, their criteria for labeling countries have been criticized for paying too much attention to foreign policy (countries aligned with the United States were more likely to be judged slightly more free than comparable states that clash with Washington), but over the years their evaluations have steadily grown more sophisticated and reliable. Although their evaluation process measures a diverse array of political rights and civil liberties, every year they produce a map of the world that sorts every country into one of three simple categories: free, partly free, or not free.[20] Using such broad blocs makes decisions about how free most countries are blunt but uncontroversial.

The cumulative result of Freedom House surveys between 1986 and 1996 sheds light on the relationship between the political regimes of countries and their incidence of violent cultural conflicts (see figure 8-2). Fully functional democracies—those that remained consistently free from 1986 until 1996—were almost totally immune to violent cultural conflict. During these years, this happy combination of political freedom and freedom from culture clashes could be found in Argentina, Austria, Australia, Belgium, Botswana, Denmark, Ecuador, Finland, Greece, Ireland, Italy, Jamaica, Japan, Mauritius, the Netherlands, New Zealand, Norway, Puerto Rico, Portugal, Sweden, Switzerland, and Uruguay. No stable democracy suffered a violent culture war. In contrast, during the same period, many of those states that had consistently unfree polities suffered from violent culture wars, including Afghanistan, Algeria, Angola, Azerbaijan, Burundi, Iraq, Rwanda, Somalia, Sudan, Syria, Tajikistan, and Zaire. While no form of government can claim to be either wholly pure or totally tainted by ethnic and civil conflict, erecting an authoritarian regime is no guarantee of internal peace.

This does not contradict the predictions of global chaos theorists, who do not argue that democracy breeds cultural violence but, rather, that democratization makes such violence more likely. In particular, they point to two aspects of the democratization process. During the early phases of democratization, as an authoritarian regime decays and "the dead hand of the state looses its grip from the throat of society," many of the restraints that the secret police once imposed on the operations of racist or nationalist and religious extremists are also lifted.[21] During the later phases of democratization, as a public sphere develops in which competing political forces use mass communications to form and expand popular constituencies, these extremists also discover how to use demagoguery and scare tactics to drum up mass support. Global chaos theorists claim that, although cultural conflict may be rare in established democracies, it grows much more common among countries that are making the transition from authoritarianism to democracy.

The upper right-hand quadrant of figure 8-3 suggests how they may have reached this conclusion. Some of the most violent conflicts of the post–cold war epoch erupted in societies that had started down the path

Figure 8-2. *Evolving Freedoms, 1986–96*

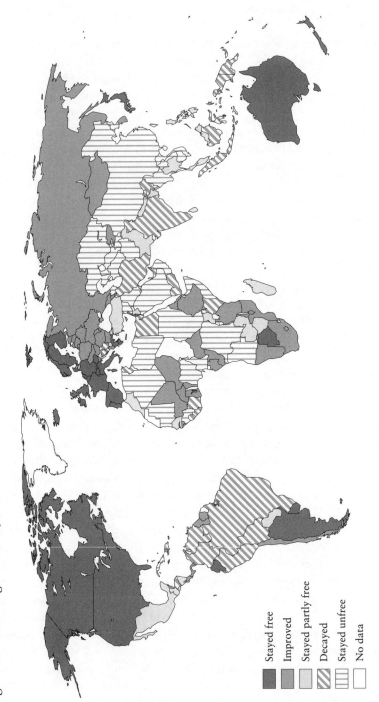

Stayed free
Improved
Stayed partly free
Decayed
Stayed unfree
No data

Source: Raymond Gastil, *Freedom in the World: Political Rights and Civil Liberties 1985–1986* (New York: Greenwood Press, 1986), various pages; Adrian Karatnycky, *Freedom in the World: The Annual Survey of Political Rights and Civil Liberties, 1993–1994* (Washington: Freedom House, 1994); and Freedom House, "Table of Independent Countries: Comparative Measures of Freedom 1995–1996," at www.freedomhouse.org/political/frtable1.html.

Figure 8-3. *Democratization and the Promotion of Culture Conflict,*
1985–96

	Without culture conflicts	With culture conflicts
Growing freer	Benin, Belarus, Burkina Faso, Chile, Costa Rica, Czech Republic, Estonia, Gabon, Ghana, Guyana, Guinea Bissau, Haiti, Hungary, Jordan, Kirghizia, Lithuania, Macedonia, Madagascar, Malawi, Mali, Mongolia, Mozambique, Namibia, Niger, Panama, Poland, Romania, South Korea, Slovakia, Slovenia, Tanzania, Ukraine	Albania, Armenia, Bulgaria, Cambodia, Central African Republic, Congo, Cyprus, Croatia, Eritrea, Georgia, Guatemala, Latvia, Moldova, Pakistan, Panama, Russia, South Africa
Growing less free	Bolivia, Colombia, Dominican Republic, Gambia, Honduras, Ivory Coast, Papua, Tunisia, United Arab Emirates, Venezuela, Yemen	Bahrain, Bhutan, Brazil, Egypt, India, Indonesia, Iran, Kenya, Peru, Sierra Leone, Swaziland, Yugoslavia (Serbia)

Source: Raymond Gastil, *Freedom in the World: Political Rights and Civil Liberties 1985–1986* (New York: Greenwood Press, 1986), various pages; Adrian Karatnycky, *Freedom in the World: The Annual Survey of Political Rights and Civil Liberties 1993–1994* (Washington: Freedom House, 1994); and Freedom House, "Table of Independent Countries: Comparative Measures of Freedom 1995–1996," at www.freedomhouse.org/Political/frtable1.html.
Note: This figure does not include countries whose pattern of government remained consistent (whether democratic or authoritarian) or that vacillated without consistent trend between the two; that is, a majority of states.

of democratization. In Albania, Armenia, Croatia, Georgia, Moldova, Russia, and South Africa, democratization and an increase of cultural violence were more or less simultaneous. In newspaper headlines after 1989, democratization and "ethnic conflict" appeared to come together. But the correlation was only a loose one. Some of the most savage internal conflicts of the post–cold war period were found in societies that were growing less free, such as the civil wars in India (which faced major secessionist challenges by Kashmiris, Sikhs, and Tamils—not to mention serious insurrections by a half dozen other groups), Egypt, and Peru. Many of the worst conflicts of the 1980s and the post–cold war years occurred in countries where the regime type was unstable, vacillating between more and less free forms, such as in Azerbaijan, Bosnia, Kuwait, Lebanon, Liberia, Nigeria, and Tajikistan.

A tempting argument is that political change per se, irrespective of the resulting regime type, was to blame for triggering or contributing to cultural violence. But a huge number of countries managed to change regimes without violence. All the countries in both left-hand quadrants of figure 8-3 managed to change their basic form of government without suffering major cultural violence—as did many others that vacillated between authoritarian and democratic tendencies: Gambia, Honduras, Kazakhstan, Lesotho, Thailand, Turkmenistan, and Uzbekistan.

Among the states whose political systems changed markedly, one subgroup deserves special attention. In 1975 both Spain and Portugal rid themselves of ancient dictatorships and evolved into surprisingly effective democracies. Together, they formed the first ripples in a steadily building "wave" of democratization that spread first to Latin America, then to Asia, and finally worldwide. (Samuel Huntington, who studied this pattern closely, dubbed this the "third wave" of global democratization, comparing it with a "first wave" that swept Europe in the nineteenth century and a "second wave" that appeared after World War II among decolonizing states.)[22] In its later stages, after 1989, when the third wave spread to sub–Saharan Africa and formerly Leninist states in Eastern Europe, it was sometimes—but hardly consistently—associated with cultural violence. But in its earlier stages, particularly in Latin America, the third wave of democratization was consistently associated with a decline of cultural violence. Argentina, Bolivia, Chile, Guyana, and Uruguay, to name only the most clear-cut cases, democratized without anything resembling culture conflict.

Democratization alone was not a sufficient condition to provoke cultural conflict.

How could democratization sometimes fuel violence and sometimes not? Some hypothesized that democratization had bred more violence in Africa than in Latin America because the latter was more culturally homogenous than the former. Huntington argued, consistent with his emphasis upon religion as the ultimate font of civilizational values, that the Catholic culture of Latin America disposed it both to democratization and social stability.[23] Ethnic or cultural violence had not been rare in sub–Saharan Africa since the decolonization of the region in the 1960s (although it was also not nearly as endemic as journalistic stereotyping implied). No one seriously suggested that internal warfare in South Africa, Liberia, or Rwanda originated with the wave of democratization that swept the region in 1989–91. Moreover, South America was a region that had shown a great potential for serious ethnic conflicts before the democratization wave of the late 1970s. In Bolivia, a majority of the population spoke Quechua and other native American tongues, not Spanish. Guyana had one of the strangest ethnic mixes in Latin America: the population was 51 percent East Indian, 43 percent black or mulatto, 4 percent native American, and 2 percent European or Chinese.[24] In Argentina, the 1970s had been a period of horrifying internal violence between Peronistas, Montoneros, and the army, yet this civil war seemed to be organized along class or ideological rather than cultural lines.

Naturally, democratization may have aggravated some of the other domestic and international trends that fostered cultural violence. But global chaos theorists have probably exaggerated its importance. "The historical behavior of individuals or of social strata seldom proceeds from a single cause."[25] This is particularly true of ethnic tensions, which a majority of experts acknowledge arise from a complex array of factors. To elevate ethnic or cultural strifes to the level of ethnic violence requires the addition of further complicating forces.

Economic Globalization

Many think that economic integration is the most powerful form of globalization. Democratization waxes and wanes, and the spread of Western culture is resisted or filtered through local traditions. But the desire to improve one's standard of living, to enjoy the goods and riches associated with involvement in world trade and technology exchange, appears to be almost universal. As the most seductive form of globalization, participation in the world economy unquestionably has far reaching (and often unforeseen) social consequences. It may, among other things, trigger culture conflict.

To test this claim, some way of measuring economic globalization is needed. At first glance, trade statistics might seem to be an appropriate index, as they tell something about how many new goods are flowing into what countries. And, despite a number of vagaries (smuggling, workers' remittances, alternative rates of exchange, and so on), governments have invested considerable effort in keeping accurate tallies of trade. These numbers do reveal some important facts, as figure 8-4 illustrates.[26]

Even the aggregated, "lump sum" numbers charted in this figure highlight the most important fact about global trade patterns: By a huge margin, the largest share of international trade is conducted among already industrialized countries. The single most important market, measured by volume of international trade, is the internal market of the European Community—which accounts for 21 percent of all international trade.

Figure 8-4. *International Trade Patterns, 1993*

Export values in $US millions, 1993

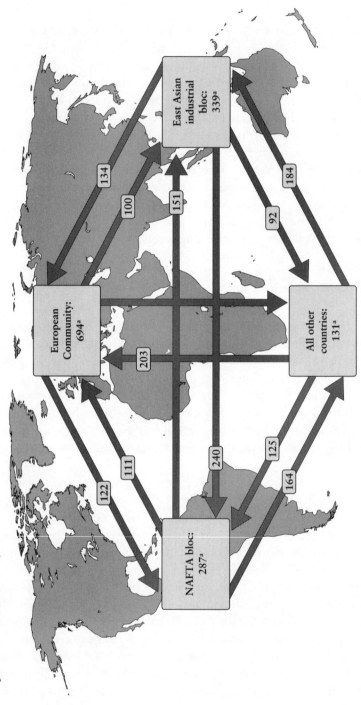

East Asian industrial bloc: 339[a]

European Community: 694[a]

All other countries: 131[a]

NAFTA bloc: 287[a]

134

100

151

184

92

203

111

122

240

125

164

Source: International Monetary Fund, *Direction of Trade Statistics Yearbook, 1994* (Washington: 1994), various pages.
a. Internal export values.

The second most important market is that linking the industrialized powers of Asia (Japan, China, Hong Kong, Korea, Singapore, Taiwan, Australia, and New Zealand), which comprises 10.3 percent of all international trade. The North American Free Trade Agreement (NAFTA) bloc (the United States, Canada, and Mexico) ranks third, with 8.7 percent of all trade.

In contrast, the combined market of trade between all other states, that is, among "the rest"—including most of the third world and the former Soviet bloc—adds up to just 4 percent of world trade.

This concentration of trade among the industrial countries says something important: Globalization has been more intense and has gone much farther in these regions than anywhere else. Yet the much smaller trade of the less developed countries may not mean that it is less significant. After all, in countries with large and developed industrial establishments, trade may provide a smaller share of the total national wealth, and thus have a weaker impact on the lives of the population, than it does in less developed countries. In the United States, for example, the value of exports in 1992 was $420 billion, which equaled only about 7 percent of the gross national product (GNP). In Saudi Arabia, the value of exports in the same year was only $41 billion, but this amounted to 33 percent of GNP.[27]

Invoking Saudi Arabia as an example highlights another problem with using trade statistics as an index of globalization. Saudi Arabia's exports consist almost entirely of petroleum (99 percent in 1992), which also happens to form the largest single commodity in international trade. Yet Saudi Arabia's status as a major petroleum exporter does not mean that the country is especially globalized. Oil production is concentrated in one part of the country and employs a small number of specialized workers. The revenue generated by the oil sector affects the lives of all Saudis, but the government has spent these funds in a manner designed to dampen globalization and to reinforce a highly conservative version of traditional Islam. In a significant number of the less developed countries, much of the value of international trade comes from similar extractive industries (copper, bauxite, diamonds) that affect only a tiny portion of the population. Even when export production involves a larger share of the population, as it does in the cultivation of cotton, jute, rubber, or coffee, international contact may be effectively monopolized by a handful of government agencies or trading firms, while the larger agricultural sector remains both traditional and insulated.

For this reason, a better index of globalization is foreign direct investment (FDI). The growth of FDI in a country is more closely linked to fundamental economic change than simple trade. Direct investment usually means hiring people, buying facilities, transferring technology, and expanding production. Until recently, no annual indices attempted to track the international distribution of FDI. But in 1991 the United Nations Conference on Trade and Development (UNCTAD) began to publish an annual report that tried to trace the growth of economic globalization in general and the activities of transnational corporations in particular. Its centerpiece was an account of the annual trends in FDI.

The pattern of FDI distribution revealed in these reports does crudely resemble the pattern of international trade in one way: The lion's share of FDI is also concentrated in the already industrialized countries. Thus, in the years 1982–89 the recipients of the largest values of FDI were (in descending order) the United States, the United Kingdom, France, Australia, Spain, the Netherlands, Germany, Luxembourg, Belgium, and Italy. All of these countries received, on average, $2 billion to $5 billion in FDI each year, except for the United Kingdom (which averaged $11 billion) and the United States ($36 billion). Not all the industrialized countries that figured prominently in trade statistics were equally receptive to FDI. Japan averaged only $162 million a year—more than Angola but less than Chile.

Even so, the less developed countries still generally ranked low on receipt of FDI, much as they did in the trade figures. Singapore, which might arguably still be considered a developing country, placed eleventh on this list, acquiring a little more than $2 billion a year. Hong Kong, Brazil, Mexico, and China also received $1 billion to $2 billion a year. The vast majority of less developed countries received far less. Another twenty developing states drew less than $1 billion but more than $100 million of FDI each year. Eighty-one received sums ranging from a high of $100 million to a low of less than $1 million. Eleven showed a net outflow of FDI during this decade.[28]

By 1994 the largest source of FDI in the United States was no longer Japanese investors, as it had been in the 1980s. Instead, the central banks of developing countries, including India, Malaysia, Taiwan, Brazil, Mexico, and Chile, had emerged as the largest sources of FDI for Washington.[29]

To what degree did the FDI figures correlate with outbreaks of culture conflict? How much correlation exists was determined by dividing the

Table 8-3. *Foreign Direct Investment and Culture Conflict*

	Quintile				
	First	*Second*	*Third*	*Fourth*	*Fifth*
Number of countries	24	25	25	25	25
Number of countries with culture strife	10	8	3	7	5
Number of countries with culture war	0	4	6	1	0
Percent of countries with culture strife	42	32	12	28	20
Percent of countries with culture war	0	16	24	4	36
Annual average foreign direct investment, 1982–95 (in millions of U.S. dollars)	–1	15	74	471	5,389

Source: United Nations Conference on Trade and Development, *World Investment Report 1994* (New York: United Nations, 1994).

149 countries for which UNCTAD provided average FDI statistics into quintiles and showing how many culture conflicts were associated with each group. The results in table 8-3 show that culture wars tend to correlate with low levels of FDI—the opposite from what chaos theorists would expect. However, the data also suggest that societies with high levels of FDI have more ethnic strifes. This contradictory pattern, with culture strife showing a positive correlation and culture war showing a positive correlation was also evident, if less pronounced, in table 8-2, which dealt with the distribution of television sets.

While this result does not lend great support to global chaos theory, its ambiguity deserves further investigation. As a first step in this direction, consider one final possible measure of economic globalization: variations in the degree of economic openness or "economic freedom."

In 1995 the Heritage Foundation, a conservative Washington think tank, published its first *Index of Economic Freedom*. This rated countries according to ten policy variables in the areas of trade, taxation, government consumption, money supply, foreign investment, banking, wage and price controls, property rights, regulation, and the black market. Each country was given an aggregate score that summarized its receptivity to the initiative of private investors.

Whether or not a country's policies reflect a high level of economic freedom does not, by itself, determine how much economic globalization it will experience. After all, some countries allow domestic investors great freedom yet insulate themselves somewhat from the global economy. Moreover, since the 1980s many developing countries have liberalized their economic policies without attracting the attention (and investment)

Figure 8-5. *Economic Freedom, 1996*

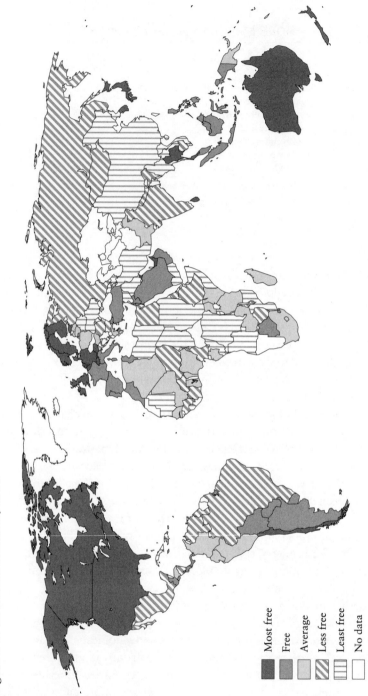

■ Most free

▨ Free

▨ Average

▨ Less free

▨ Least free

▢ No data

Source: Bryan T. Johnson and Thomas P. Sheehy, *Economic Freedom Index* (Washington: Heritage Foundation, 1997), pp. xxix–xxxii.

Table 8-4. *Economic Freedom and Culture Conflict*

	Quintile				
	First	Second	Third	Fourth	Fifth
Number of countries	28	27	28	27	28
Number of countries with culture strife	6	9	7	8	8
Number of countries with culture war	1	3	4	5	11
Percent of countries with culture strife	21	33	25	30	29
Percent of countries with culture war	4	11	14	19	39
Average economic freedom score	2.07	2.71	3.11	3.41	3.81

Source: Bryan T. Johnson and Thomas P. Sheehy, *Index of Economic Freedom* (Washington: Heritage Foundation, 1997), pp. xxvi–xxix.

they desire from world economic actors. Still, a real connection remains. Historically, countries with generally liberal economic environments tend to become enmeshed with world markets earlier and more thoroughly than those that are hostile to private capital.

Figure 8-5 presents the results of the 1996 *Index of Economic Freedom* in the form of a map. Countries have been divided into quintiles and shaded so that those with greater economic freedom are lighter than those with less. (Countries without any coloration are those for which no data were available.)

Does any correlation exist between the degree of economic freedom and the likelihood of ethnic conflict? Table 8-4 illustrates the connection.

The results for economic freedom are much more striking than those for FDI. Sri Lanka is the only country that both enjoys great economic freedom and suffers from a culture war (between Sinhala Buddhists and Tamil Hindus). A consistent correlation can be found between economic freedom and ethnic conflict—but it is an inverse correlation. That is, countries with more economic freedom are markedly less likely to suffer from culture conflict than states that score lower on the index.

This has disturbing ramifications. Countries that experience economic globalization will not be prodded into ethnic or cultural violence. Furthermore, countries that are open to the global economy may enjoy fewer culture conflicts. If this is true, the logic of global chaos theory is not just wrong but virtually backwards.

The authors of *Economic Freedom of the World* claim that economic freedom correlates with prosperity: The more liberal a country's economic policies are, the faster its rate of economic growth and the higher its standard of living are likely to be.[30] Even if this controversial claim is

only loosely true it leads to an intriguing hypothesis: Perhaps culture conflict is more common in less prosperous or less developed societies.

The idea that violence derives from poverty is ancient. It was central to
all of Aristotle's writings on politics.[31] Hundreds of thinkers subsequently
have elaborated on the diverse and distinct ways that poverty fuels violence. Among these various mechanisms, indigence, immiseration, and
inequality form a particularly sinister trinity. Indigence, the failure to ful-
fill basic human needs, leads to explosive levels of frustration and desperation.[32] Immiseration, the erosion or sudden loss of a group's former
wealth and status, is apt to breed paranoia, hatred, and aggression—as
more than one student of the decline of Weimar Germany has noted.[33]
Rousseau and his disciples maintained that inequality, simple but systematic differences in the allocation of resources among social groups, even
when none is desperately needy or downwardly mobile, is likely to breed
social conflict on its own.[34] Economic problems are probably associated
with more different mechanisms for producing violence than any other
type of factor.

All of these different ideas about how want provokes aggression form
an alternative, a countertradition, to the arguments of the global chaos
theorists and all those who stress the role of anomie.[35] The contending
claims about whether violence arises from the loss of income or the loss
of values provide starkly different ways of looking at the world. They
offer not only different visions of how conflicts arise, but also of how they
are likely to play out. If ethnic violence tends to correlate with poverty, it
suggests that the entire intellectual foundation of chaos theory may be
infirm.

How might this hypothesis be tested? Poverty, development, and economic growth are all relative terms, and major intellectual battles have
been fought over how to define each.[36] For many years, the gross national
product and the closely related gross domestic product (GDP) were
thought to be the best single indicator of levels of economic development.
But these measures have been criticized because they reveal nothing about
income distribution and, thus, the real quality of life for the bulk of the
population. Recently, new criticisms have been raised. Some think they
underreport the role of trade; others suggest they ignore environmental
factors.[37] Even the World Bank, whose definitive *World Development
Report* has ranked countries by GDP, has begun to experiment with alternative systems of accounts.[38]

Table 8-5. *Poverty and Culture Conflict*

	Quintile				
	First	*Second*	*Third*	*Fourth*	*Fifth*
Number of countries	29	30	30	30	30
Number of countries with culture strife	9	12	6	9	5
Number of countries with culture war	0	2	9	5	10
Percent of countries with culture strife	31	40	20	30	17
Percent of countries with culture war	0	7	30	17	33
Average human development index score	0.918	0.817	0.683	0.497	0.299

Source: United Nations Development Program, *Human Development Report 1996* (New York: Oxford University Press, 1996), pp. 155–57.

Perhaps the best measure currently available is the human development index (HDI) devised by the United Nations Development Program.[39] The HDI is a composite figure. Part of it measures economic wealth using factors similar to those employed to measure GDP but adjusted for differences in exchange rates into a common unit: purchasing power parity dollars. But the HDI also reflects the physical well-being of the general population—access to food, water, and medicine—by including life expectancy. Finally, it incorporates a measure of the population's skills and ingenuity as reflected in the adult literacy rate. This provides a much more rounded, if still imperfect, picture of both current standards of living and future prospects for development.

The results are different from those provided by conventional measures such as GDP, as is evident from table 8-5, which ranks the countries of the world in quintiles according to their HDI. Some countries that appear rich by narrow economic measures, such as Saudi Arabia, seem much less prosperous when HDI is employed. Other countries, such as Belize, that are notoriously poor in cash terms appear much less desperate when the well-being of the common man and woman—which is better reflected in HDI—is taken into account.

Does the level of HDI appear to have any systematic relationship to the likelihood of ethnic violence? The data in table 8-5 appear—within crude limits—to suggest that culture conflicts afflict all societies, regardless of how well developed they become, irrespective of whether people are rich or poor. This suggests that the fear of globalization among chaos theorists is misplaced. Culture conflicts can occur with or without this trigger. Yet, the news is not good. For example, pessimists such as Nathan Glazer and others who have been arguing that no amount of prosperity in the United

States will end ethnic strifes seem to be vindicated. Perhaps Ben Franklin's adage should be amended to read "Three things are inevitable: death, taxes, and strife."

The information in table 8-5 also offers an important basis for hope. Although culture conflicts seem to crop up in rich and poor countries alike, their lethality varies markedly and consistently. The reduction of poverty does not prevent conflicts, but it directly reduced the level of violence associated with them. Nasty and murderous culture wars occur in the poorest countries (such as the protracted civil wars in Sudan, Rwanda, Liberia, Angola, Burundi, Ethiopia, Afghanistan, Somalia, and Sierra Leone), while the cases of culture strife found in richer countries (the Quebec secessionist movement, the race riots in the United States, the immigrant bashing in France and Germany) involve few fatalities.

This pattern is also found, albeit less obviously, in tables 8-1 and 8-3, which dealt with television sets and foreign direct investment. In both cases, the number of culture wars appeared to be inversely proportional to the level of globalization—but the number of culture strifes showed a slight positive correlation. Perhaps these tables measure different dimensions of the same thing: real wealth, as evidenced by consumer goods, hard currency assets, or human capital. So, not surprisingly, the results are much the same in all three cases: globalization does not cause conflict and wealth does not guarantee peace, although prosperity does seem to dampen the violence of conflicts.

CHAPTER NINE

Post–Cold War
Patterns of Conflict

The claim of chaos theorists that globalization breeds culture violence is at least overstated. If anything, globalization seems more likely to promote material progress and thereby deter violence. Furthermore, chaos theorists misunderstand not only the causes of culture conflict, but also the nature of such battles themselves. Culture conflicts are not markedly different—in frequency, savagery, or much of anything else—from the other wars that have proliferated across the third world since the end of World War II. The nature of warfare during and after the cold war has remained much the same.

In considering globalization, attention here focused on the inputs and outputs of the process chaos theory describes, and the conclusion was reached that not much of a correspondence existed between globalization and culture conflict. However, chaos theory also posits a middle term that mediates between globalization and culture conflict: anomie. Perhaps globalization causes anomie, but in forms other than culture conflict? Or perhaps globalization is not the major force fueling anomie, yet anomie is still the taproot of a wave of new, savage culture wars?

Do Culture Wars Breed in Anomic Societies?

The easiest way to test whether anomie triggers culture conflicts would be to construct various indices that measure anomie and to compare them with the incidence of conflict. If culture conflicts are more common in societies that have high levels of anomie, then a causal relationship between the two is plausible—if still unproven.

A good place to start is with crime rates. In the American debate about the "culture wars," conservatives claimed that rising crime rates were the strongest evidence of widespread "moral poverty" (one of their synonyms for anomie).[1] Unfortunately, crime statistics are difficult to interpret.[2] Certain crimes (for example, spouse abuse and bestiality) are under-reported.[3] Homicide statistics are thought to be among the more reliable, because they are based on a body count instead of on the vagaries of victim testimony. But even the utility of homicide statistics varies from one country to the next. In some countries, the domain of effective police action is so circumscribed that only a fraction of all victims get counted.

Thus, comparisons of murder rates between countries becomes a hazardous business. Most Americans know that they suffer a higher homicide rate (9.4 deaths per 100,000 people in 1990) than the English or the Japanese (2.2 deaths and 1.0 deaths per 100,000, respectively). But few know that the 1990 murder rate in the Netherlands was higher (14.8 deaths). In his books and articles, Robert Kaplan has highlighted the problem of crime in West Africa, particularly in the Ivory Coast. Yet during the 1980s the homicide rate in the Ivory Coast was reportedly below 3 deaths per 100,000—less than half the rate in the United States. He should have visited Swaziland, a country with no current culture conflicts but a murder rate of 87.7 per 100,000. Or perhaps he could have focused on the Philippines, a country that during the 1980s enjoyed democratization, economic growth, and a murder rate consistently above 30 per 100,000.[4]

While such comparisons of absolute murder rates are unreliable, comparisons of change in murder rates are less problematic. A "common wisdom" shared by chaos theorists is the claim that crime rates are on the rise globally. "Crime is increasing worldwide and there is every reason to believe the trend will continue through the 1990s and into the early years of the twenty-first century."[5] But, as is so often the case, the "common wisdom" is usually a distortion and sometimes just plain wrong. Crime has certainly been on the rise in the countries that once formed the communist bloc.[6] But it has also been declining in much of the world. In 1994–95 England benefited from its largest drop in crime since the end of World War II.[7] In the same time span, major crimes in the United States fell by 3 percent.[8] And even though crime remained a source of gnawing anxiety for many Americans, murder rates in the United States have been falling steadily since 1990.[9] Between 1986 and 1990, in sixty states for

Table 9-1. *Homicide Rates and the Anticipation of Culture Conflict*

	Rank in decrease in homicide rate				
	First	Second	Third	Fourth	Fifth
Number of countries	11	11	11	11	12
Number of countries with culture strife	2	2	4	4	4
Number of countries with culture war	2	2	0	0	1
Percent of countries with culture strife	18	18	36	36	33
Percent of countries with culture war	18	18	0	0	8

Source: 1986 data from *The Economist Book of World Vital Statistics* (Random House, 1991), p. 246; 1990 data from Interpol, *International Crime Statistics for 1989 and 1990* (Saint-Cloud, France: International Criminal Police Organization, 1990).

which Interpol assembled statistics, murder rates more than doubled in the Netherlands, Peru, Burma, Italy, Sweden, Denmark, Switzerland, Norway, Germany, Greece, Libya, Fiji, Hong Kong, and Gabon. But during the same period, murder rates declined in Portugal, Malawi, Senegal, Indonesia, Japan, Jordan, Burundi, Syria, the Philippines, Malaysia, Thailand, Tanzania, Belgium, Argentina, Rwanda, Saudi Arabia, Sri Lanka, Singapore, Finland, and Luxembourg.

Crime rates do not show a single global trend. Still, they might be useful as crude indicators of anomie. Do crime rates rise before culture conflicts erupt, raising an alarm that social values are breaking down? Do they rise after culture conflict has emerged, testifying to the collapse of norms?

Table 9-1 relates another "back-of-the-envelope" test—how the incidence of culture conflict compares with that of a second variable, homicide rates. It was constructed using data on sixty countries for 1986 and 1990—the latter being the most recent date for which Interpol statistics were available. It shows the same pattern of correlation that was so common when looking at measures of globalization. Countries with sharply rising murder rates show both an increased likelihood of suffering culture tensions and a decreased likelihood of being afflicted by real culture wars. This time, however, the difference was not because cultural tensions are more likely in rich countries while culture wars are more common in poor ones. The countries that endured both increasing murder rates and cultural tensions included Burma, Germany, Libya, and Fiji, while the one that was also distressed by a real culture war was Peru. The rich, industrial countries with rapidly rising homicide rates—the Netherlands, Italy, Sweden, Denmark, Switzerland, Norway, and Greece—were not likely to suffer culture conflicts of any variety.

If homicide is used as an index of anomie, the data suggest that anomie is not a necessary ingredient in prompting culture conflicts and that, even when they suffer from anomie, more prosperous countries are less likely to suffer from culture conflict. No evidence exists that culture conflicts arise specifically in situations where anomie is growing.

Anecdotally, some connections might be drawn between homicide and conflict. For example, the high murder rates in Guatemala (27.4 in 1990) and the Philippines (30.1) could reflect the culture conflicts that had bled these countries over the preceding decade and that had disrupted values, reducing social sanctions against murder. But even this does not indicate a rise of anomie. In most countries, major wars are followed by a rise in murder rates. This was true, for example, even when the war had nothing to do with ethnicity or anomie. A general rise in murder rates occurred across the industrial world following both World War I and World War II.[10]

In El Salvador, the civil war of the 1980s was followed by a crime wave in the 1990s, which was more lethal.[11] (Yet, in neighboring Nicaragua, the unified police force that emerged at the end of its civil war won international applause for its effectiveness.)[12]

Another anecdotal association of crime with culture conflict deserves inspection. In both the Chechnya district of Russia and Xinjiang province of China, a relationship seems to exist between culture conflict and organized crime.[13] In both areas, the locally dominant ethnic group (the Chechens and the Uighurs, respectively) have long formed important criminal mafias, which have recently joined in battles for autonomy or independence. But in both these areas, this seems to be not a case of crime anticipating culture conflict but an example of social banditry. The Chechen and Uighur traditions of criminal activity had been partly ways of carrying on an armed struggle against foreign occupation.[14] In other regions of the former Soviet Union and China that have recently experienced violent culture conflict—say Tajikistan and Tibet—no special tradition of organized criminal activity can be found.

Finally, one of the most disturbing aspects of recent international trends in homicide deserves mention. In parts of Latin America, homicide rates rose dramatically during the late 1980s. The highest homicide rate in the world was found in Brazil, and the murder rate per 100,000 people in Colombia jumped from 20.5 in the late 1970s to 89.5 by the early 1980s. Crime became a major factor of life. World Bank officials estimated that the region's income would have been 25 percent higher if its level of violence had dropped to the international average.[15] Yet culture conflicts were generally rare in Latin America. It was a region where both democracy and economic growth had spread widely in recent years. Most experts thought the high murder rate in this region (and to a lesser degree even in the United States) reflected the influence of a single factor: not anomie or culture clashes but the drug trade.

If crime or murder does not seem to show any correlation between culture conflict and wider social anomie, perhaps another index might? The classic indicator of anomie, from Durkheim until today, has been suicide. If both suicide rates and the likelihood of culture conflict respond to an increase of anomie, some correlation between the two should be expected.

Unfortunately, suicide statistics are much less accurate than homicide figures. In some cultures, suicide is viewed with deep horror, and families would rather claim that a relative was murdered than admit a case of self-destruction. In others, families would prefer to have an episode counted as suicide than to admit it was murder. In India, a disturbing number of reported suicides turn out, upon investigation, to be examples of "wife burnings" in which a new bride is torched so that her in-laws can keep her dowry.[16] Countries with well-established states that support large, computerized statistics-collecting agencies survey a larger domain and create more accurate figures than poorer countries.

What figures are available suggest that internationally suicide rates correlate largely with culture—with religion being particularly influential—rather than varying as a reflection of changing levels of anomie.[17] When compared with earlier tallies, poor Hungary and Finland have something akin to national traditions of suicide. Japan and China, countries historically influenced by Buddhism, have higher suicide rates.[18] Islamic and Catholic countries (except for France) appear to have lower rates.[19]

The highest suicide rates in the world do seem to indicate anomie—but such high rates are found only under special circumstances, when people's values are not just disturbed but also displaced. When a culture is dying—not declining or fading away, but being killed—its surviving adherents often exhibit a remarkable type of despair that is attended by high suicide rates. In today's world, some of the highest suicide rates are found in the islands of Micronesia and Polynesia, where local cultures are being obliterated; the suicide rate in Samoa is twenty times higher than in the United States.[20] A similar phenomenon was observed in the nineteenth century when both the surviving Native Americans and the Xhosa in South Africa,

Table 9-2. *Suicide and Culture Conflict*

Country	Rank	Suicides per 100,000	Intensity of culture conflict
Slovenia	1	27.8	
China	2	27.7	Low
Hungary	3	27.5	
Lithuania	4	26.5	
Russia	5	26.4	Moderate
Latvia	6	23.2	Low
Estonia	7	22.8	
Finland	8	22.8	
Belarus	9	20.6	
Kazakhstan	10	18.3	
Ukraine	11	17	
Czech Republic	12	16.6	
Austria	13	16	
Switzerland	14	15.6	
France	15	15.4	Low
Poland	16	13.9	
Sweden	17	13.5	
New Zealand	18	13.4	
Bulgaria	19	12.8	
Norway	20	12.1	
Japan	21	12	
Germany	22	11.8	Low
Canada	23	11.4	Low
Australia	24	11.3	
Hong Kong	25	10.8	
United States	26	10.5	Low
Ireland	27	9.5	
Singapore	28	9.3	
Uzbekistan	29	8.2	
Puerto Rico	30	8	
Israel	31	7	Low
Argentina	32	5.6	
Spain	33	5.6	
Italy	34	5.5	
Tajikstan	35	5	High
Mexico	36	2.8	Low
Portugal	37	2.8	
Greece	38	2.5	
Albania	39	2.3	Low
Armenia	40	2.1	High

Source: World Health Organization, *World Health Statistics Annual 1994* (Geneva, Switzerland: 1995), pp. B398–B406.

after their cultures had been destroyed as living societies by white settlers, exhibited strong suicidal tendencies. The Xhosa produced a rare historical example of a real mass suicide. In the "cattle killing" of 1856–57, thousands of Xhosa slaughtered all their cattle after a prophet assured them this act of faith was the only way to ensure divine intervention against their Boer rivals. Fifty thousand Xhosa subsequently starved to death.[21]

In normal, functioning societies, suicide rates also vary under a variety of pressures: economic inflation, the weather, schedules of school exams, and even anomie.[22] However, they rotate around a level that seems to be so heavily influenced by culture that even when the darkest winters are combined with economic depression, Americans never slaughter themselves with the aplomb of Finns. The latest figures available are provided in table 9-2.

Not surprisingly, the incidence of suicide shows no particular correlation with that of culture conflict. Slovenia, the richest and most ethnically homogenous of the Yugoslav republics—not to mention the one that escaped with the least violence—has one of the highest suicide rates in the world. And Hungary, which has had consistently one of the highest suicide rates in the world, has not gone to war with Romania over the oppression of ethnic Hungarians in Transylvania—despite the expectation of many (including Robert Kaplan) that they probably would.[23]

High suicide rates, then, do not indicate the growth of anomie in any way that would allow for a prediction of (or an explanation for) the outbreak of culture conflict. But what about the related claim that culture conflicts tend to be more suicidal than "normal" wars? A claim of the global chaos theorists that had the greatest impact upon U.S. policy was the argument that anomic culture conflicts produce combatants who show little concern for human life—their own or their opponents. For this reason, some thought, deterring or disabling the Serb separatists in Bosnia would be particularly difficult, because they were driven by a culturally rooted, largely irrational, and ultimately suicidal drive for blood.

Some connection may exist between a culture's attitudes toward suicide and its likelihood to encourage death in battle. Many experts believe this is true of Japan. Japanese culture endorses suicide under certain circumstances and, at least during modern times, also expected soldiers to die rather than surrender.[24] During World War II Japanese combat behavior often appeared suicidal to Americans, who were shocked by the Japanese enthusiasm for both "banzai charges" against fortified emplacements and by the use of airplanes in "kamikaze" attacks. In a manner strikingly similar to the reasoning of chaos theorists about culture conflict, "the willingness of the Japanese to accept incredible casualties . . . persuaded many observers in the Allied camp that this was an enemy that not only deserved to be exterminated, but had to be."[25]

However, claims of a link between individual suicide and patterns of collective warfare need to be treated carefully. German troops during World War II thought that the desperate efforts of Russian troops (who, like the Japanese, were often badly outgunned by their opponents) to blunt Nazi advances were patently suicidal. German stories about Russian cavalry charges and other defensive tactics often bear an uncanny resemblance to American accounts of island fighting in the Pacific:

> the Siberian and Mongolian pillbox crews . . . did not yield an inch. Even flamethrowers did not induce them to surrender. They fought until they were shot dead, beaten dead, or burnt to death. Only a hundred prisoners were taken.[26]

Were the Russians behaving suicidally or patriotically? Soldiers prefer not to admit that participating in any form of warfare is manifestly suicidal. Moreover, admitting that an enemy is dying because of his (or her) patriotism is often a disquieting thought: Because God is always on "our" side, how could opponents' patriotism be sincere?

Just because a culture lauds death in combat does not mean it sanctions individual suicide. Islamic societies, with their strong injunctions against suicide, are a case in point. Since 1980 "suicide attacks," particularly as a means of delivering massive explosives, have grown popular among both Palestinians and Lebanese to neutralize Israel's edge in high-tech weaponry. But recruits for such suicide attacks come from a narrow subsection of the population and, even then, are rare.[27] Furthermore, Shiʿite Muslims, whose creed includes something like a cult of martyrdom, supply only a minority of the recruits for such attacks.[28]

No clear evidence is available that culture conflicts either erupt in societies that have high suicidal tendencies or that they take the form of especially suicidal warfare. Bosnia provided the classic illustration of this. Despite the alarming predictions that the Serb separatists were driven by irrational passions and were willing to destroy themselves completely in their quest for Greater Serbia, they did not—in the end—show much of a proclivity for suicide.

When Serb separatist forces overran the UN-designated "safe haven" of Srebrenica in July 1995, the scale and audacity of the attendant massacres provoked the Clinton administration (and, to a lesser extent, NATO) into bold action.[29] With at least tacit support from the Americans, the army of Croatia in August 1995 overwhelmed Serb separatist forces south of Zagreb and quickly crossed the border into Bosnia. In a coordinated attack with the Bosnian government's V Corps, Serb separatists were driven out of much of Western Bosnia. At the same time, the United States pressed its NATO allies to accept a plan for responding to the next Serb separatist provocation with a much more forceful and systematic program of airstrikes. After a Serb mortar shell killed thirty-eight people in a Sarajevo market, NATO planes spent the first two weeks of September demolishing Serb radar and anti-aircraft facilities, ammunition and fuel depots, and bridges and communication lines.[30]

Subjected to offensives on the ground and in the air, the Serb separatists behaved not like hormone-driven nationalist fanatics but as most people would under similar circumstances. Their troops in Western Bosnia retreated, some deserting and others preparing for a last-ditch defense of Banja Luka; their political leadership accepted the implications of military defeat and agreed to serious peace talks under American leadership. Interviewed after this collapse, the president of the Serb separatists, Radovan Karadžić, admitted that all through the war he had known that "if the West put in 10,000 troops to cut off our supply corridors, we Serbs would be finished."[31] By the end of the year, the Dayton accords had, at least for the moment, ended the war in Bosnia.

In the bittersweet peace that followed, there was time to reflect on how many lives might have been saved if the great powers had intervened seriously earlier, rather than invoking chaos theory to justify inaction.[32]

Are Culture Wars Unusually Savage?

If suicide and crime rates are taken as indices of anomie, then culture conflicts do not seem to occur in societies that suffer from high levels of anomie. The relationship between anomie and warfare appears, at the very least, to be more complex than global chaos theory suggests. Anomie certainly prompts individual acts of violence, particularly suicide. It probably also plays a role in various forms of crime (not just homicide), although a strong case can be made that economic conditions exert a major influence on the crime rate.[33] Some riots or spontaneous crowd actions are triggered primarily by anomie, such as soccer riots. Yet many riots are much more political affairs. For example, anomie played a minimal role in the riots and demonstrations that culminated in the Iranian revolution. Detailed social studies of the groups that participated in them show that their values and sense of morality were strong. Contrary to expectations, the movement of population from the countryside to the city had the effect of bolstering traditional values.[34] The Islamic vocabulary and icons deployed by the demonstrators were difficult for Westerners to understand, but the underlying issues that provoked them were not hard to comprehend: poverty and tyranny.

Global chaos theory overstates the role that anomie plays in causing violence as well as exaggerates its influence on the conduct of warfare. Under conditions of combat, situations arise in which normal values may break down, resulting in despair and mindless violence. But much of the worst violence is not a product of moral disorientation or culture shock. The largest killings in human history have consistently been the product of cold, rational calculation.

Consider the disturbing history of genocide. The 1994 television images of the mass killings in Rwanda, showing confused columns of weeping refugees and skulls freshly unearthed from mass graves, gave many viewers the mistaken impression that genocide is usually an act of passion, perpetrated by hysterical mobs. Nothing could be further from the truth. The killing of Tutsis was systematically organized by Col. Theoneste Bagosora, director of services in the Rwandan Ministry of Defence. The killing itself was initiated by the Presidential Guard and was carried into the countryside by the local Gendarmerie and the Interahamwe, French-trained militia units. The victims had been carefully identified in advance and, although all Tutsis—men, women, and children—were targeted, so were large numbers of Hutu who were considered politically threatening.[35] The perpetrators of the Rwandan genocide did not always wear uniforms, but they were much more in the tradition of the Nazi Einsatzgruppen than of Chingiz Khan.

Another way in which the Rwanda crisis (and reinforcing television images from Bosnia) distorted public perceptions was by conveying the idea that genocide usually occurred in the "dark places" of the world— the superstitious Balkans, primitive Africa, or the violence-obsessed Middle East. A casual review of the major genocides that have occurred

Table 9-3. *Major Genocides between 1945 and 1989*

Country	Dates	Victims	Number of deaths (in thousands)
USSR	1943–47	Repatriated nationals and ethnic minorities	780–1,600
China	1950–51	Landlords	800–3,000
Sudan	1952–72	Southern nationalists	100–500
Indonesia	1965–66	Communists and ethnic Chinese	500–1,000
China	1966–75	Cultural revolution victims	400–850
Uganda	1971–79	Opponents of Idi Amin	100–500
Pakistan	1971	Bengali nationalists	1,250–3,000
Cambodia	1975–79	Urbanites	800–3,000
Afghanistan	1978–89	Opponents of regime	1,000

Source: Barbara Harff, "Victims of the State: Genocides, Politicides, and Group Repression since 1945," *International Review of Victimology*, vol. 1 (1989), pp. 23–41.

since the end of World War II appears to confirm this impression. According to Barbara Harff, who keeps a record of this sort of thing, twenty-three clear cases of genocide took place between 1945 and 1985.[36] Table 9-3 lists only the largest of these, those where 500,000 people or more were butchered, but still captures the overall pattern. Even this short list suggests that genocide appears to have been a problem for the third world rather than for industrial societies (with the possible exceptions of the USSR in the 1940s and Yugoslavia today).

However, closer inspection of this table also reveals some more subtle patterns. First, many of the worst genocides of modern times have not been targeted primarily along ethnic lines. The genocides in the Soviet Union, China, Cambodia, Afghanistan, and even, to a great extent, Indonesia and Uganda, have focused on liquidating political dissidents; to employ the emerging vocabulary, they were politicides instead of ethnicides. The largest genocides of the twentieth century were largely politicides: the mass killings by the Maoist regime in China since 1949 (between twenty-six million and sixty-three million); by the Leninist regime in the Soviet Union between 1917 and 1959 (sixty-six million); and by the Pol Pot regime in Cambodia between 1975 and 1979 (one-third of the population of eight million died, the largest share of a single nation to fall victim to genocide).[37]

Recent culture conflicts have yet to match the record-scale genocides that attended earlier ideological struggles. Totalitarian regimes still dominate the enterprise of genocide—contributing not only the communist politicides, but also the Nazi holocaust, which set as yet unexcelled standards in the art of ethnicide. The genocides attending recent culture conflicts have not even matched another type of ethnicide: the European and American colonial wars of the nineteenth and early twentieth centuries that pioneered many of the modern techniques of mass slaughter, including the use of "scorched earth" tactics, biological warfare, and the invention of the concentration camp.[38] During the process of conquering Algeria between 1830 and 1876, French troops slaughtered 538,000 out of a total population of less then three million.[39] In the Mayan caste war of 1846–50 between Mexican settlers and natives, the population of the peninsula was cut in half.[40] Between 1883 and 1908 the Belgians managed to kill between five million and eight million Congolese just through the rapaciousness of their economic exploitation of "the heart of darkness."[41] And years before Germany discovered totalitarianism, German colonial troops in what is now Namibia suppressed a revolt among the Herero by liquidating sixty thousand of the tribe's total population of eighty thousand.[42] The American occupation of Mindanao, Brazil's conquest of Amazonia, and Australian bounties on aborigines did not kill exceptionally large numbers of people but, in percentage terms, came close to liquidating their victims as social groups.

Genocide is usually not a form of anomie.[43] It commonly results not from a spontaneous spasm of violence, but from careful organization and deliberate planning.[44] All too often, the murdering itself is done in cold blood. It occurs less when values or civilized restraints have collapsed than when they have been replaced by elaborate revolutionary or bureaucratic ideologies.[45] While perhaps the industrialized West devotes more energy to socializing its children not to kill than do other societies, the industrial West military and political organizations have honed the tools of education, advertising, and propaganda so that they are capable of reversing an individual or group's inhibitions against killing.[46]

Some people think that culture wars are more likely to be brutal because they are often fought by irregulars who do not wear uniforms or are not organized into disciplined units. But this badly underestimates the potential savagery of troops who wear uniforms and know parade drill. The German army of World War II showed a propensity for massacring prisoners, reprisals against civilians, and genocide that has rarely been equalled—and historical research has steadily implicated not just SS units but regular German troops in a growing share of these atrocities.[47] Partly in response to this, Russian troops developed such an intense hatred of the Nazis that preventing them from murdering captured Germans on sight became a major function of the political commissars attached to Soviet units.[48] American troops have better records in this area than many (at least since the cavalry stopped massacring the Sioux)—but Westerners should not feel too arrogant about this. In combat situations of any kind, barbarity is only one provocation away. Canadian troops have among the best international reputations as peacekeepers, but they were the ones caught torturing and mutilating prisoners in Somalia.[49]

Even in Bosnia, genocide was not the policy pursued by the rag-tag, hastily conscripted troops of the Bosnian army, but the forces of the Serb separatists—most of whom were disciplined, well-organized troops seconded from the regular Yugoslav army. Some of the worst massacres were perpetrated by "irregular" units of Serb nationalist extremists led by men such as Arkan and Vojislav Seselj.[50] Yet at Srebrenica and elsewhere, much of the killing was done by the same regular Serb troops that had won the admiration of United Nations Protection Force (UNPROFOR) officers for their professionalism.[51]

The brutality of the war in Bosnia has been horrifying, and the practices of the Serb separatists clearly fit the legal definition of genocide.[52] But it has probably not equalled the savagery of the battles and genocides perpetrated in the same region during World War II. The highest estimates for the number of Bosnians killed in the 1990s hover around 250,000—and some think these figures are too high. When World War II spilled over into Bosnia, the local Muslim community divided, supplying partisans for all sides. At least seventy-five thousand Bosnian Muslims died during the war, and even larger numbers of Serbs. Even Croat apologists admit that no fewer than seventy thousand Serbs were liquidated at the concentration camp of Jasenovac (in Croatia) and some estimates by Serbs run as high as one million. Immediately after the war, Tito launched a politicide that murdered another 250,000 suspected collaborators and political opponents.[53] For all that Kaplan and the Serbs themselves invoke 1389 and the Ottoman occupation as the font of Serb anger, rage in Bosnia clearly arises not from "ancient tribal rivalries" but from living memories of relatives slaughtered during World War II.

World War II has probably been underappreciated as a turning point in the history of mass slaughter.[54] It carried the practice of "total war" to new lengths, effacing the traditional distinction between combatants and noncombatants particularly through the extensive use of strategic bombing.[55]

But in many ways it was simultaneously, as George Lichtheim called it, "the European civil war," including a host of intimate feuds and guerrilla struggles between Maquis and Vichy, between partisan and Chetnik, that easily spilled over into politicide or genocide.[56] During World War I, civilian casualties constituted about 14 percent of all deaths.[57] During World War II, the percentage of civilian deaths skyrocketed to 67 percent of the total.[58] The Second World War also still holds the record for the largest number of dead in absolute terms. Recent research in the Moscow archives suggests that the long-standard estimate of twenty million Soviet war dead was inaccurate: The actual tally was more like forty million—twenty-two million soldiers and at least eighteen million civilians.[59] Added up—the Soviets plus fifteen million Chinese, six million Poles, six million Jews, four million Germans, two million Japanese, and so on—the tally runs about seventy-five million dead.[60]

World War II seems to have acted as a watershed. The number of civilian dead has constituted two-thirds or more of the total fatalities in most of the wars that followed it. According to UNICEF, the share of civilian casualties has been growing ever since 1945. During the 1980s it had risen to 80 percent and during the 1990s it appeared to reach 90 percent.[61]

Superficially, this would seem to link the recent growth of culture war to a rise in the savagery of war—with "savagery" being operationally defined in terms of percentages of civilian casualties. This would be a completely illegitimate inference, however. Since World War II the share of civilian deaths has been rising for all types of warfare, conventional or guerrilla, ethnic or not. No one would describe Operation Desert Storm and the American attack on Iraq as an ethnic war. Yet estimates of the numbers of Iraqi troops killed in combat have been continuously revised downward—some now argue only twenty-five thousand died.[62] Yet UN researchers suggest that the repercussions of the war and the economic sanctions imposed on Iraq may have resulted in the deaths of as many as 576,000 children.[63] That would mean a civilian death share of at least 95 percent.

If culture conflicts were unusually savage, they reasonably would have higher rates of civilian casualties. The available body counts for ethnic and nonethnic conflicts are provided in table 9-4. Where a breakdown of civilian versus military casualties is available for ethnic conflicts, civilians formed 73 percent of victims. In contrast, for the known data on civilian casualties in nonethnic conflicts, civilians form only 62 percent of the victims.

Table 9-4. *War-Related Deaths, 1945–92*

Country	Dates	Number of deaths Civilian	Military	Total	Civilian deaths as a percent of total
Conventional conflicts					
Algeria	1945	2,000	0	2,000	100
Indonesia	1945–46	4,000	1,000	5,000	80
Vietnam	1945–54	300,000	300,000	600,000	50
Greece	1945–49	n.a.	n.a.	160,000	n.a.
China	1946–50	500,000	500,000	1,000,000	50
Paraguay	1947	n.a.	n.a.	1,000	n.a.
Taiwan versus China	1947	0	1,000	1,000	0
Madagascar	1947–48	10,000	5,000	15,000	67
India versus Pakistan	1947–49	1,000	2,000	3,000	33
Yemen	1948	2,000	2,000	4,000	50
Israel versus Arabs	1948	0	8,000	8,000	0
Colombia	1948	n.a.	n.a.	1,000	n.a.
Costa Rica	1948	1,000	1,000	2,000	50
India	1948	1,000	1,000	2,000	50
Korea	1948	0	1,000	1,000	0
Colombia	1949–62	200,000	100,000	300,000	67
China	1950–51	1,000,000	0	1,000,000	100
Philippines	1950–52	5,000	4,000	9,000	56
Korea	1950–53	1,500,000	1,500,000	3,000,000	50
Malaysia	1950–60	n.a.	n.a.	13,000	n.a.
Bolivia	1952	1,000	1,000	2,000	50
Kenya	1952–63	3,000	12,000	15,000	20
Tunisia	1952–54	3,000	0	3,000	100
Morocco	1953–56	3,000	0	3,000	100
Guatemala	1954	n.a.	n.a.	1,000	n.a.
Taiwan	1954–55	n.a.	n.a.	5,000	n.a.
Algeria	1954–62	82,000	18,000	100,000	82
Argentina	1955	2,000	2,000	4,000	50
Cameroon	1955–60	n.a.	n.a.	32,000	n.a.
Hungary versus USSR	1956	10,000	10,000	20,000	50
Egypt versus Israel	1956	1,000	3,000	4,000	25
Lebanon	1958	1,000	1,000	2,000	50
Indonesia	1958–60	n.a.	n.a.	30,000	n.a.
Cuba	1958–59	2,000	3,000	5,000	40
Vietnam	1960–65	200,000	100,000	300,000	67
Laos	1960–73	18,000	12,000	30,000	60
Angola	1961–75	30,000	25,000	55,000	55
China versus India	1962	1,000	1,000	2,000	50
Algeria	1962–63	1,000	1,000	2,000	50
Yemen	1962–69	n.a.	n.a.	15,000	n.a.

(continued)

Table 9-4. War-Related Deaths, 1945–92 (Continued)

Country	Dates	Number of deaths Civilian	Military	Total	Civilian deaths as a percent of total
Guinea-Bissau	1962–74	5,000	10,000	15,000	33
Zambia	1964	n.a.	n.a.	1,000	n.a.
Pakistan versus India	1965	13,000	7,000	20,000	65
Dominican Republic	1965	1,000	2,000	3,000	33
Vietnam versus United States	1965–75	1,000,000	1,058,000	2,058,000	49
Mozambique	1965–75	n.a.	n.a.	30,000	n.a.
Egypt and Syria versus Israel	1967–70	50,000	25,000	75,000	67
China	1967–68	450,000	50,000	500,000	90
China versus USSR	1969	0	1,000	1,000	0
El Salvador versus Honduras	1969	3,000	2,000	5,000	60
Jordan	1970	5,000	5,000	10,000	50
Cambodia versus United States and Vietnam	1970–75	78,000	78,000	156,000	50
Pakistan versus India	1971	0	11,000	11,000	0
Sri Lanka	1971	5,000	5,000	10,000	50
Chile	1973	n.a.	n.a.	5,000	n.a.
Zimbabwe	1972–79	n.a.	n.a.	12,000	n.a.
Philippines	1972–92	20,000	20,000	40,000	50
Israel versus Egypt and Syria	1973	0	16,000	16,000	0
Chile	1974	20,000	0	20,000	100
Cyprus versus Turkey	1974	3,000	2,000	5,000	60
Cambodia	1975–78	750,000	250,000	1,000,000	75
West Sahara	1975–87	3,000	13,000	16,000	19
Argentina	1976–79	12,000	3,000	15,000	80
Ethiopia versus Somalia	1976–83	15,000	24,000	39,000	38
Turkey	1977–80	n.a.	n.a.	5,000	n.a.
Uganda versus Tanzania	1978–79	0	3,000	3,000	0
Nicaragua	1978–79	25,000	25,000	50,000	50
Cambodia versus Vietnam	1978–89	14,000	51,000	65,000	22
Afghanistan	1978–91	1,000,000	500,000	1.500,000	67
China versus Vietnam	1979	9,000	26,000	35,000	26
El Salvador	1979–91	50,000	25,000	75,000	67
Jamaica	1980	1,000	0	1,000	100
Brazil	1980	n.a.	n.a.	1,000	n.a.
South Korea	1980	1,000	0	1,000	100
Chad	1980–87	2,000	5,000	7,000	29
Iran versus Iraq	1980–88	50,000	450,000	500,000	10
Uganda	1981–87	300,000	8,000	308,000	97
Nicaragua	1981–88	15,000	15,000	30,000	50
Mozambique	1981–92	1,000,000	50,000	1,050,000	95

(continued)

Table 9-4. War-Related Deaths, 1945–92 (Continued)

Country	Dates	Civilian	Military	Total	Civilian deaths as a percent of total
Argentina versus UK	1982	0	1,000	1,000	0
Lebanon versus Israel	1982–90	n.a.	n.a.	144,000	n.a.
Zimbabwe	1983	2,000	0	2,000	100
China	1983–84	5,000	0	5,000	100
Liberia	1985–88	5,000	0	5,000	100
Colombia	1986–92	14,000	8,000	22,000	64
South Yemen	1986–87	7,000	4,000	11,000	64
Chile	1987	3,000	0	3,000	100
China	1989	1,000	0	1,000	100
Panama versus United States	1989	1,000	0	1,000	100
Romania	1989	1,000	0	1,000	100
China versus Vietnam	1987	0	1,000	1,000	0
China	1990	1,000	0	1,000	100
Kuwait and United States versus Iraq	1990–91	100,000	100,000	200,000	50
Nigeria	1991–92	5,000	0	5,000	100
Kenya	1991–92	n.a.	n.a.	1,000	n.a.
Afghanistan	1991–92	n.a.	n.a.	5,000	n.a.
Iraq	1991–92	n.a.	n.a.	10,000	n.a.
Croatia	1992	n.a.	n.a.	2,500	n.a.
Bosnia	1992	n.a.	n.a.	125,000	n.a.
Georgia	1992	n.a.	n.a.	2,000	n.a.
Moldova	1992	n.a.	n.a.	1,000	n.a.
Tajikistan	1992	n.a.	n.a.	20,000	n.a.
Rwanda	1992	2,000	0	2,000	100
Culture conflicts					
India	1946–48	800,000	0	800,000	100
Taiwan	1947	20,0000	0	20,000	100
Burma	1948–51	n.a.	n.a.	8,000	n.a.
Indonesia	1950	n.a.	n.a.	5,000	n.a.
China versus Tibet	1950–51	2,000	0	2,000	100
Indonesia	1953	n.a.	n.a.	1,000	n.a.
Tibet	1956–59	60,000	40,000	100,000	60
Rwanda	1956–65	102,000	3,000	105,000	97
Iraq	1959	1,000	1,000	2,000	50
Zaire	1960–65	n.a.	n.a.	100,000	n.a.
Iraq	1961–70	100,000	5,000	105,000	95
Sudan	1963–72	250,000	250,000	500,000	50
Indonesia	1965–66	500,000	0	500,000	100
Uganda	1966	1,000	1,000	2,000	50
Guatemala	1966–92	100,000	40,000	140,000	71

(continued)

Table 9-4. War-Related Deaths, 1945–92 (Continued)

		Number of Deaths			Civilian deaths as a percent of total
Country	Dates	Civilian	Military	Total	
Nigeria	1967–70	1,000,000	1,000,000	2,000,000	50
Pakistan	1971	500,000	500,000	1,000,000	50
Uganda	1971–78	300,000	0	300,000	100
Burundi	1972	100,000	10,000	110,000	91
Philippines	1972–92	20,000	15,000	35,000	57
Pakistan	1973–77	6,000	3,000	9,000	67
Ethiopia	1974–92	500,000	75,000	575,000	87
Lebanon	1975–76	75,000	25,000	100,000	75
Indonesia	1975–82	100,000	50,000	150,000	67
Angola	1975–92	n.a.	n.a.	300,000	n.a.
South Africa	1976	1,000	0	1,000	100
Iran	1978–89	70,000	18,000	88,000	80
Burma	1980	n.a.	n.a.	5,000	n.a.
Nigeria	1980–81	n.a.	n.a.	5,000	n.a.
Ghana	1981	n.a.	n.a.	1,000	n.a.
Syria	1982	20,000	0	20,000	100
Zimbabwe	1983–84	2,000	0	2,000	100
India	1983–92	13,000	5,000	18,000	72
Peru	1983–92	20,000	6,000	26,000	77
South Africa	1983–92	15,000	0	15,000	100
Nigeria	1984	n.a.	n.a.	1,000	n.a.
Turkey	1984–92	n.a.	n.a.	5,000	n.a.
Sri Lanka	1984–92	18,000	14,000	32,000	56
Sudan	1984–92	500,000	6,000	506,000	99
Burma	1985–92	n.a.	n.a.	7,000	n.a.
Burundi	1988–92	8,000	0	8,000	100
Somalia	1988–92	350,000	5,000	355,000	99
Armenia versus Azerbaijan	1989–92	n.a.	n.a.	7,000	n.a.
Liberia	1990–92	10,000	10,000	20,000	50

Source: Ruth Leger Sivard, *World Military and Social Expenditures 1993* (Washington: World Priorities, 1993), p. 21.
n.a. Not available.

This 11 percent difference between the civilian death ratios in culture and nonculture conflicts is significant if not dramatic. However, it does not show that culture conflicts are more savage than nonculture. The figures for civilians killed in nonculture conflicts has been distorted by a few unusual cases. For example, the Iran-Iraq war looms large in casualty statistics but was unusual in a variety of ways. The battle between the legions of Ayatollah Khomeini and Saddam Hussein was virtually a

Middle Eastern rerun of World War I in its use of gas and trench warfare and in the low percentage of civilian casualties (10 percent).

The great majority of wars since 1945—culture and nonculture alike—have been what the Pentagon calls "low-intensity conflicts" (LICs). In a LIC, at least one major group of combatants is not a state with a regular army but an insurgent force organized as guerrillas or militias.[64] All the culture conflicts included in table 9-4 are, by definition, LICs but so are the great majority of nonculture conflicts. If the Iran-Iraq war and a handful of similar old-fashioned "conventional wars" (Vietnam versus Cambodia and China; Israel versus Egypt and Syria; India versus Pakistan) are subtracted from the tally of nonculture conflicts, the difference between culture and nonculture conflicts disappears. Civilian casualties have formed 69 percent of all those killed in nonculture LICs since 1945. The difference between this figure and the 73 percent civilian casualties killed in culture LICs is statistically insignificant. The idea that LICs result in higher civilian casualty rates than conventional wars is hardly novel. But the absence of evidence that civilian casualties in LICs are higher when culture quarrels are involved is more surprising.

In terms of casualties or anything else, virtually no difference exists between culture conflicts and other forms of LICs. The similarity between culture and nonculture LICs is reinforced by the data in figure 9-1, which show that, while it has temporarily bobbed up or down, the number of deaths from wars of all kinds in the developing countries has consistently hovered around 400,000 per year since 1945.[65]

This suggests that no dramatic change has taken place since World War II in the savagery—or at least the lethality—of war. This fact is hard to reconcile with the assertions of chaos theory. Global chaos theorists assert that culture warfare grew during the 1980s and 1990s, replacing the less savage ideological wars of earlier decades. The absence of any dramatic change in the death counts related in figure 9-1 suggests that a fairly steady stream of LICs can be found throughout the postwar epoch.

The information in figure 9-1 also implies another problem for chaos theory. According to chaos theorists, culture wars are not only more savage than conventional wars, but they are also becoming more common, more frequent. If culture wars are dramatically more numerous, why is the global death toll from war not rising? How can wars get more savage, increase in frequency, and yet the total number of casualties remain the same?

Figure 9-1. *War Mortality, 1945–92*

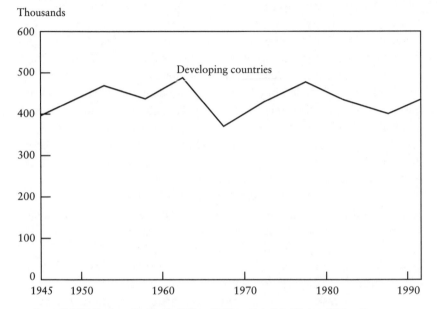

Thousands

Source: UNICEF, *The State of the World's Children, 1996* (New York: United Nations, 1996), p. 33.
Note: The number of deaths from wars and related causes has averaged around 400,000 per year for all developing countries, with little change between 1945 and 1992.

Are Culture Conflicts Becoming More Frequent?

The answer to this conundrum seems to be: it cannot. Something is fundamentally wrong with global chaos theory's claims about the world. Culture wars are not more savage than other forms of LICs. Moreover, culture conflicts are not appearing with accelerating frequency.

While in 1992 a number of new culture conflicts burst upon the world scene—such as in Bosnia, Chechnya and Tajikistan and Georgia and Moldova—the great majority of culture conflicts raging that year were already old. They were examples of "persistent" culture conflicts: wars that explode for a few years, lapse into dormancy, and then reappear again. The battle between the Turkish and Iraqi governments and the Kurds were good examples of this, as was the clash of Tutsi and Hutu in Rwanda and Burundi, Tajik and Pathan in Afghanistan, Arab and Dinka in the Sudan, Sinhala and Tamil in Sri Lanka, Kashmiris and the Indian government, and Shans and the Burmese government. These battles were not new, and they were largely unaffected by globalization, the end of the cold war, changing levels of anomie, or any of the other forces to which chaos theorists assign such importance.

Equally important, and much less noticed, is that in 1992 a number of the conflicts that had plagued the world during the 1980s were terminating. This was most evident in Central America, where the end of the cold war created auspicious conditions for ending the civil wars in Nicaragua and El Salvador. But it was also true in Africa, where the vortex of conflicts that had engulfed Ethiopia and Eritrea ended dramatically and the deadly civil war in Mozambique gave way to peace. In many other places, LICs and culture conflicts may not have definitively terminated but at least they lapsed into dormancy. The fighting in Moldova ended quickly, the long agony of South Africa gave way to impressive civility, and even the angry factions in Angola arranged for a long cease-fire and a power-sharing arrangement.

The net effect of these changes on the world's population is illustrated in figure 9-2. While the majority of people have to live with persistent culture conflict or tension, they are not enduring Bosnia-style horrors. (The United States, for example, is a society with persistent culture tension. A history of racial discrimination periodically produces riots and assassinations without exploding into full-scale warfare.) A fortunate fifth of the global population live in countries free of violent culture problems—from Sweden to Lesotho.

For real experts on culture conflict—a category in which not many chaos theorists claim membership—this result is not surprising. Those who make their living measuring this sort of thing have never claimed that a sudden explosion of culture conflict occurred at the end of the cold war. Instead, most consistently argued that the number of culture conflicts had been rising steadily but gradually since the end of World War II.[66] This fact is well documented by the data in in figure 9-3, which was prepared by Ted Robert Gurr, a political scientist famous throughout his discipline for the elaborate quantitative databases on culture conflict he has assembled. Viewed against this long-term background, the new culture conflicts that appeared in 1992 were not the beginning of a new trend but a spike—not a tendency but an incident.

If this is the case, then why did Americans generally—not just global chaos theorists—become so alarmed about culture conflict in 1992 and 1993? The number of newspaper articles about culture conflict in the *Washington Post,* for example, rose from eleven in 1990 to twenty-nine

Figure 9-2. Global Populations Involved in Culture Conflicts

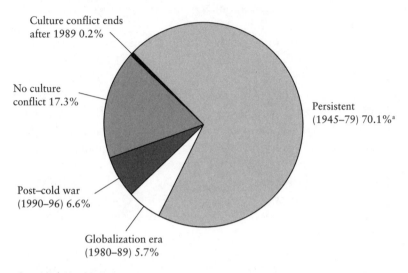

Culture conflict ends
after 1989 0.2%

No culture
conflict 17.3%

Persistent
(1945–79) 70.1%[a]

Post–cold war
(1990–96) 6.6%

Globalization era
(1980–89) 5.7%

Source: Author's estimates.
a. Conflicts beginning before 1980 and persisting to the present, at least intermittently.

in 1991 then jumped to forty-three in 1992 and thirty-seven in 1993.[67] Chaos theory developed because the wider American public was already convinced that culture conflict was an emerging problem.

A series of factors were at work. Perhaps the most important was a change in the geographic distribution of culture conflict. The new culture conflicts of 1992 were located primarily in the former Yugoslavia and the former Soviet Union; that is, close to the West and within easy reach of television cameras. In contrast, the many persistent and the few terminating culture conflicts were much more distant and less visible. For example, Americans rarely saw pictures of the conflict in Eritrea. And after the war was over, journalists had even less incentive to lug their videocameras to Asmara.

The effects of this change in the geographic distribution of culture conflicts were reinforced by a shift in the focus of attention among Americans and Westerners generally. From the 1940s until 1989 overseas news coverage for Western audiences had been riveted on the cold war—a focus well justified by the possibility of universal nuclear holocaust. They attended to the various "brush fire" wars in the developing countries, culture conflicts among them, only to the extent that they threatened to

Figure 9-3. *Long-Term Trends in Ethnic Conflict*

Intensity of conflict, aggregated from numerical scores

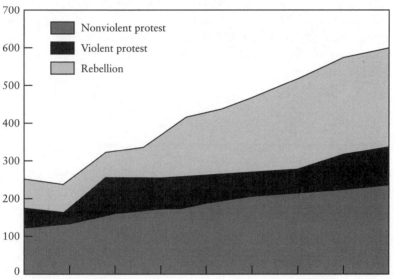

1945–49 1950–54 1955–59 1960–64 1965–69 1970–74 1975–79 1980–84 1985–89

Source: Ted Robert Gurr, *Minorities at Risk: A Global View of Ethnopolitical Conflicts* (Washington: U.S. Institute of Peace, 1993), p. 101.

involve the superpowers or tip the global balance of power. And even when these conflicts momentarily attracted attention, they were viewed overwhelmingly in cold war terms. Thus, when an American news crew risked their lives to haul their cameras into Afghanistan on muleback, the story they sent home was likely to focus upon the dramatic efforts of the Mujahadin to bring down Soviet helicopters with American-supplied Stinger missiles—rather than upon the much more seedy business of how Mujahadin warlords who represented different communities and sects murdered each other's followers in a quest for primacy. Then, abruptly, the cold war ended. As a result, all the little wars in the developing countries had less competition for the limelight (and, if they happened to lie within easy flying distance of Vienna or Rome, they were especially likely to become newsworthy).

Finally, culture conflicts attracted attention partly because they stung. In 1989 Americans from Francis Fukuyama to George Bush had hoped they were seeing the fulfillment of the American century. They dreamed of a new world order based on law and civility instead of force and terror. When their campaign to bring the rule of law to Iraq degenerated into civil strife, not only leaving Saddam Hussein in power but also allowing him to massacre the Shiᶜa and Kurdish insurgents who had struggled to overthrow him, the injustice rankled. Culture conflicts were newsworthy because they provided a ruler for measuring America's disappointed aspirations for world peace.

CHAPTER TEN

The Mythology of Ethnic Conflict

Ethnic conflicts are not much different from other forms of low-intensity conflict. They are certainly not any more savage or irrational. Their number is increasing slowly, not exploding in some post–cold war spasm. Still, their number is increasing. They form a real problem that deserves serious attention.

Most of the "culture clashes" that global chaos theorists worry about turn out, on close inspection, to be varieties of ethnic conflict. Although many of the claims made by global chaos theorists have been dubious, perhaps their early attention to the problem of ethnic conflict means they still have lessons to teach. Perhaps the value of this school lies not in its sweeping claims about globalization and anomie, but in its detailed advice about concrete ethnic conflicts?

The evidence suggests that even in this particularly important facet, the global chaos theorists mislead more often than they guide. They present a one-sided picture of how ethnicity functions. They make inaccurate claims about how ethnic conflicts start. And they present an upside-down picture of the circumstances in which ethnic conflict is most likely to become a serious policy problem—when states collapse.

The 'Moynihan Thesis'

The idea that ethnic conflicts can destroy states has been popularized by Daniel Patrick Moynihan, the Harvard University professor turned U.S. senator.[1] Moynihan's favorite example of the power of ethnic forces is the breakup of the Soviet Union. He notes that already in the 1970s, when he was serving as U.S. ambassador to the United Nations, Moscow's policy clashes with Israel led him to suspect that an ethnic revival among Soviet Jews was already occurring and that ethnic tensions were on the rise in the USSR. "Why should [the Soviets] have commenced a massive, systematic effort to delegitimize the state of Israel, if not because a mass movement had formed within the Soviet Union to go there? A movement of persons defined by religious affiliation stamped on internal passports. If religion was alive among Jews, would it not be alive among Gentiles? If religion, then language; if language, then nationality."[2]

This speculative chain of reasoning led Moynihan in 1979 to write an editorial for *Newsweek* entitled "Will Russia Blow Up?" He sketched a picture of a declining economy and claimed "the infrastructure of the Soviet state" had sickened. This fueled internal tensions that would inevitably assume ethnic form. "Since 1920 the Communists have rather encouraged ethnic culture, while ruthlessly suppressing ethnic politics. It won't work. By the year 2000 one-third of the population will be Muslim. Less than half the population will be great Russian. They will no longer be able to rule from the center."[3] In his 1993 *Pandaemonium*, Moynihan, with an impressive lack of modesty, devotes a half dozen pages to trumpeting the news that this made him the only man in America to have foreseen the demise of the Soviet Union. He further claims that his ability to predict this event vindicates the importance of studying ethnic forces as a roadmap to world history.[4]

This claim is, to be polite, disingenuous. In a 1979 essay, Moynihan did not anticipate the demise of the Soviet Union; he predicted that Moscow would take dramatic action to relieve the build up of domestic tensions.

The problem is that the internal weaknesses of the Soviet Union have begun to appear at the moment when its external strength has never been greater. . . . Soviet arms and Soviet-trained Cubans are deployed all over Africa, and now, increasingly, in the Middle East. This can't last. So long as the economy was growing, the system could put up with the 'waste' of armaments. But that time is past. And oil is running out. The move is obvious: into the oil fields of the Persian Gulf in order to reverse the decline at home and preserve national unity.[5]

But what Moynihan prefers to remember having argued, not what he said, is of concern here.

The argument Moynihan claims he made certainly was presented by a French scholar, Hélène Carrère d'Encausse, whom he admits shared his "prescience." In 1979 she published a book entitled *Decline of an Empire: The Soviet Socialist Republics in Revolt,* which argued that simmering ethnic conflicts were undermining communist rule. In 1993 the English translation of her *The End of the Soviet Empire: The Triumph of the Nations* appeared. The book provided a blow-by-blow history supporting the idea that nationalist forces had destroyed the "Red Empire." In this account, the first serious threat to Gorbachev's efforts to reform the USSR were the December 1986 riots by ethnic Kazakhs in Alma-Ata, which she portrays as the most noteworthy mass demonstration since 1927.[6] From this beginning, nationalist movements erupted in a long succession of riots and clashes: In February 1988, thousands of Armenians began demonstrating for the union of their republic with the Armenian-majority district of Nagorno-Karabakh; in the fall of 1988, nationalist "popular fronts" formed not only in several Transcaucasian states but also in all three Baltic republics; by January 1989, demonstration and counterdemonstration had escalated into a pogrom by Azeris against Armenians in which at least sixty died; in April, at least twenty Georgians were killed by Russian troops during independence demonstrations in Tblisi; in May, riots broke out in the capitals of several Central Asian republics; and so on.

Through this chronology, Carrère d'Encausse provides an explanation for the end of the cold war that makes no reference to "star wars," the Reagan defense buildup, liberalizing tendencies among provincial Soviet bureaucrats, failing grain harvests, Yuri V. Andropov's love of jazz, the collapse of the Berlin Wall, or any other historical commonplace.

The sudden defeat of communism under the combined blows of national communities determined to decide their own destiny first occurred in the USSR. That it started there was natural: communism began in Russia, and the Soviet Union that succeeded Russia set about imposing it from the outside; the general crisis of the system it embodied could come only from its weakening. The solidarity of peoples, that community of states ever willed and extended by Moscow—one day turned against the system and finished it off.[7]

In her account, nationalist resentment of Russian domination essentially bred opposition to Moscow, fueled the rise of militant ethnonational movements, battered the power of the Soviet state, and simultaneously destroyed communism and the USSR.

This interpretation of "the Leninist extinction" assigns a central part to the collapse of state power. Moynihan and its other proponents admit that this collapse was accelerated by economic factors, but they argue that the primary force sapping state power was nationalist resistance.[8] As an explanation of the collapse of the Soviet Union, this monocausal nationalist explanation remains controversial. But as a picture of a widespread process by which ethnic violence destroys political order, it was a popular idea—not new, but popular.[9] Robert Kaplan invoked it repeatedly in *Balkan Ghosts*. David Fromkin probably learned the idea from similar sources (his *End of Empire* reads as if it were written by a British colonial historian), and he helped to make the same idea popular among amateur students of the Middle East. Through a diverse series of assignations and transferences, the idea became a sort of nostrum.

Was War in Bosnia the Result of 'Ancient Tribal Rivalries'?

Whether or not he predicted the demise of the Soviet Union, Moynihan deserves much of the praise or blame for propagating this idea. For many years, he had been the leading spokesperson in the United States for an influential school that claimed ethnic identity and the disposition to ethnic conflict were not symptoms of "deeper" social structures, but autonomous forces in world history. Adherents of this school are often called "primordialists" because they believe something akin to an instinct makes people identify with their ethnic kin and loathe ethnic out-groups.[10]

By a primordial attachment is meant one that stems from the "givens"—or, more precisely, as culture is inevitably involved in such matters, the assumed "givens"—of social existence: immediate contiguity and kin connection mainly, but beyond them the givenness that stems from being born into a particular religious community, speaking a particular language, or even a dialect of a language, and following particular social practices. These contiguities of blood, speech, custom, and so on, are seen to have an ineffable, and at times overpowering, coerciveness in and of themselves. One is bound to one's kinsman, one's neighbor, one's fellow believer, ipso facto; as the result not merely of personal affection, practical necessity, common interest, or incurred obligation.[11]

Drawing on the same conservative psychology of Erik Erikson that inspires other global chaos theorists, primordialists argue that "if one looks down the dark ravines of history, one sees that men in social groups need some other group to hate. The strength of a primordial attachment is that emotional cohesion derives not only from some inner 'consciousness of kind,' but from some external definition of an adversary as well."[12] People are loyal to their ethnic groups even when it is individually self-destructive to do so, or, as one primordialist wag put it, "MAN IS A *K*NATIONAL ANIMAL."[13]

Moynihan and the primordialists recognized that their claims contradicted the traditional hopes of liberals and Marxists alike that, as society develops, the hold of ethnicity will weaken and all groups will assimilate to a common, cosmopolitan culture. The persistence of ethnic and race issues in the United States, despite great progress in productivity and rights, convinced Moynihan—and much of the American public—of the autonomy of ethnic forces.[14]

Long before the end of the cold war and the birth of global chaos theory, primordialists united behind the idea that the current epoch is characterized by "a massive retribalization running sharply counter to all the globalizing effects of modern technology and communications. . . . [Tribalism] is the refuge to which, in any case, great masses are retreating and withdrawing in the face of the breakdown or inadequacy of all the larger coherences or systems of power and social organization."[15] Some, including Moynihan, did not dwell on the question of why the urge to ethnicity is so strong—they just take it as given. Others thought that the foundations of this urge were genetic, instinctive.[16] In the 1990s the popularity of primordialism grew apace with the wider resurgence of interest in the genetic foundations of social behavior, a movement evident in the rebirth of social Darwinism, sociobiology, or what is now called "evolutionary psychology."[17]

Primordialism has become increasingly popular among the general public—but not among experts on ethnicity. Today only a minority of experts would accept the primordialist claim that ethnicity is primarily a product of instinct or an urge so powerful that it easily prevails over material calculations and even desire for self-preservation.[18]

Even when first made, the primordialist claim that ethnic loyalties were prerational or outright irrational seemed extreme to many scholars. (Most scholars thought that the intellectual antithesis of primordialism, "instrumentalism," that is, the belief that ethnicity is always reducible to underlying antagonisms of social structure—usually to class conflict—was also extreme and one-sided.)[19] Over the years, research seemed to show that the allure of ethnicity varies enormously from one society to the next and one period to another. Serious scholars increasingly realized that a complex variety of forces could accelerate or retard, aggravate or suppress, the expression of ethnic identity and the likelihood of ethnic antagonism. In most cases, ethnic, communal, or national identity is not primordial at all: It is a social construct with a distinct history, something that people built in much the same way that they build cities or states.[20]

The conflicts in the former Yugoslavia provide excellent examples of how clashes over "ethnic" identity have interacted with struggles over the distribution of wealth and power in complex and subtle ways—and not at all as Moynihan or Kaplan thought. These examples show that ethnicity is not some atavistic force that bubbles away in darkness until it explodes in a fury of irrational violence. Instead, ethnicity is one pattern around which people can organize—and its appeal must constantly compete with many other ways that people might group themselves.

For example, Serb nationalism is the oldest in the Balkans—but even it is not ancient, much less primordial. Although Serb nationalists insist their forebears were a united people at the time of their defeat by the Turks in the 1389 battle of Kosovo, this is pure mythology. Both sides in that battle fielded polyglot hordes, not national armies. Christians, including many Serbs, probably formed the majority of the troops who took the field on behalf of the Ottoman Sultan Murad.[21] Serb nationalism—the belief that people who spoke Serbo-Croat and practiced the Orthodox faith not only shared cultural traits in common but also formed a discrete political unit that deserved its own state—only began to develop late in the eighteenth century and blossomed in the nineteenth century after a successful 1804 revolt against the Ottoman forces headquartered in Belgrade.[22]

Serb nationalism was not always the dominant ideology among Serbs. At various times, it was eclipsed by pan–Slavic sentiments, Yugoslav nationalism, and even the Marxist philosophy of history.[23] In the 1980s, after forty years during which it had been marginalized and largely dormant, Serb nationalism began to revive again. Two main forces were responsible for its resurrection. First was the structural crisis of the Yugoslav economy and state, which increasingly pitted the citizens of each republic against the others. Second was the deliberate effort of Slobodan Milošević and his allies to promote and employ Serb nationalism to construct an autonomous power base for themselves.

No evidence exists that Milošević felt any personal interest in Serb nationalism until his famous visit to Kosovo in April 1987, when he seized headlines by his outspoken defense of the province's angry Serb minority.[24] (Although the province contained the ancient battlefields and monasteries that played a central role in Serb history, an influx of Albanians that began in the eighteenth century meant that by the 1980s Serbs formed only 10 percent of the population.)[25] He quickly formed an alliance with radical Serb nationalists and, by combining their underground networks with his own control over the transportation and communication facilities of the Serb republic, was able to engineer a series of mass, "spontaneous and popular," demonstrations that allowed him to shake up the ruling nomenklatura and to place his own clients in every important position of power.[26] By June 1989 he was able to arrange for one million Serbs to assemble for the six hundredth anniversary of the battle of Kosovo amidst a massive orgy of nationalist symbols.

Milošević used this combination of nationalist propaganda and street demonstrations to dominate the government of the Serb republic as well as the governments of several neighboring republics. In the summer and fall of 1988 he organized demonstrations in the autonomous districts of Vojvodina and Kosovo that toppled their governments and installed his clients. In January 1989 he successfully repeated this strategy and gained effective control over the government of Montenegro. This meant that Milošević then controlled half of the votes (those of Serbia, Vojvodina, Kosovo, and Montenegro) in Yugoslavia's eight-member collective presidency. Not surprisingly, this alarmed the other republics (Slovenia, Croatia, Bosnia, and Macedonia) where the development or revival of local nationalisms often appeared to be the natural defense against fears of Serb domination.[27]

Milošević had not invented Serb nationalism. But in his quest for power, he had systematically sponsored it, cultivated it, and put the instruments of the state apparatus in Belgrade to work promoting it. In the process, he violated the taboos and crippled the apparatus that the Yugoslav state had created to check local nationalisms in every region of the country. Perhaps the very existence of all these contending nationalisms shows that some deep human instinct exists to form groups and exclude outsiders. But Milošević's actions show clearly that how strong nationalist sentiments become, and what particular form they take, is something that can be affected or even determined by conscious political action and for personal advantage.[28]

Just how pliable and subject to political engineering nationalist or ethnic identity is becomes evident when examining the reaction to Milošević among the Muslims of Bosnia. When Milošević triggered a rebirth of nationalism after 1989, most Bosnian Catholics were quick to identify themselves as Croats and many Bosnian Orthodox renewed their fealty as Serbs. Bosnian Muslims, however, had common traditions as an ethnic group, but not as a nation.[29] That is, they shared an identity rooted in common cultural traits but no conviction that they deserved—or even wanted—the creation of a state for themselves.[30]

Throughout the modern period, Muslims formed the largest confession in Bosnia but never an absolute majority. (In 1991 they constituted just under 44 percent of the Bosnian population.)[31] They were not settled in discrete or compact areas within Bosnia that might easily be partitioned off; they were found in nearly all the towns and in villages widely scattered over the countryside. Politically active Bosnian Muslims, regardless of their personal ideological orientation, acknowledged the implications of this fact: They could not form a state of their own (unless they were willing to try to impose their rule over the majority of the population and trigger a civil war—which they were not). Both avowed secularists such as Adil Zulfikarpašić and religious reformers such as Alia Izetbegović agreed that, in any desirable future, Bosnia's Muslims would have to share a state with their Serb and Croat neighbors.[32]

For many years, this meant that Bosnia's Muslims refused to be Muslim nationalists—but it did not mean they could not be nationalists. Some became ardent Yugoslavs, seeing in the Yugoslav state a decent vehicle for sharing power with their neighbors without risking total subordination to them. They feared that the dissolution of Yugoslavia would probably leave them a minority divided between Croatia and Serbia. And they had learned during World War II that any war between Serbs and Croats was most likely to be fought out on their land. Thus, when the federal government began to dissolve, even men such as Izetbegović, who had spent years in Yugoslav prisons and who favored greater Bosnian autonomy, fought hard to find a formula that would keep Yugoslavia alive.[33]

Even when the secession of Slovenia and Croatia clearly had doomed Yugoslavia, Bosnia's Muslims did not become Muslim nationalists. They called for the creation of a Bosnian state in which Muslims, Serbs, and Croats would have equal rights as citizens. Instead of resurrecting the Bosnian flag that had flown over the region during its occupation by the Ottomans or the Austro-Hungarians—both of which featured the Islamic symbol of the crescent moon—they adopted the banner of the medieval kingdom of Bosnia, with its confessionally inoffensive fleurs-de-lis.[34] Many Bosnians took great joy in various events and institutions that symbolized the multiconfessional nature of their new republic: the makeup of the collective Bosnian presidency (which had to include two Muslims, two Croats, two Serbs, and one "Yugoslav"); the participation of thousands of Serbs (including the deputy commander of the Bosnian army, Col. Jovan Divjak) in the defense of Sarajevo against the siege imposed by their separatist coreligionists; and the aggressively pluralist staffing and editorial policies of the Sarajevo daily, *Oslobodjenje,* which also defied the siege.[35]

But Bosnian nationalism, with its multicultural character, proved difficult to promote in the midst of a civil war.[36] Treason, suspicion, and competition for diminishing resources strained the fraternity of the communities that supported Bosnia. The siege of Sarajevo led much of the population to flee; but those who remained in the city often felt betrayed by the emigrants, particularly if they went to stay with relatives in Zagreb or Belgrade. An increasing share of the population of the city was formed by rural Muslims who had been driven from their villages by ethnic cleansing and lacked the cosmopolitan traditions that sustained the multiculturalism of the original Sarajlije.[37] As the city's character became less multicultural, so did the politics of its Muslim community.

This was no accident. Primary objects of ethnic cleansing had been to seize land and to win recruits for the nationalist cause by poisoning relations between communities.

It was one thing to lay siege to Sarajevo, but in the ethnically mixed villages of Bosnia, the [Serb separatist] fighters could not pursue ethnic cleansing successfully on their own. They had to transform those local Serbs who were either still undecided about joining the fight or frankly opposed to it into their accomplices. The natural impulse for self-preservation was the fighters' greatest ally, providing they could summon up the necessary ruthlessness. One common method used was for a group of Serb fighters to enter a village, go to a Serb house, and order the man living there to come with them to the house of his Muslim neighbor. As the other villagers watched, he was marched over and the Muslim was brought out. Then the Serb would be handed a Kalashnikov assault rifle or a knife—knives were better—and ordered to kill the Muslim. If he did so, he had taken that step across the line the Chetniks [a colloquial term for Serb nationalists] had been aiming for. But if he refused, as many did, the solution was simple. You shot him on the spot. Then you repeated the process with the next Serb householder. If he refused, you shot him. The Chetniks rarely had to kill a third Serb. As a fighter in Bosanska Krupa, who, to my astonishment, boasted of the tactic, informed me gleefully, "By the third house, they're shitting themselves and asking you where you want the Muslim shot, and how many times."[38]

Ethnic cleansing thus worked two ways. Serbs who may have had no personal animus against Muslims became implicated in the process, even if they were only bystanders, and were thereafter more likely to endorse the separatist ideology. Many Muslims, meanwhile, gradually lost faith in the country's tradition of civility.

Being victimized by their neighbors not only made Bosnian Muslims angry, but it also gave them a common identity that they had lacked. For the first time, some began to think that they would be better off if they had a state of their own, in which Serbs and Croats would be the tolerated minorities.[39] This new variety of nationalism labored to create a state, not for Bosnians—a community in which Catholics, Orthodox, and Muslims all participated—but for Bosniaks, that is, Bosnian Muslims alone. This idea appeared increasingly logical as the war concentrated more and more of the country's Muslims into the tiny central corridor that was controlled by the Bosnian government.

Bosniak nationalism developed a following among the senior ranks of the Bosnian army. They began to form all-Muslim units, such as the Black Swan commandos and the Krajina Brigade, recruited from the survivors of ethnic cleansing.[40] A large following also developed inside the majority party, Izetbegović's Party of Democratic Action (known by its local acronym, SDA). As early as 1993 some of the party's leaders convened a "Bosniak assembly," at which only Muslims could vote, to discuss the country's future.[41] By 1994 the party-controlled Ministry of Culture was trying to press both radio stations and newspapers to propagate Bosniak sentiments.[42] In 1995 the SDA split in two: former prime minister Haris Silajdzić seceded to form his own party dedicated to a multicultural Bosnia while Izetbegović's wing drifted slowly toward Bosniak nationalism.[43]

Many Serbs and some Westerners have ranted that Bosnia is falling under the control of "Islamic fundamentalists." Nothing could be further from the truth.[44] The real tragedy in Bosnia is that a civic type of identity, Bosnian nationalism, which accords citizenship without distinguishing on the basis of an inhabitant's religion or culture, is slowly being edged out by a narrower, single-community ideology, Bosniak nationalism. Bosniak nationalism is no monstrosity and, despite its emphasis upon the common Islamic heritage of the Bosniaks, is much more a secular than a religious movement. It is much like the type of nationalism that Milošević culti-vated in Serbia and more recently developed in Croatia. Still, outside of the Balkans, few would applaud the development of any of these exclu-sionist, adversarial, and generally seedy ideologies—if only because they provide an open invitation to future warfare.

In ten years then, the identity of some Bosnian Muslims had evolved from being non-nationalist Muslims to Yugoslav nationalists to Bosnian nationalists to Bosniak-Muslim nationalists.[45] The speed of these transi-tions is impressive—particularly, perhaps, to Americans who have never had to change their identity in their lifetime.[46] The anthropologist Tone Bringa and a British film team caught the process on camera. Their doc-umentary, *Bosnia: We Are All Neighbors,* showed what happened to a mixed Muslim-Catholic village in central Bosnia as the fighting swept closer to them in 1992. The inhabitants had lived together amicably for as long as anyone could remember. Particularly among the women, close friendships that cut across confessional lines were commonplace. When war broke out, people initially swore that they would not let the battles in neighboring towns affect their own community. But when fighting spread to where the villagers could hear the artillery and when the factory where many of them worked in a nearby town was closed by combat, fear engulfed the whole community with shocking speed.[47]

Within a forty-eight-hour period, Catholics and Muslims stopped speaking to one another and became suspicious that anyone who did con-tinue communication across confessional lines must be a spy. When local Catholics took in family members from distant villages who had been made refugees by the fighting, they were distraught with anger, terror, and grief. They rallied to the local Croat militia. When that militia began to dig machine-gun emplacements above the village, local Muslims formed their own armed neighborhood watch. The two factions eyed each other warily for a few weeks; friendships faded, commerce halted, doubts and misgivings thrived. Then a single shot triggered a devastating clash. At the end of one day's fighting, the entire local Muslim community was driven from their homes. In private, individuals on both sides hoped that the prewar harmony might be restored; but in public, the two communities now appeared to be implacable enemies. If one did not know the history of the town, the hostility could easily be seen as the product of "ancient tribal rivalries."

Primordialism, for all its pessimism about the possibility of intercommunal harmony, presents a vision of the world that is more reassuring than the reality. It presumes that ethnic hatreds take years to develop, mature, and take root. In this, it echoes the language of nationalists and ethnic separatists themselves, who commonly try to bolster the legitimacy of their cause by claiming that their identities are rooted in ancient traditions and their hatreds are founded on long-standing grievances. In reality, both traditions and grievances often turn out to be very modern inventions.[48] How quickly people can turn against their neighbors, how rapidly civility can evaporate and be replaced by a frighteningly strident loathing, is disturbing.

Intense violence does not require an ancient pedigree; it can develop almost overnight. The age of a national or ethnic identity is no measure of its appeal or "authenticity." Converts are notoriously passionate, and the newest ideologies often attract the most fanatical followers.

However, a glint of hope can be found in these gloomy facts. Identities, loyalties, and hatreds are not eternal facts but social constructs. They come into being when conditions are right, and often only with the conscious decision of men such as Milošević (and women such as his wife, Mirjana, who by most accounts devised much of his political strategy) who see a way to derive personal benefit from their triumph. To sustain an ethnic hatred—even when conditions are favorable, even when it has the benefit of resting on "tradition"—takes effort.

The assumption of inertia, that cultural and social continuity do not require explanation, obliterates the fact that both have to be recreated anew in each generation, often with great pain and suffering. To maintain and transmit a value system, human beings are punched, bullied, sent to jail, thrown into concentration camps, cajoled, bribed, made into heroes, encouraged to read newspapers, stood up against a wall and shot, and sometimes even taught sociology. To speak of cultural inertia is to overlook the concrete interests and privileges that are served by indoctrination, education, and the entire complicated process of transmitting culture from one generation to the next.[49]

If constructing an ethnic hatred takes effort, then counterefforts can deconstruct (or demolish) one.

Serb nationalism is a couple of hundred years old. But the current form of Serb nationalism, with its emphasis upon separatism, its bitter resentment of Slovenes, Croats, and Bosnians, is much newer and shallower. It prospered when political elites, for rational (if hardly admirable) reasons, decided to lend it the support of state power, which had previously been dedicated to Yugoslav nationalism. Serb separatism has bolstered the power of these elites but has not yet delivered either economic or political benefits for the great majority of Serbs. Tempering the separatist element and promoting a more "neighborly" form of Serb nationalism would probably cost less and demand less social engineering than most people think.[50]

State Collapse: Cause or Consequence?

Recognizing that ethnic and national identities grow and dissolve, and change from active to passive, has policy implications—at several different levels. First, ethnic forces need not be accepted as immutable or inevitable; they can be used, altered, or combated. Second, schools of foreign policy thought that fail to recognize the mutability of ethnic forces—such as the version of global chaos theory promoted by Moynihan—are flawed as analysis and usually misleading as a guide to practice.[51]

The Moynihan thesis, that ethnic conflict causes instead of reflects the decay of the state, needs to be reevaluated in this light. Some cases exist in which the order of causation is much as Moynihan predicts. The Serb "awakening" that began in 1804 posed a real challenge to the Ottoman Empire and contributed to its downfall.[52] In a similar fashion, the growth of Croat nationalism in the years just before World War I helped to contribute to the collapse of the Habsburg empire. (In both cases, other factors, ranging from the Ottoman provincial reform movement of Selim III to the Bolshevik Revolution, also played a role.)

But in recent years, the Moynihan thesis has seemed much less applicable. In the dissolution of Yugoslavia, the upsurge of Albanian nationalism—particularly the violent demonstrations in Kosovo during 1981—was one of the events that helped to trigger the country's problems.[53] But the crisis of the Yugoslav state was clearly much more an autonomous product of economic pressures. In turn, the revival of Serb nationalism after 1987—not to mention the sudden explosion of Croat nationalism after 1989—followed, not caused, the crisis of the state.[54] And the invention of Bosnian and Bosniak nationalism was virtually unthinkable until after the Yugoslav state had already collapsed.

When the state decays, the process can, up to a certain point, enhance certain formal freedoms—it can appear to parallel the process of democratization. The growth of freedom often entails imposing limits upon the power of the state: curbing its ability to search and seize, requiring due process, swathing individuals and organizations with certain rights. But past a certain point it undermines democracy; there is no power to be publicly controlled.[55]

Even before state decay reaches this point, it is likely to foster civil strife. The state no longer holds in check criminal elements or secessionist minorities. New local organizations are revived or invented to deal with the tasks that the state no longer serves. And the division of territory and responsibility among these local organizations is not clear, making competition and eventually conflict among them likely. (And this conflict makes sustaining anything like democracy difficult.)

The dissolution of Yugoslavia provides a good example of this. The taproot of state decay in Yugoslavia was unquestionably economic (a point that even Robert Kaplan emphasizes in his later reflections upon *Balkan Ghosts*).[56] Susan L. Woodward, in her *Balkan Tragedy*, provides an excellent account of how the country's accumulating economic problems in the 1980s steadily translated into political decay.[57] Like many developing countries, Yugoslavia borrowed heavily in the aftermath of the 1973 oil price shock and then suffered repayment problems when interest rates rose sharply in the late 1970s.[58] To deal with this crisis, the federal government—working in close consultation with the International Monetary Fund—devised a series of austerity programs that sought to accumulate funds for debt service by cutting national consumption. As a result, real net personal income declined rapidly and steadily after 1978 (falling 24 percent in 1988 alone), dropping back to the levels of the 1960s.[59] The austerity measures, however, hit various parts of the country differently. Slovenia, whose economy was export-oriented, maintained full employment while in the district of Kosovo, whose products were largely marketed domestically, unemployment reached 50 percent.[60]

The economic crisis and the unequal burdens it imposed on different republics triggered a series of debates. Some, led by the republican government of Slovenia, argued that the restraints of the federal government should be loosened, allowing each republic to seek its own economic niche (an approach favored by the more prosperous republics). Others, who found champions in the republican government of Serbia, favored strengthening federal institutions, an approach that offered the prospect of both greater financial discipline and greater integration of the Yugoslav national market. As the argument between these alternatives grew more heated and desperate, some republics began to take preemptive action—a process that steadily eroded the powers of the federal state.

The austerity program adopted by the federal government had a noxious effect on its own budget: Revenue from customs duties and sales tax declined. This effect was aggravated by the growing debate among the republics, many of which defaulted on their payments to the central government. Since more than half of the federal government's budget was devoted to the armed forces, nasty debates took place about how much the country needed its military apparatus anyway.

The system hit a showdown over Kosovo in 1987.[61] Milošević discovered that appealing to Serb nationalist sentiments and pressing for tighter control of Kosovo by Belgrade could be used to promote both his personal power and his program for strengthening federal institutions.[62] The Slovene leadership opposed these actions, supporting Kosovar autonomy.

For decades, economic reform in Yugoslavia had revolved around the idea of decentralization and involved shifting powers and responsibilities away from the federal government and down to its constituent republics. By the late 1980s economic reform had decentralized state functions to the point where the republics increasingly operated on their own, and republican leaders began to bolster their claims to autonomous power by resurrecting local nationalist sentiments.[63] Croat, Slovene, and Serb nationalism had old histories, but their sudden revival in the late 1980s was made possible because they began to receive energetic support from the republican governments.[64] The 1987 "conversion" of the Leninist functionary Slobodan Milošević into a militant Serb nationalist was only the most famous instance of a process repeated across Yugoslavia and throughout the former Leninist states.[65]

Under these influences, most of the Yugoslav republics evolved into independent states with surprising speed. They beefed up their "home guards" into serious armies and restructured their ruling party bureaucracies into modern civil services. Unlike so many states in the developing countries, the Yugoslav successor states quickly proved that they were more than mere "quasi-states," ruling cliques with a flag and a seat at the UN General Assembly.[66] They were fully functional organizations that could provide public security and a framework for economic action—or organize ruthless campaigns of war and terror.

But in Bosnia the political devolution of Yugoslavia followed a different pattern. The local republican government proved much weaker, much less statelike, than its peers in Slovenia, Croatia, and Serbia. When the power of the federal state began to collapse, Bosnians turned not to the government of the republic but to other, even more local and diverse, institutions. Some authorities have dubbed these institutions, "boasting certain essential attributes of a normal state but grotesquely lacking in others," as "parastates."[67]

A variety of factors combined to prevent the republican government of Bosnia from following the straightforward path to statehood found in Serbia or Croatia. In August 1987 a major economic scandal led to a broad purge of the Bosnian nomenklatura. The local branch of the League of Communists, the ruling party, was left decimated—and was thus in no position to "convert" to nationalism and to provide a leadership role for the new republic.[68] Partly because of this, as Yugoslavia began to decay, the leaders of other republics were much quicker than the Bosnians to snatch control of the federal government's assets—even when they were located on Bosnian territory. Bosnia had been, for example, the locale for many of Yugoslavia's most important military bases and arms industries. But when the country began to fall apart, the officer corps of the federal army (which was 54 percent ethnic-Serb) conspired with the republican government in Belgrade to seize many of these assets and transferred control of them to Serbia or its local allies.[69] Where they could not sustain such control, facilities were stripped or sabotaged. This was the fate of $50 million worth of equipment at the gigantic Bihać airbase and of the central telephone exchange in Sarajevo.[70]

Because the republican government was crippled, the next most obvious candidate to act as a protostate were the political parties. The Bosnian branch of the ruling party, the League of Communists, never recovered from the scandals of 1986–87 and had effectively ceased to function by 1989. New parties, however, had begun to develop. The most effective were the Serb Democratic Party (known by its local acronym as the SDS) and the Croatian Democratic Alliance (HDZ). Both originated in Croatia (the former was founded to represent the demands of the Serb minority within Croatia) and then spread to Bosnia in 1989.[71] They quickly grew into highly effective organizations, a transformation that was greatly facilitated by the funds, technical advice, and arms they received from the states of Serbia and Croatia. They quickly created their own assemblies, militias, logistics, and so on.

The Bosnian Muslims were also quick to form their own nationalist vehicle, the Party of Democratic Action (SDA).[72] The SDA, however, lacked the sponsorship of any strong state. Moreover, it was internally divided between one faction that supported creating a state for Bosnian Muslims and another that favored preserving Bosnia as a multiethnic state in which Muslims, Croats, and Serbs each played a role. The SDA worked to slowly repair the republican government of Bosnia and to build it into an effective state structure, but it took them years of struggle. The outbreak of war in April 1992 complicated the task, although it also lent the Bosnians the energies of sheer desperation.

During this struggle, the fabric of the Bosnian state had to be stiffened by seeking support from a series of other entities, particularly local organizations. This is a common development whenever states come close to collapse. People, abandoned by the failing structures of the state, look increasingly to local, sometimes previously nonpolitical, institutions to provide the services and security that they once expected of their central government.

Even before the dissolution of Yugoslavia, it was common throughout Bosnia for a single local industry to dominate the politics of a town or region. For example, life in Maglaj revolves around its giant paper mill and in Zenica around its huge steel plant.[73] These industries provided most employment as well as medical care, housing, investment capital, and a host of other public services for the surrounding communities. (This was a common pattern in many Leninist states, including the Soviet Union.)[74] When the state collapsed, these firms were quickly saddled with additional responsibilities.

For example, in the northwest Bosnian region of Bihać, the trade organization Agrokomerc acted as a parastate, organizing both economic and political life.[75] Ironically, the shady finances of Agrokomerc had been at the center of the 1987 corruption scandal that wrought such havoc among the Bosnian political elite.⁷⁶ The firm, which had employed thirteen thousand people, had lost many of its productive assets, but its director, Fikret Abdić, survived the purges with much of his local political influence intact. His patronage was still potent enough to allow him to erect a local political machine, which proved the most effective single vote-getter for the SDA. Abdić had enough power to hold off the spread of civil war to Bihać for several years, personally supervising the removal of barricades erected by fearful local Serbs and Muslims.⁷⁷ Playing up the neutrality of his enclave, he turned it into a profitable center for smuggling and trade in war materials. Eventually he even recruited his own ten thousand-man militia.⁷⁸ In 1993, however, he overplayed his hand. He declared Bihać independent of the rest of Bosnia and formed an alliance with Serb separatists against the government in Sarajevo. By 1995 his forces were defeated and he found himself in exile.⁷⁹

One of the more unusual (but potent) parastatal organizations that played a role in Bosnia was a community association. The Sarajevo suburb of Dobrinja grew up during the 1970s and 1980s, a large section of it having been constructed as part of the Olympic village for the 1984 Winter Games. Its forty-five thousand inhabitants were largely "yuppies," engineers, architects, and doctors in their late thirties, and, though they represented every ethnic community in Yugoslavia, they shared a common loyalty to secular government and civic institutions. Although Dobrinja was surrounded by Serb militias from the earliest hours of the war, it quickly recruited its own highly effective "neighborhood defense" militia. As the siege of Sarajevo dragged on for months and then years, Dobrinja set an example (rarely emulated) for the entire city by carefully organizing the distribution of food, water, and other scarce resources along collectivist lines. Each apartment building elected its own representative to a neighborhood council that included militia leaders.⁸⁰ The example of ethnic fraternity in Dobrinja helped the Bosnian government to retain the loyalty of many of the 200,000 Serbs who continued to live within the territories it controlled even after the SDS had led many others to secede.⁸¹

Nowhere is the role of parastates more striking than in the Bosnian defense forces. Most of the Yugoslav military assets—troops, officers, tanks, munitions—located in Bosnia in 1991 wound up under the control of Serbia or Serb separatists. Only a handful of regular soldiers (and a slightly larger number of police) chose to follow the orders of the Bosnian government. To supplement these forces, the SDA organized its own all-volunteer militia, popularly known as the "Green Berets."⁸² These forces, however, would hardly have been adequate to withstand the onslaught of the heavily armed Serb separatists had it not been for two other sources of troops. First, many veterans who had served as conscripts in the Yugoslav army banded together spontaneously to defend their villages or neighborhoods. Second, organized crime, which already had weapons and knew how to use them, rushed to the aid of the government.[83]

In Sarajevo in April 1992, during the critical first days of the Serb siege, Musan Topalović and Ramiz Delalić, the "dons" of two local mafias that had once organized local protection rackets and loan sharking, led the erection of barricades, created neighborhood defense networks, and impressed citizens with their personal courage.[84] In the Drina Valley enclave of Srebrenica, where forty-four thousand Muslim refugees were surrounded by Serbs for more than three years, the local defense was organized by Nasir Orić, a local tough who had once served as a bodyguard to Serbia's president Milošević.[85] Criminal gangs led the organization of parastates in several Bosnian communities—Muslim, Croat, and Serb alike.[86] The most aggressive forces among the Serb separatists—and the most loyal defenders of their local chieftain, Radovan Karadžić—were "the Serb Tigers." These irregulars, who committed some of the worst atrocities of the war, were led by Arkan, the nom de guerre of Zeljko Raznjatović, a gangster who before the war was wanted by Interpol for a trail of murders and robberies across Europe.[87]

But in Bosnia, the power of these mafias and parastates was eventually curbed—and in the process the regional decay of state power was arrested and slowly reversed. The central government slowly asserted some control over the profiteers in Bihać and the gangsters in Sarajevo and gradually built its own army into a professional—if still poorly equipped—organization. President Izetbegović and his supporters showed no special talent for state formation, but their efforts were reinforced by two factors. First, the external threat of Serb ethnic cleansing, which in places such as Srebrenica meant simple physical extermination, compelled Bosnians to band together and seek central coordination of their efforts. Second, once it received international recognition as the legitimate government of Bosnia, the Izetbegović regime qualified for various forms of foreign support: weapons from Iran, food deliveries by the Americans, economic aid and advice from the UN and the European Community, and so on.[88] As of 1995 the government in Sarajevo seemed likely to succeed in building a state with some of the same strengths— and many of the same problems—as its neighbors.

The reach of the Sarajevo government will probably prove much shorter than the advocates of a multicultural Bosnia originally envisioned. It was only one of three states that had put down roots in the country. Its writ ran only to the largely Muslim districts of central Bosnia (and was not always honored there). It was supposed to be joined in a federation with the Croats who predominated in the southwestern part of the country, Herzegovina, but this alliance was always tenuous and the Bosnian Croats seemed to be edging steadily closer to union with Croatia. Similarly, under the Dayton accords of 1995, the Serb separatists were supposed to stay part of a wider Bosnian state but in practice remained self-governing. And wherever the claims of these three nascent states overlapped, the potential for violence remained high.

In the light of what is now known about Bosnia, the Moynihan thesis—that ethnic conflict led to the collapse of the Soviet Union—seems increasingly dubious.[89] The great majority of post–cold war culture and ethnic conflicts erupted in the territories of the former Soviet Union. Exactly what led to the crisis of the Soviet regime in the early 1980s is a topic that scholars will debate for decades to come. Like the debate over the causes of the decline of the Roman Empire, the quest for the "ultimate" cause of the "Leninist extinction" is likely to go on interminably.[90] The moral decadence of marxism, the inherent illegitimacy of totalitarianism, the economic challenge of China, the debilitating burden of sustaining a grossly inefficient military, the "clever plan" of Ronald Reagan to force Moscow into an exhausting competition; these and many other explanations have their advocates.[91] But, with the exception of Moynihan and a handful of primordialists, virtually all participants in the debate agree that the Soviet system was already in deep trouble by 1985—before anything resembling systematic nationalist resistance to the regime began to develop. Most students agree that the first example of nationalist revolt adduced by Hélène Carrère d'Encausse—the riots in Alma-Ata, the capital of Kazakhstan, in December 1986—testified to how corrupt and decayed Soviet government structures had already become in the provinces long before that date.[92]

The Varieties of State Collapse

In the early 1990s the problem of state collapse attracted the attention of policymakers. It was a problem not only in Yugoslavia but also across the territories of the former Soviet Union and in many other places, such as

Zaire and Afghanistan. A pair of American diplomats penned an influential article arguing that such "failed states" should be administered as trusteeships ("conservatorships") by the United Nations.[93] Samuel Huntington and his colleagues devoted long seminars to trying to develop alternative solutions to the problem.[94]

One of the first things those grappling with this problem discovered was that it came in many different forms. Even within the former Yugoslavia, the state could collapse in more than one way. In Kosovo, for example, the experience was dramatically different from that of Bosnia. In Kosovo,

> the anarchist dream has been realized at least for a moment. Kosovo, like Bosnia, is the site of ethnic conflict between Albanians (90 percent of the population) and Serbs (guarding their holy shrines). Since Milošević took away Kosovo's autonomy several years ago, a few Serb Stalinists have occupied the government's offices and, on paper, ruled the province. But the Albanians simply seceded from the state without leaving the territory. They do not pay taxes, rent, or utility bills to the provincial government. Instead, the Albanian parliamentarians reassembled secretly, elected their own government, and assessed informal taxes on their community. Now, the Albanians obey their informal government, apparently without coercion. They live by smuggling and remittances from Germany. They attend informal schools in houses and mosques and are all learning English, and quite well.[95]

Saying that Bosnia and the states of the former Yugoslavia were in any sense lucky, given the recent history of massacres, systematic rape, plunder, torture, and concentration camps, is perverse. Yet a discomfiting fact remains that, as terrible as their sufferings were, other countries in similar situations have experienced worse—because they could not match the effectiveness of the parastate structures that provided a foundation for rebuilding public order in Bosnia, or constructing "underground" parastates in Kosovo.

Consider the unhappy story of recent Somali history. In their excellent monograph, *Somalia: State Collapse, Multilateral Intervention, and Strategies for Political Reconstruction,* Terence Lyons and Ahmed Samatar show that the Somali state dissolved in 1989–90 under the impact of forces that were remarkably similar to those that demolished Yugoslavia.

The declining value of Somalia's cattle exports in the early 1980s forced the country to borrow heavily abroad.[96] Becoming one of the most colossal debtors in sub–Saharan Africa (by 1989 its external debt total was twenty-six times the total annual value of its exports of goods and services), it, too, was forced into negotiations with the International Monetary Fund, which advocated a series of austerity programs that drastically undercut the living standards of the man and woman on the street.[97] Again, this aggravated both class and regional differences inside the country. Inhabitants of the northern districts (formerly united as the British colony of "Somaliland") felt that they bore more than their share of the burden of economic adjustment.[98] These problems were compounded by political mismanagement. The regime of President Siad Barre not only excluded northerners from his government but, as a result of his irredentist efforts to liberate the Ogaden district from Ethiopia, also provoked a war and a series of guerrilla battles that afflicted the north.[99] In 1981 the northerners formed the Somali National Movement (SNM) to oppose Siad Barre.[100] In 1988–89 the fighting between the regime and the movement escalated into a full-scale civil war, which drew in growing numbers of southerners who also had grievances against the regime.

Siad Barre was defeated and fled the country in January 1991. But the collapse of the ancien regime had different effects in each region of the country. In the northern "Somaliland" provinces, the SNM leadership declared its intention to secede from the rest of Somalia. Despite tensions between factions in the SNM military, traditional political elites managed to negotiate solutions to conflict and restore public order. This, in turn, permitted a slow recovery of the economy.[101] Somaliland's success was thus analogous to that of Slovenia, which emerged relatively unscathed from the dissolution of Yugoslavia.

But the rest of Somalia neither emulated Slovenia nor imitated Serbia or Bosnia. In the south and central portions of the country, the civil war bred a host of contending authorities, most of which were in no position to replace the services once performed by the evaporating state. There were exceptions; for example, in the southern port of Merca, a diverse coalition of Islamists calling themselves the Islamic Union seized local control and imposed a Qur'anic version of law and order.[102] But across most of the south, warlords and their militias held sway. During the civil war, the Somali army had dissolved unit by unit, with colonels and generals leading their troops off and then setting themselves up in power in one district or another. These warlords—Gen. Mohamed Said Hersi "Morgan,"

Mohamed Farah Aideed, Col. Ahmed Omar Jess, Ali Mahdi Mohamed, and others—reinforced their authority by making appeals to their "clans," the segmentary lineages that had provided the foundation of social organization in precolonial Somalia. While clan loyalties still retained effectiveness, the traditional clan leadership had attenuated across much of the country. Traditional elites were prevented from playing the moderating role they had in the north, leaving the warlords with final political authority.[103]

Fundamentally, the authority of the warlords was not based on their clan standing but on their ability to deliver booty. In a familiar "protection racket," they hired their troops out to the various multinational charities that were moving food to curb famine in Somalia. They routinely pilfered the supplies they were supposed to be guarding. The warlords paid their forces primarily by means of pillage; their troops stole cars, occupied apartment buildings, sold off blank passports looted from government offices, and so on.[104] The warlords were thus not acting as quasistates or parastates. Their dependence upon booty put them at odds with the reassertion of any form of property rights or public order.[105]

But this was not the worst of it. Each militia looked after its own—at the expense of everyone else. The militias raided each other constantly and killed thousands of civilians in their attempts to seize territory. This warfare, and not any "natural" calamity, triggered the famines that racked Somalia during the 1990s.[106] Exactly how many people died will remain a matter of controversy. When the Somalia state collapsed, so did the ability to collect even rudimentary statistics. Hunger alone had probably killed between 500,000 and one million people by the time the famine peaked in the summer of 1992.[107] No reliable numbers are available on those killed in the fighting itself, but the battles—which leveled significant parts of towns as far flung as Boosaaso and Kismaayo—certainly claimed tens of thousands.[108]

While the casualty totals in the former Yugoslavia are debated, too, more people probably died in Somalia than in Bosnia.[109] Whether the slow death of Somali children in the Baidoa famine is somehow less horrible than the genocidal spasms visited on Muslim Bosniaks at Omarska and Srebrenica is a judgment best left to Munkir and Nakir, the angels that Islamic tradition claims record the book of the dead. Whatever their bottom line, this much is clear: The existence of a state in Bosnia meant that at some point the killing could be curtailed and public services gradually restored. Even if the Dayton peace accord unravels, Bosnians already knew more security in 1995 than their Somali counterparts.

Despite a $1 billion-per-year intervention by eighteen thousand UN troops, of whom more than one hundred were killed, the war in Somalia lingers and the killing continues—albeit at a slower rate.[110] Many years will pass before the violence is brought under control, and an effective, unified Somali state may never develop.

With the examples of Bosnia and Somalia in mind, appreciating how state decay might contribute to ethnic conflict is easy. In the 1990s the world was littered with the relics of states that were wrecked during the cold war, such as Afghanistan, Angola, Cambodia, and Ethiopia. In all of these former states, as in Somalia, state decay was prominent among the variety of factors that combined to promote ethnic conflict.

Conclusion

The primordialist image is behind one of the most misleading policy claims of global chaos theory: the notion that the United States cannot deal with ethnic conflicts because they are rooted in "ancient tribal rivalries" that are ultimately irrational and not pliable by conventional political or military techniques. This council of despair is unwarranted. Ethnic rivalries may have some deep, dark foundation, but the bulk of the energies driving them are contemporary. These energies can be awesome. Just because they are recent does not mean they are false or superstructural, any more than their being based on inaccurate history makes them inauthentic. But just how powerful they are deserves serious study, for sometimes they are transparent and transient.

State collapse is not the only cause of ethnic conflicts, but today it is one of the major forces that fuels the growth of ethnic militancy, nationalism, and religious radicalism.

At its heart, state collapse involves the breakdown of a system of power. The modern state is a specific coterie of institutions that creates a new order of power by pooling and coordinating the energies of subgroups and individuals.[111] As the state grows weaker, abuses its powers, or fails to deliver services, persuading people to contribute to it becomes harder. Such decay may be long and slow (as in the Chinese and Ottoman Empires), but often it is terrifyingly sudden. At some point, the process crosses a threshold, cascade effects set in, and state power collapses.

Often this is marked as a revolution. People, uniformly eager to restore order, transfer their loyalty to a new regime. As Alexis de Tocqueville noted, revolutions that begin with the collapse of state power often have the paradoxical consequence of dramatically strengthening the state.[112] In many ways, this happened in much of the former Yugoslavia and the former Soviet Union. An old state died, but its citizens quickly transferred their loyalties to parastates and then to new states.

But this is not always the case. Sometimes the state dies and is not replaced by different states, but by chaos. When state power evaporates in this manner, the results are terrifying for modern societies. At least, the provision of many services on which people have come to depend comes to an end—from the post office to public order, including the guarantee of property rights, the adjudication of contract disputes, and physical security.

One of the great experts on modern China, Franz Schurmann, showed an acute understanding of how people react to the collapse of authority in his discussion of what happens when empires collapse. In his critique of the American war in Vietnam, Schurmann was forced to admit that "the American Empire" had stronger support worldwide than he would have expected.

> Looking at the history of mankind, it is not surprising that there are so many unexpected sources of support for the American Empire. Empires by and large have been seen as of great benefit, and their passing is regretted. The Roman Empire finally crumbled but the empire lived on in Western Europe as the Holy Roman Empire, which only Napoleon finally ended. In the East it lived on as Byzantium and then as the Ottoman Empire, which only ended after World War I. The Chinese Empire of two millennia created, maintained, and spread one of the greatest of the world's civilizations, which even its enemies on the peripheries have always admired. . . . History shows that darkness and war follow the collapse of empires. In 1973 a whole array of nations, once intent upon restraining America's violent adventurism, came to fear what could happen if the world order, for which America was the core, collapsed.[113]

The collapse of empires, which are loosely bound polities over great areas, is far less disruptive than the collapse of states. Is it any wonder then, that the fear of state collapse provokes violent responses?

CHAPTER ELEVEN

From Chaos
to Complexity

Most of the available evidence suggests that global chaos theory is wrong about most of its major claims. Globalization does not seem to be a major cause of culture clashes. Conflicts among cultures seem to be fairly evenly distributed throughout human societies. Anomie or the collapse of values does not seem to be an important cause of collective violence (although it may play a role in disposing individuals to murder, suicide, and so on). Wars today appear to be caused by the same mixture of forces that have propelled combat throughout history: fear, desperation, want, arrogance, foolishness, and myriad other forces. Finally, neither the number of conflicts nor their savagery seems to have increased dramatically. This is not to say war is not a nasty business—but that is hardly news.

What lessons for the conduct of U.S. foreign policy can Washington draw from the shortcomings of global chaos theory? The most obvious lessons are negative. If global chaos theory fundamentally misunderstands the dynamics of contemporary politics, it is legitimate to treat its own policy recommendations warily. President Clinton would have been well advised not to base his Bosnia policy on a reading of *Balkan Ghosts*. Americans need not gird themselves for a looming clash of civilizations because battles of this kind are not the dominant form of conflict in today's world.

Some of the negative lessons that can be drawn from the critique of global chaos theory are more specific and concrete. For example, some chaos theorists have suggested that, because (they claim) globalization causes culture conflict, everyone should be cautious about anything that promotes globalization. They argue that America should be cautious about rushing to encourage the development of democracy or free speech in other societies because this can breed nationalist backlash. They worry that immigration and multicultural education or anything else that forces alien values into contact may ignite tensions. Whether or not democratization or multicultural education are good ideas can be debated, but the evidence suggests that culture conflict ranks low among the problems they are likely to cause.

In balance, over the short term, globalization does appear to disrupt societies, and sometimes this can produce conflict. Yet over the long term globalization also seems to often promote prosperity, political legitimacy, and even greater intercultural understanding. Even if someone could figure out a way to hold back or reverse globalization, this approach would probably indirectly fuel more culture conflicts than it would suppress.

A second negative lesson that can be drawn from the critique of global chaos theory concerns America's pattern of alliances or engagement with other countries around the world. Samuel Huntington has called for Washington to construct a system of alliances that ensures the victory of "the West against the rest." Although few global chaos theorists have endorsed this slogan, they, too, generally favor an alliance of the industrial countries of the "zone of peace" to face the threats and trouble that seem to characterize the third world. Nothing in the critique suggests that anything is wrong with strong alliances among the Western or industrialized states—but to view this as directed against the bloc of less developed countries could be dangerous.

The countries of "the global South" are diverse. They include some of the world's fastest growing economies and some of the fastest decaying ones. They include states of great stability, some with impressive democratic credentials, and other states that either exist only on paper or are formed from the stuff of nightmares. About all these countries share in common is that they are industrializing later, historically, than the West. That has never been enough to make them a single bloc—and any effort to lump them all together and treat them as if they were the same will fail. Even the countries that seem to share a common culture or civilization cannot be pigeonholed together. For example, Malaysia and Indonesia, which have Muslim majorities, have a great deal more in common with other newly industrializing countries such as Singapore than they do with other Muslim nations such as Afghanistan or Egypt.

American stockholders have already discovered that some of the best investments in the world today are in "emerging markets." Potentially and in fact, some of Washington's best allies—loyal, strategically positioned, influential—can also be found in the third world. Differences of culture rarely prevent states from understanding when they have common interests. America can judge its allies on their merits, without worrying that differences of religion or lifestyle will inevitably drive a wedge between them.

A final negative lesson from the critique of global chaos theory concerns the organization and application of the U.S. military. Many chaos theorists thought that the fanaticism and bloodlust of combatants in culture conflicts made them impervious to normal calculations of deterrence, pressure, and force majeure. They argued that either America should avoid intervening in such battles wherever possible or, when it was forced to engage, it might need to deploy large numbers of troops and be prepared for a long frustrating battle with high casualties on both sides.

War is a grave, ugly business, but ethnic or cultural wars are not substantially different from ideological or venal wars. Some culture wars are fought by irregular or guerrilla combatants who are hard to distinguish from the civilian population and must be rooted out in protracted, often grotesquely violent campaigns. (Anyone who thinks that regular armies cannot defeat guerrilla fighters should study what the Iraqis did in Kurdistan during the 1980s—although this is an example one hopes few democracies will emulate.) Others are fought by regular armies, commanded from centralized capitals, that can be defeated by entirely conventional means. (The Bosnian Serbs fell into this category, despite their experience with guerrilla warfare during World War II.)

Nothing changed at the end of the cold war that, by itself, requires America to develop a new form of military organization. The enemies, threats, and nuisances Washington faces today resemble those it has dealt with in the past. Perhaps it can afford a smaller military (perhaps it never needed the huge one it fielded during the cold war). America (like other democracies) has some problems prosecuting guerrilla wars in which the Pentagon's insistence upon applying overwhelming force conflicts with the political interest in minimizing casualties among the civilians who live cheek-to-jowl with enemy troops—but this was as much of a problem in Vietnam as it was in Somalia. Ethnic or cultural wars are won by much the same means that lead to victory in other battles.

Perhaps the most egregious myth about ethnic conflict that global chaos theory helped to propagate was the idea that Washington will be generally powerless to deal with ethnic conflict. Clinton thought he had learned this lesson from reading *Balkan Ghosts*—that America could not bring peace to Bosnia unless it was prepared to obliterate the fanatics of Serb separatism and to absorb the massive casualties that mission would require. But ethnic wars are not markedly different from other types of warfare. Washington had at least as many different options about how to deploy U.S. power to end the conflict in Bosnia as it did in 1990 when it decided to "liberate" Kuwait.

Ethnic conflicts are much less chaotic than they often seem in Western press accounts. They often appear when economic competition increases and political institutions decay. They are not usually started or fought by sociopaths, victims of atavism, anomie, or other crazy people. Even the wildest fringe elements in most ethnic conflicts are more like Mafia dons than serial killers. They are good family men, as popular and respected within their own local community as they are feared and hated outside of it. And many of the worst atrocities in ethnic wars—as in nonethnic wars—are conducted by people who, for good or ill, resemble Lt. Col. Oliver North—people who think they are "doing their duty" or serving "a higher cause."

Chaos is not a strategic threat, certainly not in the way that global chaos theorists would have people believe. It cannot be legitimately invoked to justify maintaining the Pentagon's inflated budgets or compel European allies to keep their wagons in the circle of the Atlantic alliance's laager. Despite all the din to the contrary, a global explosion of new and menacing ethnic conflicts has not occurred. What ethnic conflicts do exist are not markedly more savage or deadly or less tractable than other types of warfare in the developing countries.

Structural Lessons

The proponents of global chaos theory may have been wrong about many things, but they were not stupid or foolish. They were trying hard to see beyond today's headlines into the trends that would dominate the future. They were attempting to dig beneath the deceptive surfaces of events to unearth the deeper structures of history. They were not primarily interested in the tactical mechanisms that might be useful for resolving ethnic and cultural conflicts: patterns of negotiation, leadership, compromise, and small-group psychology. Instead, they looked for the strategic concepts that might help them to anticipate, prevent, or remedy many disparate culture conflicts.

The focus upon grand strategy has left its mark upon this critique as well. This manuscript has concentrated upon structural mechanisms that produce and shape culture conflicts, not upon the tactics that policymakers might use when dealing with them in "crisis management" mode. The development of such tactics is extremely important: brilliant strategy cannot help win a war if battlefield tactics are so poor that troops are routed in every concrete engagement. But this has not been a book about tactics, and to suddenly introduce a discussion of tactics in the conclusion could only be a jarring, unsupported departure from its earlier themes—a kind of op-ed piece tacked onto the end.

However, in the discussion of the strategic thinking of the global chaos theorists, certain positive ideas about how to deal with culture conflicts have emerged organically, flowing naturally from the analysis. They have not been the kind of paradigm-shift insights that suggest a whole new way of dealing with the problem. But they do provide some concrete pointers about how to cope with the problem of culture conflict. They may not provide one with a blueprint for eliminating ethnic conflict, but they provide a decent sketch of where people might focus their efforts.

One real surprise emerged from the "back-of-the-envelope" sketches: The common expectation among contemporary scholars (and almost anyone who has been influenced by the ideas of the eighteenth century Enlightenment) was that culture conflicts would be concentrated among societies that are poorer, politically unstable, and at the early stages of socioeconomic development. Even global chaos theorists share a version of this idea. They understand that the forces of globalization are strongest among the fully industrialized countries of the West. But they believe that the modern cultures of the West have had time to adapt to these forces and now insulate people from the most painful intrusions of globalization. In contrast, less developed societies have had less time, and fewer resources, with which to adapt and thus seem more likely to be susceptible to culture conflicts.

But the tally of culture wars and culture strife showed a different picture. Culture conflict appeared to be distributed randomly among more developed and less developed societies. This seemed to confirm the claim of Daniel Patrick Moynihan and Nathan Glazer that ethnic identity and ethnic conflict would not just fade away as modernization proceeds. But the tally also showed that the lethality of culture conflicts varied according to the general level of development in society. In countries that were more rich, more politically stable, and more familiar with the forces of globalization, culture conflicts were far more likely to take the form of strife than of war. In countries that were less prosperous, less stable, and less familiar with globalization, culture conflict often involved the large casualties and organized military slaughter associated with full-scale culture wars.

Optimists may see in this pattern evidence of the existence of something that deserves to be called "civilization"—not in the sense of a group of people bound together by values that make them disposed to clash with other civilizations, but in the sense of groups of people who have developed alternatives to organized violence as a means of resolving their internal disputes.[1] (This is the broad conclusion that experts on the evolution of values in industrial cultures, such as John Mueller and Ronald Inglehart, have reached.)[2] There may not be a unitary problem of culture conflict. Instead, two discrete problems may exist: one of culture strife and another of culture war.

The riots and oppression associated with culture strife are not generally a pressing problem for the international community. In an era of growing concern for human rights, incidents of culture strife may provoke sympathy from the international community, but they are not much of a threat to international order. They do not usually produce the cross-border repercussions associated with culture wars—sudden influxes of large mobs of terrified refugees; strong demands for arms imports that can destabilize local military balances; pressure for the export of drugs and contraband to finance arms imports; and the horror of genocide that challenges the rule of law internationally.

Culture strife may persist for generations; racial violence in the United States is an example. Yet most countries seem to slowly develop their own mechanisms for containing and ameliorating such disputes. Certainly little reason exists to expect that the international community could do a better job. Thus, if German skinheads attack ethnic Turks (or Kurds), the problem is probably best left for the German government (perhaps with some collaboration from Turkey) to deal with. More controversial, if Uighurs and Tibetans occasionally riot against rule by Han Chinese, international action probably cannot be sustained, much less prove effective.

International action seems to be called for primarily in those cases where culture conflicts have escalated to the level of culture wars. But this does not always follow. Culture wars may produce the type of border-hopping repercussions that elicit international concern—but they may not. The international community may develop an interest in a particular culture war or it may not. International interests (like national ones) are not objective facts, deducible with some scientific certainty. Instead, they are political constructs that develop through a process of haggling, pressure, and compromise among subjective assessments. Whether or not the international community had an interest in or mandate for intervening in the tragic war in Bosnia was not a fact waiting to be discovered but an artifact waiting to be invented.[3]

What can be said with greater certainty is that, when Washington or the international community gets involved in culture wars, both the strategic and tactical aspects of the problem must be attended to. Culture strife tends to be a problem with largely tactical solutions. It is not a reflection of the general poverty of society or of crises such as state collapse. Culture wars, in contrast, are bred by deeper structural problems. Thus, something can legitimately be said about what Washington—or the international community—might fruitfully do to deal with the structural aspect of culture wars.

Assessing the Risk of State Collapse

The absence of material prosperity and political stability seem to be the two major structural problems that are most closely associated with the outbreak of ethnic or culture wars. So to prevent such wars all one needs do is promote economic growth and good government. Simple, no?

No. Both economic and political development remain daunting tasks, and limited expert agreement exists about how to foster them. Perhaps, greater hope can be found that they are more widely attainable now than twenty years ago. The success of the green revolution in countries such as Bangladesh and of export-led industrialization in countries such as South Korea have penetrated the gloom of the "limits to growth" pessimists. The spread or revival of democratic institutions throughout Latin America and in parts of Asia and Africa holds out the prospect of more civil governance. But there is little reason to believe that economic growth and good government will become universal any time soon.

Yet, efforts in these two areas can make a contribution to reducing the number of ethnic and culture wars. Sometimes a culture war can be prevented by marginal improvements in an economy or by maintaining a minimal level of political order.[4] Even when no immediate means are available to influence the economic and political forces that may be breeding a culture clash in some country, appreciating their role may enable policymakers to better deal with the situation.

One consistent conclusion of analyses of ethnic and culture conflicts is that they are easiest to resolve when they are addressed early, before fear has dissolved intercommunity bonds and violent incidents have bred a desire for revenge. This has helped to fuel the recent vogue of "preventive diplomacy."[5] Even most of those who opposed military intervention in Bosnia agree that, if Washington and the West had acted more forcefully in 1990 or even 1991, the entire conflict could have been smothered before it got going.[6] Intervention is cheaper before anything resembling an act of ethnic cleansing has a chance to inflate passions on all sides. A focus on social structure can contribute by allowing one to anticipate where such conflicts are most likely, by providing some early warning of emerging "hot spots."

For example, the ability of Washington or the international community to deal with the crises in the former Yugoslavia and Somalia would have been greatly enhanced if the likelihood of state collapse could have been anticipated. Such a warning might have given policymakers a chance to prevent state collapse or, if that proved impossible, at least to make early preparations for the disorder that would follow.[7]

A crude idea of where state collapse is most likely can be found in the data in table 11-1, which shows when various contemporary states began their independent existence. States can take decades or centuries to fully establish their authority, to instill a degree of public trust or at least acceptance. Many of the newest states are only "quasi-states," bureaucracies with little reach beyond their capital cities, whose main claim to authority comes from their having a flag and a seat at the UN.[8]

Statemaking is not something that happens every day. It is a process that has occurred in waves, and some evidence is available that states that emerged from the same wave share common characteristics, imprinted upon them by the international environment at the moment of their birth. Thus, the Latin American states born during the Bolivar wave share a dedication to "order and progress," while those that emerged in Eastern Europe from the Leninist extinction share a common obsession with "civil society." However, longevity is hardly a guarantor of state survival. Many of the regimes and countries that disappeared during the Leninist extinction had respectable histories of survival. Old states can and do collapse. To anticipate the breakdown of political order, more sophisticated tools need to be deployed.

Table 11-1. Waves of State Making

1800 The Westphalia system	1810–49 The "Bolivar" wave	1850–1914 The emergence of central Europe	1915–39 Collapse of empires
Great Britain	Argentina (1810)	Liberia (1847)	Finland (1917)
Portugal	Paraguay (1811)	Italy (1860)	Estonia (1918)
Spain	Chile (1818)	Germany (1870)	Latvia (1918)
France	Colombia (1819)	Romania (1877)	Lithuania (1918)
Switzerland	Mexico (1821)	Bulgaria (1878)	Poland (1918)
Belgium	Guatemala (1821)	Serbia (1882)	Czechoslovakia (1918)
Netherlands	El Salvador (1821)	Australia (1901)	Austria (1918)
Luxemburg	Honduras (1821)	Cuba (1902)	Hungary (1918)
Sweden	Nicaragua (1821)	Panama (1903)	Yugoslavia (1918)
Denmark	Costa Rica (1821)	Norway (1905)	Egypt (1922)
United States	Peru (1821)	New Zealand (1907)	Turkey (1923)
Morocco	Venezuela (1821)	Albania (1913)	Saudi Arabia (1927)
Abyssinia	Ecuador (1822)		Iraq (1932)
Ottoman Turkey	Brazil (1822)		
Yemen	Bolivia (1825)		
Persia	Uruguay (1828)		
Siam	Greece (1829)		
Japan			
China			
Mongolia			
Afghanistan			
Montenegro			

Source: Author's estimates.

1940–59 *Decolonization of Asia*	1960–66 *Decolonization of Africa*	1967–89 *The latecomers*	1990 forward *"The Leninist extinction"*
Lebanon (1945)	Mauretania (1960)	South Yemen (1967)	Namibia (1990)
Philippines (1946)	Mali (1960)	Equat. Guinea (1968)	Slovenia
Syria (1946)	Niger (1960)	Swaziland (1968)	Croatia
Jordan (1946)	Chad (1960)	Nauru (1968)	Bosnia
India (1947)	Senegal (1960)	Fiji (1970)	Macedonia
Pakistan (1947)	Ivory Coast (1960)	Tonga (1970)	Belarus
Israel (1948)	Upper Volta (1960)	Bhutan (1971)	Moldova
Ceylon (1948)	Togo (1960)	Bangladesh (1971)	Ukraine
Burma (1948)	Dahomey (1960)	Bahrein (1971)	Russia
Korea (1948)	Nigeria (1960)	United Arab	Georgia
Indonesia (1949)	Central African	Emirates (1971)	Azerbaijan
Libya (1951)	Republic (1960)	Qatar (1971)	Armenia
Laos (1954)	Congo-Zaire (1960)	Guinea-Bissau (1974)	Kazakhstan
Vietnam (1954)	Congo (1960)	Comoros (1975)	Kirgizia
Tunisia (1956)	Cameroon (1960)	Sao Tome (1975)	Turkmenistan
Sudan (1956)	Gabon (1960)	Angola (1975)	Tajikistan
Ghana (1957)	Madagascar (1960)	Mozambique (1975)	Uzbekistan
Guinea (1958)	Somalia (1960)	Papua (1975)	
	Cyprus (1960)	Djibouti (1977)	
	Kuwait (1961)	Tuvalu (1978)	
	South Africa (1961)	Solomons (1978)	
	Algeria (1962)	Kiribati (1979)	
	Uganda (1962)	Brunei (1984)	
	Rwanda (1962)	New Caledonia (1987)	
	Burundi (1962)	Cook Islands (1987)	
	Samoa (1962)		
	Malaysia (1963)		
	Kenya (1963)		
	Cambodia (1963)		
	Zambia (1964)		
	Tanzania (1964)		
	Rhodesia (1965)		
	Cape Verde (1965)		
	Gambia (1965)		
	Maldives (1965)		
	Lesotho (1966)		

Unfortunately, no standard index of political decay exists. No one can pinpoint which states are collapsing with the same facility with which one can speak about numbers of television sets per one thousand citizens. Such an index could be constructed, though. Data on taxation would help, revealing something about which governments were running out of money to pay their troops. Maps of political corruption would also be valuable, providing some indication of where provincial bureaucracies were surreptitiously beginning to assert their independence from the central government.[9]

An example of the types of data that would be helpful can be found in table 11-2, which appeared in the British newsweekly the *Economist* in 1986. The purpose of the table was "not to predict which countries are going to fall into chaos by 1990. It is to guess, based on a dozen-and-a-half signs of things going wrong, how much risk there is for each of the 50 countries on our list that its condition will deteriorate over the next few years and it will become a seriously (or more seriously) unstable place." The predictions implicit in this table did not prove to be either impressively accurate nor wildly mistaken. (Choices about which countries would be either "hyper-risk" and "low-risk" proved generally accurate. Surprises are found among the middle cases. Some countries to which the table assigned medium-risk—such as Yugoslavia and Algeria—drifted off into terrible internal wars, while others rated as very high-risk—such as Uganda, Chile, and Vietnam—have been stable.) But of interest here are the criteria the table's authors employed.

Predictions about political stability remain much more guesswork than science, but the better studies employ criteria similar to those in the *Economist* table.[10] They rely heavily upon economic indicators: trends in economic growth and inflation, capital flight and debt service, volatility in food supply, or the prices of major exports. But they temper these with a host of political variables: Is the regime aging, unpopular, dictatorial? Taken together, these criteria provide a better-than-subjective basis for guessing whether a government is likely to repay its creditors or protect foreign investors—which is the reason most political risk assessments are made. Such political risk indices are not meant as gauges of how likely a state is to collapse. But they are as close an index as is likely to be constructed. At least for the purposes of crude argument, the group of countries that bankers and investors think of as very high political risks overlaps to a great extent with those that are most likely to experience state collapse.

Perhaps because political risk analysis is an expensive (and often fruitless) business, the *Economist* never published an update of its 1986 table.[11] Fortunately, for a decade the bankers' journal *Euromoney* has been publishing its own annual survey of the risk associated with lending to the different countries in the world. *Euromoney*'s criteria emphasize economic factors more than the *Economist*'s did. *Euromoney* attaches great weight to whether or not a country's economy is lively enough to generate the hard currency necessary to repay a loan. But since 1992, *Euromoney* has been disaggregating its annual country risk figures, showing how much of the uncertainty associated with loaning to a particular government arises from more narrowly political factors.[12]

Like the *Economist* figures, the *Euromoney* numbers include things that are unrelated to the likelihood of state collapse. However, they do provide an important indication of how likely a government is to become corrupt and unstable, its revenues failing, its police disobedient if only for one reason: *Euromoney*'s political risk numbers influence how likely a government is to be able to borrow abroad. And the ability to borrow hard currency, in a world where a majority of states are recent creations barely able to sustain themselves on the basis of domestic revenues alone, is a critical indicator of the likelihood of state decay.

Figure 11-1 is a map of the world showing *Euromoney*'s political risk ratings for 1996. Some problems associated with trying to employ bankers' ideas about political risk as a shorthand for the likelihood of state decay immediately become apparent. *Euromoney* has consistently rated North Korea and Cuba as among the riskiest potential debtors on earth, not because they have been in decay but because they were "rogue states," insensitive to international conventions and pressures, and thus unusually likely to default on obligations to foreign capitalists.[13] Similarly, the governments of Indonesia and Turkey are rated as very low risk—even though they confront violent internal wars in some regions. Their high level of creditworthiness may reflect more that their governments are respected players in the international system—with high levels of support from Washington—than their level of domestic stability would seem to justify.

Political risk analysis provides insight into how state collapse might be anticipated. A wide array of variables might be incorporated to improve the sensitivity of such a warning system. Measuring the amount of capital flight from a country might reveal when its government was evolving into a kleptocracy, a predatory regime that many social groups would like to see replaced. Measuring income inequality might indicate when

Table 11-2. Countries in Trouble, 1986

	Economics (33 points)						Politics (50 points)
	Falling GDP	Inflation	Capital flight	Foreign debt	Low food output	Commodity dependence	Bad neighbors
Algeria	0	2	1	2	4	6	1
Argentina	5	3	0	4	1	5	0
Bangladesh	2	4	0	4	2	2	0
Bolivia	8	3	0	6	3	6	0
Brazil	1	3	0	3	1	3	0
Burma	1	4	0	3	0	6	1
Chile	5	3	0	6	2	4	0
China	3	2	0	0	0	2	3
Colombia	4	3	0	1	2	5	0
Ecuador	0	5	0	4	3	6	1
Egypt	3	5	0	4	3	6	3
El Salvador	6	5	0	2	3	3	3
Ethiopia	8	5	0	4	2	6	2
Ghana	6	4	0	1	4	6	0
Greece	2	2	0	4	2	3	2
Guatemala	0	5	0	1	2	5	2
Hong Kong	1	1	1	5	2	0	3
India	1	4	0	1	1	3	2
Indonesia	2	0	3	2	0	6	1
Iran	8	5	2	0	2	6	3
Iraq	8	3	2	1	3	6	3
Kenya	2	4	0	5	2	5	1
Korea (south)	2	1	0	3	1	0	3
Malaysia	3	1	0	3	1	5	1
Mexico	1	5	1	5	2	4	3

tensions between regional subdivisions or between the urban and rural populations were reaching dangerous levels. And a host of political variables that it would be useful to include as well.

Efforts to anticipate (and allay) the danger of state collapse, whether by field observers or office-bound number-crunchers, will succeed only by cultivating a new understanding of the mechanisms involved. Throughout the cold war, Americans focused on the question of whether a state was "democratic," "authoritarian," or "totalitarian"—a question that often meant little more than "whose side are they on?" They need to learn that, in terms of the provision of political order, other, much more fundamental differences exist between states. In the 1960s one of America's leading

Politics (50 points)					Social (17 points)				
How authoritarian	Stale- ness	Illegiti- macy	Generals in power	War	Urbani- zation	Islamic fundamen- talism	Cor- rup- tion	Ethnic tension	Total
4	3	2	0	4	0	2	2	1	34
4	2	0	4	5	1	0	2	0	36
5	3	5	5	5	1	1	6	2	47
5	3	4	3	5	1	0	6	1	54
2	1	2	0	2	0	0	2	2	22
5	5	3	3	10	0	0	4	2	47
7	4	9	6	10	1	0	3	1	61
3	1	2	1	4	0	0	2	1	24
0	0	2	1	10	1	0	6	3	38
3	2	3	2	5	1	0	3	0	38
3	2	5	4	8	1	4	5	2	58
4	1	5	4	17	0	0	5	3	61
6	3	6	6	17	1	1	6	4	77
5	2	5	6	7	1	1	6	4	58
2	0	0	2	3	2	0	4	0	28
3	2	3	2	14	1	0	4	3	47
2	0	5	0	1	3	0	1	0	25
2	3	2	0	7	0	0	5	4	35
6	5	5	5	8	0	3	6	3	55
6	2	5	2	20	1	4	6	3	75
6	4	5	5	20	2	2	6	4	80
5	3	4	2	7	2	0	6	3	51
3	0	4	5	6	1	0	1	0	30
4	0	4	0	5	1	1	3	4	36
5	5	4	0	5	1	0	5	1	47

(continued)

experts on comparative politics understood this and made a point that remains good advice today:

> The most important political distinction among countries concerns not their form of government but their degree of government. The differences between democracy and dictatorship are less than the differences between those countries whose politics embodies con- sensus, community, legitimacy, organization, effectiveness, stability, and those countries whose politics is deficient in these qualities.[14]

The author of this wisdom was Samuel Huntington.

184 / From Chaos to Complexity

Table 11-2. Countries in Trouble, 1986 (Continued)

	Economics (33 points)						Politics (50 points)
	Falling GDP	Inflation	Capital flight	Foreign debt	Low food output	Commodity dependence	Bad neighbors
Morocco	2	4	0	6	3	4	2
Nigeria	4	4	2	2	2	6	0
Pakistan	2	4	1	3	2	2	3
Peru	2	3	1	6	3	5	0
Philippines	2	0	1	6	1	3	0
Poland	2	2	0	3	2	2	3
Portugal	1	2	2	3	3	1	0
Saudi Arabia	4	0	0	0	2	6	3
Singapore	3	0	0	1	4	2	0
South Africa	7	5	1	3	3	1	3
Sri Lanka	2	4	0	3	0	4	0
Sudan	5	3	4	6	2	6	3
Taiwan	1	0	0	1	0	0	3
Tanzania	3	5	0	5	2	6	2
Thailand	3	0	0	1	1	4	3
Tunisia	2	4	3	4	3	3	2
Turkey	2	3	0	3	2	3	3
Uganda	1	5	1	1	2	6	1
Uruguay	2	5	0	6	1	4	0
Venezuela	4	4	3	0	3	6	1
Vietnam	4	5	0	4	0	6	3
Yugoslavia	1	5	0	3	1	1	3
Zaire	3	3	3	6	3	6	2
Zambia	7	5	0	6	4	6	3
Zimbabwe	5	5	0	2	4	4	3

Source: "Countries in Trouble—1986," *Economist*, December 20, 1986, pp. 69–72.
Note: GDP = gross domestic product.

'Structural Adjustment' without State Collapse

If the degree of economic hardship and political vulnerability in societies can be assessed more accurately, it can also reshape the measures taken to prevent or forestall potential culture conflicts.

Ever since Aristotle, the linkage between economic pressures and collective violence has been apparent.[15] The "back-of-the-envelope" tables in this book suggest a clear connection between the level of economic misery in a society and the likelihood of high-casualty, militarily organized

Politics (50 points)					Social (17 points)				
How authoritarian	Staleness	Illegitimacy	Generals in power	War	Urbanization	Islamic fundamentalism	Corruption	Ethnic tension	Total
5	3	3	2	9	1	3	2	1	50
6	3	5	6	9	0	3	6	4	62
4	3	4	4	7	0	4	5	3	51
5	0	4	3	12	1	0	4	2	51
3	4	4	3	10	1	2	4	3	47
4	5	5	5	4	0	0	3	1	41
2	0	1	1	5	1	0	1	1	24
7	5	5	2	3	0	3	3	1	44
5	5	3	0	0	3	0	0	2	28
4	3	7	3	12	0	0	2	4	58
3	0	6	2	15	0	0	1	4	44
5	3	4	3	16	1	3	5	4	73
4	4	4	2	3	0	0	1	3	26
6	5	3	1	5	1	0	6	1	51
3	2	3	6	10	2	0	3	1	42
5	5	3	2	5	1	3	4	1	50
4	1	3	4	8	0	1	2	2	41
5	4	6	6	15	2	1	6	4	66
3	2	4	2	3	2	0	2	0	36
2	0	1	1	3	1	0	1	0	30
4	5	4	6	15	0	0	3	2	61
5	5	5	3	5	0	1	3	4	45
6	5	5	3	7	0	0	6	3	61
6	5	4	3	7	1	0	5	2	64
4	2	5	2	10	1	0	3	4	54

violence, that is, war. Promoting development in such countries is thus a legitimate national security issue. Some of the most visionary proposals for American foreign policy after the cold war have focused on this idea:

It is a remarkable feature of American strategic leadership of the Western alliance that the U.S. enthusiastically financed and supported the progress of Japan and Western Europe to become economic superpowers, without ever quite realizing what a miracle was being performed: in the light of most human history, neither Japan

Figure 11-1. *Political Risk Rankings, 1996*

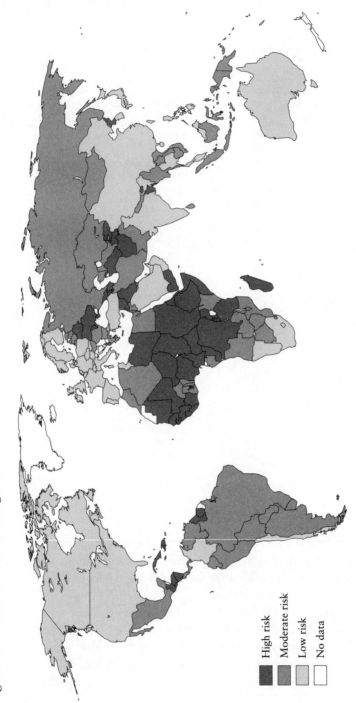

High risk

Moderate risk

Low risk

No data

Source: Rebecca Dobson and Cara Solomon, "Asia's Economies Start to Slip," *Euromoney* (September 1996), pp. 200–205.

nor Europe sought to use its economic prowess to become the military behemoth its wealth would justify.

The world could be embarking on a twenty-year window of opportunity—before China becomes a military and economic superpower, and while Russia reconstructs—in which the U.S. will remain the only superpower worthy of that name. It will have the capacity to keep the peace, and to foster that golden age of global growth that could follow if the vastness of Eurasia—from Eastern Europe to Korea, from the Arctic to India and Indonesia—becomes as stable, as prosperous, and as democratic as have the members of the Western alliance that prevailed during the Cold War. The building of that tripartite global economy of Japan, Europe, and North America was the real achievement of American strategy during the Cold War. Its extension to Latin America, the Middle East, and Asia—and, one trusts, eventually to Africa—must now be its goal.[16]

This is an extremely attractive vision, but one must not underestimate the challenge involved. Despite some heartening developments in the last couple of decades (the green revolution, the emergence of the newly industrialized countries), most of the world remains painfully underdeveloped. "A fifth of the developing world's population goes hungry every night, a quarter lacks access to even a basic necessity like safe drinking water, and a third lives in a state of abject poverty—at such a margin of human existence that words simply fail to describe it."[17] In much of the world, economic growth has lagged behind population growth or stagnated outright. As of 1996, thirty countries have per capita incomes that had not risen since the 1980s, thirty-five where it had not risen since the 1970s, and another thirty-five where it had not risen since the 1960s or before.[18]

A majority of the world's economists share a common understanding of how this immense weight of underdevelopment might be lifted. This understanding has been dubbed the "Washington consensus," and it urges the developing countries to reform their policies in ten key areas:

1. Fiscal discipline (cut budget deficits)
2. Public expenditure priorities (redirect funds to health, education, and infrastructure)
3. Tax reform (cut marginal rates)
4. Financial liberalization (market-determined interest rates)

5. Exchange rates (cut to promote exports)
6. Trade liberalization (low tariffs)
7. Foreign direct investment (encourage it)
8. Privatization (dismantle white elephants)
9. Deregulation (abolish monopolies)
10. Property rights (define and defend them)[19]

During the 1980s a growing number of countries adopted the Washington consensus. Probably the primary impetus behind this trend was the combined force of the International Monetary Fund (IMF) and the global debt crisis. If a developing country wished to refinance or reschedule its debts through the London Club or Paris Club, it had to first seek an endorsement from the IMF. And the IMF only endorsed countries that either met the ideals of the Washington consensus or were revising their policies to conform with that ideal through a "structural adjustment program."

Structural adjustment programs may lay the foundation for long-term economic growth, but they usually require a measure of short-term economic pain. They usually involve devaluing the currency, which raises the price of all imports; in the developing countries, this often includes basic foodstuffs. Privatization often closes down large plants, contributing to unemployment. Cutting the fiscal deficit usually means eliminating consumer subsidies, again affecting the price of staples. No one at the IMF, the World Bank, or the other institutions that promoted structural adjustment ever said that this process would be easy. But failure to implement these reforms makes growth almost impossible and ensures the long-term erosion of the economy.

That implementation of a structural adjustment program could trigger bread riots, strikes, and other violence by suddenly threatened consumers has long been known. In the Middle East, for example, IMF-inspired structural adjustment programs led to government-threatening riots in Egypt in 1977, in the Sudan in 1986, in Algeria in 1988, and in Jordan in 1989. But governments and the IMF continued to press structural adjustment programs in the conviction that the economic growth they generate would soon dampen consumer anger.

By the mid-1990s, however, this conviction had begun to change subtly. Dozens of evaluations of structural adjustment programs did not shake the consensus that they were a necessary condition for economic growth.[20] But they did seem to confirm that growth would take much longer to materialize than economists had originally hoped. Paul Krugman, one of America's most influential economists, put the new understanding this way: "The point is not that the policy recommendations [of the Washington consensus] are wrong, but that their efficacy—their ability to turn Argentina into Taiwan overnight—was greatly oversold."[21] A World Bank consultant who worked on Africa put the problem even more poignantly: "We didn't believe that the human cost of structural adjustment programmes would be so high, and economic gains so slow in coming."[22]

This realization may not have required a basic economic rethinking of structural adjustment, but it had important implications for its political impact. Upon realization that adjustment was a process that might take decades instead of months or a few years, the calculus of how much human suffering they imposed and how much violence they were likely to trigger rose. If structural adjustment took a decade or more, it might spur not only food riots but also a wider process of political polarization, class or culture conflict, or even civil war. Structural adjustment programs were consciously designed to reduce the activities of the state, lessening the likelihood that governments would obstruct private economic action.[23] But after a decade of adhering to such programs, a real danger arose that some states would not just shrink but be pushed to the brink of collapse—or beyond. This appeared to be what had happened in Yugoslavia as well as in a number of African states including Algeria. Not surprisingly, in 1995 a kind of "brush-fire rebellion" of African governments took place against the prescriptions of the IMF and World Bank.[24]

The Washington consensus thus led to a dilemma: How can economic growth be encouraged without igniting the tendency toward political violence that growth was supposed to dampen?

Several ways out of this dilemma seem to exist. A variety of economists and political scientists advocated more flexibility in the application of structural adjustment programs and greater diversity in their design. Even the most orthodox economists had, over time, become sympathetic to the idea that structural adjustment programs should include an element of "income policy" or at least some type of "social welfare" fund that would assuage the pain of the poorest and most vulnerable populations in the adjusting country.[25] Others argued that to make adjustment programs sustainable, the already industrialized countries would have to set aside larger funds to use as investment incentives or to provide debt relief for adjusting countries.[26] A growing number doubt the viability of "shock therapy"—which tries to impose all the features of the Washington consensus in a brief, forced march—and favor instead sequencing the various

Figure 11-2. *Total Debt Stocks as a Percent of Exports, 1995*

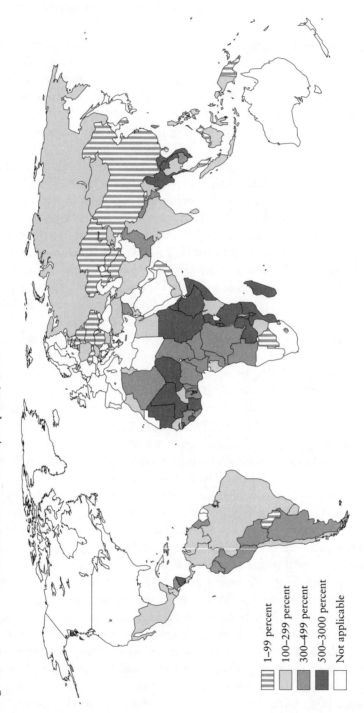

1–99 percent

100–299 percent

300–499 percent

500–3000 percent

Not applicable

Source: World Bank, *World Debt Tables 1996* (Washington: 1996), various pages.

elements of adjustment in a carefully designed series of phases.[27] Finally, even the World Bank had begun to argue that certain very poor countries needed immediate debt relief, to ease the pressures of onerous debt service and to release funds for sustaining a long-term adjustment process.[28]

The reformers did not propose that every adjustment process need incorporate any of these revisions. If a country such as Poland could implement a traditional structural adjustment program, it would benefit in a number of ways. Rapid, successful implementation would reduce the overall cost of the process and improve the country's credit rating internationally. However, countries that faced more adverse conditions could benefit from incorporating one or more revisions in their adjustment program. The poorest, most vulnerable countries might have to plead for debt forgiveness, a request that would certainly damage their future ability to borrow but might be necessary to avoid immediate political and economic collapse.

Which country should avail itself of which revisions? If economists had to paint a quick-and-dirty picture, they would usually point to the level of indebtedness among developing countries. The total debt stock of Estonia equals the value of only 13 percent of its annual exports of goods and services. Ceterus paribus, then, the Estonians would probably have a much easier time implementing a straightforward, "orthodox" structural adjustment program than would Sudan, with debts equal to the value of twenty-nine years of its annual exports. The Sudanese would be better candidates for immediate debt relief. The data in figure 11-2 give an overview of which countries (divided roughly into quartiles) suffer how heavily from their debt service and thus provide a sort of prima facie indicator of which societies are candidates for orthodox structural adjustment, revised structural adjustment, or emergency debt relief programs.

Other economic indicators should be consulted in determining what kind of adjustment program is appropriate for a country. More important, political indicators need to be kept in mind as well. In a state whose debt problems were not terrifying but whose political system was fragile (say, for example, Russia), one of the less traumatic versions of adjustment might be desirable.

Adjustment programs need to be varied to match specific political and economic circumstances. In nature, some species are diverse and others are homogenous. Dogs constitute a single species but exhibit enormous diversity, varying from chihuahuas to mastiffs. Cheetahs, meanwhile, not only look alike; each individual is so genetically similar to every other that they are having trouble reproducing in the wild. In this context, states are clearly dogs.

Global Complexity

Grappling with the structural conditions that promote ethnic and culture conflict will be a learning process. Few policymakers (and fewer intellectuals) seem to appreciate that all policies are experiments. Given the limits of knowledge about society, they can be nothing else. Policymakers should imitate Napoleon, who said before battle, "On s'engage et puis s'on voit." ("We will engage the enemy and then see what happens.") Policies begin with a plan, which has to be ruthlessly revised as its strengths and shortcomings become clear.[29]

Tinkering with the structures that foster ethnic and culture conflict, policymakers will inevitably learn a great deal. Despite the current prevalence of the Washington consensus, understanding of the mechanisms of economic development is still crude. No subfield of economics is more prone to fashion or exhibits such lurching variations over time. The Washington consensus replaced an earlier international consensus that emphasized the need for planning and state intervention, which had replaced an earlier consensus, and so on.[30] Understanding of the process of state formation is not even this advanced. The academic literature on state formation is of high quality, but scarce and recent.[31] (America's own experience with state building is particularly alarming. Neither Liberia, the Philippines, nor South Vietnam testify well on behalf of its ability to export political institutions.)

Although many surprises will arise as understanding of these problems advances, one thing is already clear. "The world is not only queerer than we think it is, it is queerer than we can think it is."[32] The international environment is not chaotic (most of its behavior has structural underpinnings that make it rationally understandable if not exactly predictable), but it is certainly complex. Learning to recognize, acknowledge, and deal with complexity may be the hallmark of successful diplomacy in the coming years.

The world, though, has always been complex. The subtle mechanisms that fuel the Hutu-Tutsi conflict in Rwanda today are not different from those that triggered their first great massacres in the 1960s. At least since 1945 the United States has had the luxury of ignoring these complexities. Instead, American eyes were epoxied in close focus on the struggle with the Soviet Union. Until 1989 the only aspect of Somali politics that concerned Washington was whether the incumbent regime was leaning toward or away from Moscow. The stakes in the international struggle against totalitarianism seemed to be so high that they justified a realpolitik that neglected other issues.[33] Thus, America aligned itself with "friendly tyrants," misunderstood or recast ethnic conflicts (such as violence against Indians in Guatemala) as if they were battles with "communist insurgents," and clashed with nationalist leaders (such as Nasser) who were never dupes of the Soviets.[34]

But—barring a Martian invasion or a massive return to isolationism—Americans no longer have this luxury. Most wars in the next decade are likely to be caused (and, no less important, be seen to be caused) by highly complex local factors rather than by easily understood international ideological crusades. The current debate about whether or not to impose trade sanctions on China (Does trade give tacit approval to Chinese government oppression or does it lay the long-term foundation for its amelioration?) is probably more typical of the type of issue policymakers will face. And many will be much more complex.

Americans are not well prepared for this sort of complexity. At the height of the war in Bosnia, as their government contemplated military intervention, a majority of Americans could not name which group was besieging the city of Sarajevo.[35]

A newspaper cartoon beautifully captured the dilemma of Americans confronting the naked complexity of the world. A single uncaptioned drawing shows a man scratching his chin and glancing between two maps. One is entitled "Old World Order," and it shows two countries, one white and one black, and labeled "good" and "evil." The second map is entitled "New World Order," and it shows dozens of countries, with their borders squiggling like mealy worms, and labeled into seven discrete categories: "ok," "not-so-bad," "bad," "worse," "even worse," "wretched," and "unspeakable."[36]

A new mental map of the world is needed that does a better job of capturing its complexities. A bilateral vision of the world, one that pits East against West, is hopelessly simplistic. A trilateral vision, one that apportions the world into West (former) Communists, and "the third world," is only marginally better. To his credit, when Samuel Huntington suggested his readers reconceptualize the world in terms of nine clashing civilizations, he was trying to get them to embrace a more complex—and, to that degree, more accurate—vision of the world.[37]

Figure 11-3. *International Misery Index*

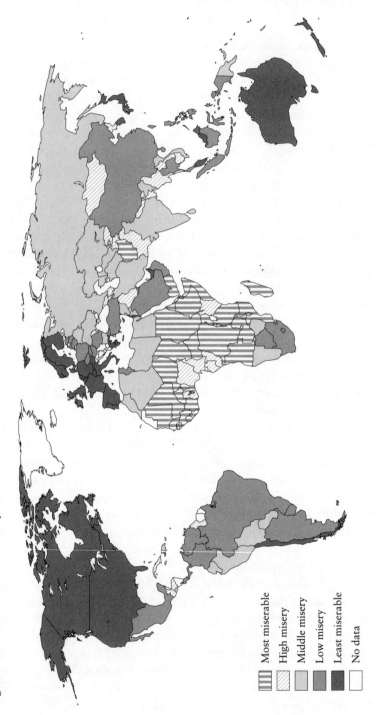

Most miserable

High misery

Middle misery

Low misery

Least miserable

No data

Source: Author's calculations.

How might the problems of a complex world be disaggregated into more manageable units? A good place to start might be with those structural factors that so strongly shape the pattern of international conflict: prosperity and political stability. The United Nations Development Program (UNDP) human development index and the *Euromoney* political risk ratings have already been used to sketch how these qualities are distributed internationally. What would happen if they were merged? The results would show which countries enjoyed prosperity and stability, and which enjoyed neither. This ranking system can be labeled the "international misery index," in memory of the domestic American "misery index" that President Reagan did so much to popularize.[38]

A graphic representation of the international misery index, subdivided into quintiles, is found in figure 11-3. Although the division into quintiles is more or less arbitrary, it does focus attention on some intriguing features of the international scene.

The least miserable countries include the states that traditionally formed the West as well as a number of recently industrialized countries— not only the East Asian Tigers (South Korea, Taiwan, Hong Kong, and Singapore) but also Malaysia and Chile. This highlights an important fact: Over the next few decades, these new industrial nations are likely to press for, and deserve, inclusion in the counsels of the major powers. They may not be ready to join the G-7, but they deserve the same level of consultation and respect currently enjoyed by other countries such as Spain and New Zealand. Despite their cultural diversity, the countries in this quintile are probably natural allies.

The next quintile (second from the top) includes much of Latin America, the Baltic States and Eastern Europe, China and Indonesia (some of the fastest growing economies in Asia), and an important swath of southern Africa that is all too often lumped in with its more troubled neighbors to the north. These are the countries with real potential, likely to be the new powers of the twenty-first century.

The middle category is even more diverse. It includes states with real problems, but also real hopes. The handful of them scattered in Latin America (El Salvador, Peru, Bolivia, and Paraguay) may benefit from the rapid growth of their neighbors. Iran and India are heirs to ancient cultures, enjoy impressive reserves of human capital, and have already shown some success at bucking global political trends. And the future of Russia is up for grabs. A country that combines so much human talent with such lavish resources cannot be held back for long. The issue of how to reintegrate a reviving Russia into the world system will probably form the new "German question" of the twenty-first century.

Below this come two quintiles whose futures are much more cloudy. In many ways, distinguishing between the two is hard: Nepal is in the fourth quintile and Malawi is in the fifth, but neither is expected to become industrialized or a regional power in the twenty-first century. A few states in the fourth quintile (Nigeria and Iraq) might worm their way upward into the third quintile over the next decade or so, but these are a distinct minority. These countries are not hopeless, but the improvement of economic and political conditions will proceed slowly and require great patience.

Coming up with names for these four categories is a delicate matter. Some names work, and some do not. The term "third world" caught on, while the term "second world" never did. In the late 1970s Zbigniew Brzezinski became known for coining the phrase "crescent of crisis" to describe those states wedged between the Indian Ocean and the Soviet Union where some of the hottest battles of the cold war were about to be fought. Twenty years later his words sank like a stone when he tried to argue that the great contests of the post–cold war epoch would be fought in "the Eurasian oblong of maximum danger."[39]

The least miserable countries might be called "the North," the Atlantic Community, the first world, Panglossia, the Winner's Circle, or just "us." This group includes most of what is called "the West," as well as a significant number (the four East Asian Tigers, Chile, the United Arab Emirates, Malaysia, and Israel) that do not strictly belong in that cultural category. It resembles the idea of a "zone of peace" endorsed by some global chaos theorists, inasmuch as its members are unlikely to make war against each other (although they are often at war with states from other categories). This group of states is also probably those whose support American statesmen have in mind when they make moralizing pronouncements in the name of "the world community."

The remaining countries of the world might be distinguished into three broad groups: the flyers, the floaters, and the flops. The second least-miserable quintile of states, those who rank just after the North, constitute the flyers. These societies, scattered across Latin America, southern Africa, Eastern Europe, and Asia, have made a good start at the process of building modern market economies and stable political institutions. Many are growing so rapidly that over the next few decades they are likely to close the gap between themselves and the countries of the industrialized North. The group of flyers overlaps with that of the emerging economic power centers that Jeffrey E. Garten has dubbed "the big ten": Mexico, Brazil, Argentina, South Africa, Turkey, Poland, South Korea, China, Indonesia, and India.[40] Over the next century, China is likely to emerge as the most potent member of this group.

The middle quintile of countries can be called the floaters. They may play the same contested role that the third world did during the cold war, only, instead of leaning toward Washington or Moscow, some will become more developed while others will decay.

The combination of the fourth and fifth quintiles constitutes the flops. While all of these countries are capable of progress, they are going to have to fight hardest for it. This region is also where, with or without advances in globalization, structural conditions are likely to breed the most violent ethnic wars. To the extent that the idea of a "zone of turmoil" applies anywhere, it is here.

What does the international misery index say? Of the groups it identifies, only one—the North—is likely to form a real political bloc, with its members collaborating and forming durable alliances. The rest are only categories, whose members are unlikely to feel any sense of common identity, much less work toward common ends.

Some might use the index for crude forms of triage. Those countries that are flyers can, given enough time, handle most of the crises they are likely to face relying primarily upon domestic resources. The problems of the flops, in contrast, are so overwhelming that even very high levels of international support cannot guarantee success. Applying the logic of triage, this might be used to justify focusing international assistance efforts, whether in the form of economic aid or military intervention, on the countries of the floaters. However, before trying to implement any such idea, the crude nature of the index should be remembered. It is a simple merger of two other indices, both of which are only modest measurements of prosperity and stability.

Besides, triage is a technique justified only under the pressure of immediate emergencies. A more sophisticated application of the international misery index would be in deciding what type of policies are most appropriate for what type of country. For example, regular IMF austerity programs might be appropriate in the flyers; straightforward debt relief would be more apposite for the flops; and so on.

But the most important policy implication of the international misery index is what it reveals about the complexity of the world. The old categories no longer capture the new realities. The old second world (socialist bloc) no longer exists, and many of its members have in effect joined the third world. And the old third world amalgamates countries so dramatically different in their political and economic development that almost no valid generalizations can be made about them. The quintiles identified by the international misery index at least share certain cultural features. But how diverse is each of them internally? The constituents of the flyers speak languages from the Romance, Bantu, Semitic, Slavic, Sinic, and Malay groups, and they include followers of all the world's major religions. And yet the flyers are probably less internally diverse than the floaters.

In a world of global complexity, U.S. foreign policy will have to become more flexible. It will have to be tailored more to local particularities rather than relying upon global maxims. It will have to be informed more by knowledge about local cultures and structural conditions than by visions of grand strategy. It will have to abandon the idea of the "magic bullet"—the single solution that solves all problems.

To give credit where it is due, one of the first people to realize this was the global chaos theorist Robert Kaplan. In some of his early writings about the Balkans, Kaplan suggests that America needs to rely more upon "area specialists" such as Rebecca West, who wrote about Yugoslavia in the 1930s. In her writings

> every church and mountain vista, every person met along the way, becomes an excuse for an exposition into some aspect of history or local myth. Study the language, culture, and history of a place, and always keep your strategy attuned to those realities, she seems to repeat, over and over again. This book is a plea for knowledge over mere opinion. Yugoslavia, because it completely resists simplification and condensation on op-ed pages, is potent ammunition for this argument.[41]

The need to develop expertise is good advice—even though one should be careful about embracing Kaplan's decisions about who is and is not an expert.

The suggestion here is not that America let experts make its foreign policy decisions, although policymakers might profit from listening to them more often than they have in the recent past. But, far more important, better experts are needed. Rebecca West, Kaplan's ideal, spent only six weeks in Yugoslavia and never learned any of the local languages. America remains desperately short of real experts who speak the languages, have lived in the countries, struggled through rigorous formal academic training, and have invested the time to ripen their analyses.

Attending to the debate of real experts can strengthen American foreign policy in a number of ways, particularly if an understanding is reached of what experts are good at and what they are not. Experts are not decisionmakers. The purpose of their research and study in the social crafts (no such thing as a social science exists) is not to determine laws, make predictions, and identify recipes for success. The purpose of such study is to train minds so that they will recognize dangers before they arise and opportunities before they slip away, to broaden imaginations, to lift the blinders of old metaphors and nostrums so that responses can be confident yet supple.

CHAPTER TWELVE

Conclusion

This book has focused on the social structures that undergird culture conflicts. Not all of the forces that drive and shape these conflicts are structural, however. One nonstructural factor is so important that it deserves to be singled out for attention at the end of this inquiry. Given the lives at stake, to do anything else would be morally irresponsible.

In *Balkan Ghosts,* Kaplan buttresses his argument about the inexorability of culture conflicts by quoting the most famous modern Greek novel, *Zorba the Greek* by Nikos Kazantzakis. Kaplan notes that while Zorba is familiar in the West largely as a spontaneous, drunken dancer, he was a character with a darker past. Zorba hailed from Macedonia, where he had spent his youth among groups of nationalist comitadji, "irregulars" who looted, raped, and murdered any Turks or Bulgars who fell into their hands.[1]

Kaplan is right about Zorba's noisome past—but he fails to mention the epiphany that divided Zorba's youth from his maturity. The great turning point of Zorba's life occurred when he killed a Bulgar priest who had been leading opposition to the Greeks. He slit the man's throat and cut off his ears. Then, a few days later, he encountered five children sitting in the village:

> They were all dressed in black, barefoot, holding one another by the hand and begging. Three girls and two boys. The eldest couldn't have been more than ten, and the youngest was still a baby. The eldest girl was carrying the youngster in her arms, kissing him and caressing him so that he shouldn't cry.

Zorba began to question them and was devastated to discover that they were the family of the priest he murdered. He wept, gave the children all his money, and ran from the village. "And I am still running," he lamented.

Years later, recounting his epiphany, Zorba erupted with a speech that says volumes about the potential for change in countries plagued by ethnic and cultural violence.

> There was a time when I used to say: that man's a Turk, or a Bulgar, or a Greek. I've done things for my country that would make your hair stand on end, boss. I've cut people's throats, burned villages, robbed and raped women, wiped out entire families. Why? Because they were Bulgars, or Turks. "Bah! To hell with you, you swine!" I say to myself sometimes. "To hell with you right away, you ass." Nowadays I say this man is a good fellow, that one's a bastard. They can be Greeks or Bulgars or Turks, it doesn't matter. Is he good? Or is he bad? That's the only thing I ask nowadays.[2]

Kazantzakis's insight is true: If Zorba could have a change of heart, so can any other nationalist extremist. Cultural conflicts, like all forms of violence, ignite passions. But passions are feeble, fickle things. They rise quickly, burn out fast, and change into their opposites with shocking facility.[3]

Thus, there is some good news and some bad news. The good news is that most of the conflicts around the world are not rooted in thousands of years of history—they are new and can be concluded as quickly as they started. The bad news is that intense, genocidal hatreds can (with support from political organizations) be generated almost overnight—they do not require centuries of incubation.

Appendix

The basic procedure for the "back-of-the-envelope" tests of global chaos theory presented in chapter 8 is as follows: A series of different measures of globalization are compared with the international distribution of "culture conflicts" to see if any correlations emerge.

Data on globalization were assembled for all the countries of the world that have populations larger than 500,000. (Smaller countries were excluded partly for reasons of parsimony and partly because the World Bank *World Development Report,* one of the major sources of the data, no longer presents full data on such small countries.) An effort was made to construct data series that focused on the period from 1980 to 1996, that is, the years in which the chaos theorists claimed globalization became a dominant force in international affairs.

Data on "culture conflicts" were assembled for the same countries and for the same period. Each conflict was labeled either a "culture war" or a "culture strife," depending upon the number of casualties and the level of military organization involved. An attempt was made to emulate the judgments of the global chaos theorists themselves about whether a particular form of violence was culturally rooted, and thus a symptom of post–cold war chaos. Thus, insurrection by UNITA (National Union for the Total Independence of Angola) in Angola was labeled a culture war, but the insurrection by RENAMO (National Resistance of Mozambique) in Mozambique was not. When in doubt, conflicts were usually included in the database rather than excluded. For example, the "narcoterrorism" in Colombia was listed as a culture strife, even though many would find such labeling dubious.

In addition to the texts of the global chaos theorists themselves, the culture conflicts database draws heavily upon certain third party resources that thinkers such as Samuel P. Huntington and Robert D. Kaplan cite as authorities. These include various editions of Ruth Leger Sivard's *World Military and Social Expenditures* and the Stockholm International Peace Research Institute's *SIPRI Yearbook,* Ted Robert Gurr's *Minorities at Risk: A Global View of Ethnopolitical Conflicts* (Washington: U.S. Institute of Peace, 1993), and various stories from the *New York Times.* In addition, the following sources were consulted to refine the database: Christer Ahlstrom, *Casualties of Conflict: Report for the World Campaign for the Protection of Victims of War* (Uppsala University, Department of Peace and Conflict Research, 1991); and Ylva Nordlander, ed., *States in Armed Conflict 1993* (Uppsala University, Department of Peace and Conflict Research, 1994).

Notes

Chapter One

1. In the summer of 1947, "Mr. X"—a pseudonym for George Kennan, who had just become the first director of the policy planning staff at the Department of State—published an article entitled "The Sources of Soviet Conduct" in *Foreign Affairs*. This article laid out certain theses about Soviet behavior, American interests, and the character of international relations that, over the next few years, not only assumed the status of the "conventional wisdom" among pundits and intellectuals but also were enshrined as the foundation of America's grand strategy for dealing with the Soviet Union. Kennan's strategy was soon dubbed "containment," and his philosophy was called "realism." See John Lewis Gaddis, *Strategies of Containment: A Critical Appraisal of Postwar American National Security Policy* (New York: Oxford University Press, 1982), pp. 25–53.

2. For an impressive effort to account for the overall costs of the war in Bosnia, see Michael Cranna, ed., *The True Cost of Conflict: Seven Recent Wars and Their Effects on Society* (New York: New Press, 1994), pp. 164, 166.

3. A few thought it might be lower; see George Kenney, "The Bosnia Calculation," *New York Times Magazine*, April 23, 1995, pp. 42–43.

4. Tony Horwitz, "Balkan Death Trip: Scenes from a Futile War," *Harper's*, March 1993, p. 36.

5. On the systematic nature of the rape campaign, see Amnesty International, *Bosnia-Herzegovina: Rape and Sexual Abuse by Armed Forces* (New York: January 1993); and Paul Lewis, "Rape Was Weapon of Serbs, U.N. Says," *New York Times*, October 20, 1993, p. A1. For important background information on the politicization of the concept of rape in Serbia during the period of Yugoslavia's dissolution, see Silva Meznaric, "Gender as an Ethno-Marker: Rape, War, and Identity Politics in the Former Yugoslavia," in Valentine M. Moghadam, ed., *Identity Politics and Women: Cultural Reassertions and Feminisms in International Perspective* (Boulder, Colo.: Westview Press, 1994), pp. 76–97.

6. Lewis, "Rape Was Weapon of Serbs." For detailed accounts of the rape campaign, see Peter Maass, "The Rapes in Bosnia: A Muslim Schoolgirl's Account," *Washington Post*, December 27, 1992, pp. A1–A32; and Maggie O'Kane, "Bosnia Crisis: Forgotten Women of Serb Rape Camps," *Guardian*

Weekly, December 19, 1992, p. 9; and Alexandra Stiglmayer, ed., *Mass Rape: The War against Women in Bosnia-Herzegovina* (University of Nebraska, 1994). For a dispassionate overview, see Cheryl Benard, "Rape as Terror: The Case of Bosnia," *Terrorism and Political Violence,* vol. 6, no. 1 (Spring 1994), pp. 29–43.

7. UN International Children's Emergency Fund (UNICEF) press release from Edward J. Mitchell, April 22, 1993.

8. The best account of the camps is Roy Gutman, *A Witness to Genocide* (Macmillan, 1993). Gutman won a Pulitzer prize for the series of stories in which he followed up rumors of the camps, pinpointed their locations, and eventually forced entry. For additional details, see Roger Cohen, "Secrets of Susica: How Muslims Died in Bosnia; Ex-Guards for Serbs Tell of Grisly 'Cleansing' Camp," *New York Times,* August 1, 1994, p. A1; Roger Cohen, "Secrets of Susica: How Muslims Died in Bosnia; Bosnian Camp Survivors Describe a Random Death," *New York Times,* August 2, 1994, p. A1; and Steven Coll, "In the Shadow of the Holocaust," *Washington Post Magazine,* September 25, 1994, pp. 23ff. The State Commission for Gathering Facts on War Crimes in the Republic of Bosnia and Herzegovina estimates that the Serb separatists interned 260,000 people in their network of camps at one time or another, but this figure is probably inflated (Online Bulletin 1-1). The network of camps had a maximum holding capacity, at any one time, of 130,000. Casualty figures are even harder to pin down. However, in 1996 experts still suspected that as many as 11,500 of the internees at the Omarska camp alone were still missing, their fate unknown. See Andy MacIntyre, "Suspected Mass Grave Is Found," *Washington Post,* March 22, 1996, p. A30.

9. For an overview of the international institutions involved, see Lawrence J. LeBlanc, *The United States and the Genocide Convention* (Duke University Press, 1991).

10. Laura Silber and Allan Little, *Yugoslavia: Death of a Nation* (New York: TV Books, 1996), p. 26.

11. See the definitive account of this development in James Gleick, *Chaos: Making a New Science* (Viking Penguin, 1987). In the 1993 movie *Jurassic Park,* millions of Americans were exposed to a bastardized form of chaos theory that suggested the movement revolved around Murphy's Law: "Anything that can go wrong will go wrong." By this time, physical scientists had begun to rename their theories, calling it the study of "nonlinear dynamics" or "complexity." (See Roger Lewin, *Complexity: Life at the Edge of Chaos* (Macmillan, 1992); and George Johnson, "Researchers on Complexity Ponder What It's All About," *New York Times,* May 6, 1997, p. C1.) For one of the few direct attempts to apply chaos theory to the social sciences, see Bernice Cohen, *The Edge of Chaos: Financial Booms, Bubbles, Crashes, and Chaos* (London: John Wiley and Sons, 1996).

12. The choice of a name for a movement matters. The word "chaos" had become evocative by the early 1990s, so many different thinkers were laying claim to it. See Stephen S. Hall, "Scientists Find Catchy Names Help Ideas Fly," *New York Times,* October 20, 1992, p. C1. See also Al Kamen, "Counting on Chaos to Save the Day for Dole," *Washington Post,* September 16, 1996, p. A17.

Chapter Two

1. *Balkan Ghosts: A Journey through History* (Vintage Books, 1993) was Robert D. Kaplan's first book to attract national attention. It benefited from a major marketing and publicity campaign, attracting the sponsorship of Paul Kennedy, a Yale historian, and Jason Epstein, a highly influential publisher. Kennedy and Epstein knew a great deal about how to market works of this kind. Together they had turned Kennedy's *The Rise and Fall of Great Powers: Economic Change and Military Conflict from 1500–2000* (Random House, 1987) into one of the few works of social science to ever attain best-seller status. (For the history of efforts to promote *Balkan Ghosts,* see Paul Elie, "Robert D. Kaplan: This Political Journalist Has a Passion for Adventure," *Publishers Weekly,* vol. 240, issue 13 (March 29, 1993), pp. 30–31. For the Kennedy-Epstein team, see Kenneth L. Woodward, "The New Class Warriors," *Newsweek,* October 5, 1992, pp. 40–41.)

2. "Since Croats are ethnically indistinguishable from Serbs—they come from the same Slavic race, they speak the same language, their names are usually the same—their identity rests on their Roman Catholicism." Kaplan, *Balkan Ghosts,* p. 16.

3. Kaplan, *Balkan Ghosts,* p. 25.

4. Kaplan, *Balkan Ghosts,* p. 50.

5. Kaplan, *Balkan Ghosts,* p. 22.

6. Kaplan, *Balkan Ghosts,* p. 7. Kaplan claims this vision was implicit in remarks made to him by the Croatian journalist Slavenka Drakulic. But Drakulic has gone to some lengths to dissociate herself from this kind of language, which implies the dissolution of Yugoslavia was rooted in a "clash of civilizations." For example, in her book *Balkan Express: Fragments from the Other Side of War* (W. W. Norton, 1993), she complains that through use of this language "the West tells us, 'You are not Europeans, not even Eastern Europeans. You are Balkans, mythological, wild, dangerous Balkans. Kill yourselves, if that is your pleasure. We don't understand what is going on there, nor do we have clear political interests to protect.'" Quote on pp. 2–3.

Kaplan used virtually identical language in an earlier article, without crediting Drakulic for its inspiration: "No story demonstrates the limits of conventional journalism like Yugoslavia. Here is the ultimate East-West struggle, where capitalism and communism are code words for deeper historical forces: Christendom against Islam; Western Catholicism, as represented by the Croats and Slovenes, battling Eastern Orthodoxy, as represented by the Serbs and Macedonians; the modernist traditions of Habsburg Austria-Hungary colliding with the despotism of Ottoman Turkey." Robert D. Kaplan, "Bloody Balkans," *New Republic,* April 8, 1991, pp. 14–15.

7. Robert D. Kaplan, "The Clairvoyance of Rebecca West," *National Interest* (Winter 1991–92), p. 66.

8. In 1936 Rebecca West spent six weeks in Yugoslavia, returned to England, and wrote a 1,181-page tome that interwove anecdotes of her travels with a history of the Balkans: *Black Lamb and Grey Falcon* (Viking Press, 1943). West,

who had been the companion of H. G. Wells, was one of the great prose stylists of twentieth century English literature, and *Black Lamb* remains a masterpiece of travel writing. It is not, however, *pace* Kaplan, a good analysis of the Balkan question. Kaplan, *Balkan Ghosts,* p. xiv.

9. Steven J. Woehrel, *Yugoslavia's Kosovo Crisis: Ethnic Conflict between Albanians and Serbs* (Congressional Research Service, November 2, 1989), p. 11.

10. Kaplan, *Balkan Ghosts,* p. 35.

11. Kaplan, *Balkan Ghosts,* p. xvii.

12. Kaplan, *Balkan Ghosts,* p. 30.

13. Kaplan, *Balkan Ghosts,* p. 42.

14. Kaplan, *Balkan Ghosts,* p. 25. Kaplan makes this point several times: "Fear of the East, as manifested by Constantinople—whether Byzantine or Turkish—swept the Croats willingly into the arms of Catholic popes, Hungarian kings, and Austrian-Habsburg emperors" (p. 24).

15. Robert D. Kaplan, "A Reader's Guide to the Balkans,"*New York Times,* April 18, 1993, section 7, p. 1.

16. Kaplan, *Balkan Ghosts,* p. 32. Emphasis in the original.

17. Kaplan, *Balkan Ghosts,* p. 74.

18. The image of Eastern Europe as a "haunted" land became popular in the early 1990s. But Tina Rosenberg and Eva Hoffman employed the metaphor for different purposes. They emphasized how the immediate past weighed down on the present—and did not suggest that anything especially irrational existed about this. See Tina Rosenberg, *The Haunted Land: Facing Europe's Ghosts after Communism* (Random House, 1995); and Eva Hoffman, *Exit into History: A Journey through the New Eastern Europe* (Viking, 1993).

19. Elizabeth Drew, *On the Edge: The Clinton Presidency* (Simon and Schuster, 1994), p. 157.

20. For an excellent analysis of how Herodotus pioneered the "familiar" versus "alien" tradition in Western historiography, see Francois Hartog, *The Mirror of Herodotus: The Representation of the Other in the Writing of History,* Janet Lloyd, trans. (Berkeley, Calif.: University of California Press, 1988). Herodotus did not use the idea of Occident versus Orient; that only emerged under the Romans. See Walter Burkert, *The Orientalizing Revolution: Near Eastern Influence on Greek Culture in the Early Archaic Age* (Harvard University Press, 1992), p. 153. See also the brilliant analysis of Herodotus and the debate over ethnicity in Neil Ascherson, *Black Sea* (New York: Hill and Wang, 1995).

21. "And once Uzbeks, Turkmens, Mongols, the advance guard of 'les Chinois,' begin surging westward, it will be the Russians whose historic task will be to hold them up. Russia, the new frontier of what remains of Western civilization." John Lukacs, *The End of the Twentieth Century and the End of the Modern Age* (New York: Ticknor and Fields, 1993), p. 46.

22. Zbigniew Brzezinski, "Post–Communist Nationalism," *Foreign Affairs,* vol. 68 (Winter 1989–90), pp. 1–25. For Brzezinski's flirtation with global chaos theory, see his *Out of Control: Global Turmoil on the Eve of the Twenty-First Century* (Charles Scribner's Sons, 1993), where he argues that *"the global relevance of the West's political message could be vitiated by the growing tendency in*

the advanced world to infuse the inner content of liberal democracy with a life-style that I define as a permissive cornucopia. The priority given to individual self-gratification, combined with the growing capacity of the human being to reshape itself through genetic and other forms of scientific self-alteration—with neither subject to moral restraint—tend to create a condition in which little self-control is exercised over the dynamics of the desire to consume and to tinker with the self. In contrast, outside the richer West, much of human life is still dominated by fundamental concerns with survival and not with conspicuous consumption. These divergent trends undermine and inhibit global consensus and enhance the dangers inherent in a deepening global cleavage." Quote on pp. xii–xiii.

23. William Pfaff, "The Absence of Empire," *New Yorker*, August 10, 1992, pp. 59–69. Pfaff may deserve recognition for being the first person to argue that chaos was the major foreign policy issue confronting America. In 1983, a decade before anyone else showed an interest in the term, he wrote: "The enemy is the Soviet Union, but behind that can be seen another—chaos. Mr. Reagan spoke with feeling about chaos when he announced the invasion of Grenada. He said that he did it to forestall further chaos; chaos, the void—in Greek, χαοσ ('unformed matter'). Our struggle is with disintegration itself. The challenge is very great, but it is in the American grain. We have always conceived of ourselves as the bringers of order, givers of light. But the risk is equally imposing—that chaos wins, when, to turn to a dark meaning what Pope lightly wrote,

Light dies before thy uncreating word;
Thy hand, great Anarch! lets the curtain fall,
And universal darkness buries all."

William Pfaff, "Order, Chaos, and the National Interest," *New Yorker*, November 14, 1983, p. 113.

24. Samuel P. Huntington is one of America's most prominent and accomplished political scientists. He wrote perhaps the most influential single study of comparative politics, *Political Order in Changing Societies* (Yale University Press, 1968). His study of civil-military relations, *The Soldier and the State: The Theory and Politics of Civil-Military Relations* (Vintage Books, 1964), was also considered definitive. Over the years, he had authored a string of influential studies of U.S. strategy, including Samuel P. Huntington, ed., *The Strategic Imperative: New Policies for American Security* (Cambridge, Mass.: Ballinger Publishing, 1982). Most recently, he had penned a major study of the global democratization trend, *The Third Wave: Democratization in the Late Twentieth Century* (University of Oklahoma Press, 1991). In between, he had found time to serve on diverse government committees, lending his name to controversial studies of everything from the Vietnam War to U.S. strategic planning. He was, for example, one of the authors of the 1987 report *Discriminate Deterrence: Report of the Commission on Integrated Long-Term Strategy* (Department of Defense, 1987), an early attempt to project a strategy for the United States that might work after the cold war ended. His nomination for membership in the American Academy of Sciences led to an unusual debate about the relationship between his politics and scholarship (see George F. Will, "Professors Who Play Politics,"

Washington Post, May 7, 1987, p. A27; and Amy E. Schwartz, "Science by the Numbers," *Washington Post,* June 25, 1987, p. A17). At least in private, however, even his most fervent opponents concede he is a scholar of exceptional range and brilliance.

25. Samuel P. Huntington, "The Clash of Civilizations?" *Foreign Affairs,* vol. 72, no. 3 (Summer 1993), pp. 22–49; quote on pp. 30–31. Huntington took this map from a monograph by William Wallace about the forces that might give the European Union a common sense of identity. Wallace did not, however, attribute any special importance to the extension of "Western Christianity" in 1500. He noted that this was one among several criteria that different states deployed to justify their own particular claims to admission to the community. "Each claimant to full European participation attempts to draw the boundaries of Europe around and behind it: to include all the countries of the Western tradition, of Catholicism and the Enlightenment, for Austria, Hungary and Poland; of the broader Christian tradition, for the southern republics of Yugoslavia, Romania, Bulgaria and Russia; of the secularizing and modernizing tradition, for Turkey." William Wallace, *The Transformation of Western Europe* (New York: Council on Foreign Relations for the Royal Institute of International Affairs, 1990), pp. 17–18.

26. Huntington, "The Clash of Civilizations?" p. 22.

27. Huntington, "The Clash of Civilizations?" pp. 40–41.

28. Huntington, "The Clash of Civilizations?" p. 40.

29. Huntington, "The Clash of Civilizations?" p. 25.

30. In 1995 *Baywatch,* a one-hour television series renowned for its display of hunky male and nubile female lifeguards, uncluttered by too much plot or unnecessary clothing, was the most watched show in the world—the latest in a string of American cultural triumphs that also included *Dallas* and *The Fugitive.* See Bill Carter, "Stand Aside CNN; America's No. 1 TV Export Is—No Scoffing, Please— 'Baywatch,'" *New York Times,* July 3, 1995, p. A41.

31. Susan Woodward, senior fellow, Brookings Institution, oral communication, 1996.

32. Owen Harries, "Power and Civilization," *National Interest,* no. 35 (Spring 1994), p. 109. The original article was Owen Harries, "Clash of Civilisations," *Australian,* April, 3, 1993. For sample replies, see Greg Sheridan, "'Culture Wars,' A Product of the Conspiracy Junkies," *Australian,* April 7, 1993; and Richard Woolacott, "We Must Be the Odd Man In," *Weekly East Australian,* April 17, 1993. I am grateful to Mr. Harries for these citations.

33. Samuel P. Huntington, "The Coming Clash of Civilizations: Or, the West against the Rest," *New York Times,* June 6, 1993, p. D19.

34. Huntington, "The Clash of Civilizations?" The next issue of *Foreign Affairs* was devoted to replies to Huntington, which were then collected and republished with the original article as a book: Samuel P. Huntington, *The Clash of Civilizations: The Debate* (New York: Council on Foreign Affairs, 1993).

35. R. C. Longworth, "On the Record," *Chicago Tribune,* February 16, 1997, section 2, p. 3.

Chapter Three

1. The casualty figures are from Joe Rosenbloom III, "Waco: More Than Simple Blunders?" *Wall Street Journal*, October 17, 1995, p. A20.

2. Hans Magnus Enzensberger, *Civil Wars: From L.A. to Bosnia* (New York: New Press, 1993), p. 20. For some measure of Enzensberger's influence in the United States, see the sympathetic review he got from his intellectual opponent, Francis Fukuyama, in "The New World Disorder," *New York Times Book Review*, October 9, 1994, pp. 12–13; and the long review by Nader Mousavizadeh, "Hearts of Darkness," *New Republic*, November 28, 1994, pp. 70–73.

3. Enzensberger, *Civil Wars*, p. 21.

4. Almost a quarter of Robert D. Kaplan's essay "The Coming Anarchy: How Scarcity, Crime, Overpopulation, Tribalism, and Disease Are Rapidly Destroying the Social Fabric of Our Planet," *Atlantic Monthly*, February 1994, is devoted to expounding on the ideas contained in Martin van Creveld, *The Transformation of War* (Free Press, 1991).

5. Van Creveld, *The Transformation of War*, p. 20.

6. Van Creveld, *The Transformation of War*, p. 197.

7. Van Creveld, *The Transformation of War*, p. 198.

8. Van Creveld, *The Transformation of War*, p. 196

9. For some fascinating musings on this theme from the period under discussion, see Edward O. Wilson, "Is Humanity Suicidal?" *New York Times Magazine*, May 30, 1993, pp. 24–29.

10. Thomas Emmert, "Why Serbia Will Fight for 'Holy' Kosovo; And the Peril for Western Armies Approaching the Balkan Tripwire," *Washington Post*, June 13, 1993, p. C1. For the related discussion of the Kosovo myth, see John Kifner, "Through the Serbian Mind's Eye," *New York Times*, April 10, 1994, pp. E1–E5. Even articles that did not emphasize the suicidal nature of Serbian nationalism often dwelt on the isolation from reality that made it potentially self-destructive. "Serbia's political leaders also reflect an other-worldly quality. The shadowy President, Slobodan Milošević, rarely appears in public, and citizens are left to divine his views from cryptic statements. Radovan Karadžić, the psychiatrist who is the Bosnian Serbs' leader, insists in the midst of Serbian offensives that Serbs never launch offensives. . . . 'Gangsterism and criminality are so rampant here that we are now like some Latin American country, Paraguay perhaps,' mused one Serbian official. 'But it isn't just the criminal aspect that is overwhelming our society. There is a drifting away from reality into a bizarre kind of fantasy world, like the world in Garcia Marquez novels.'" Stephen Kinzer, "The Nightmare's Roots: The Dream World Called Serbia," *New York Times*, May 16, 1993, section 4, p. 1.

11. Henry Kissinger, "Bosnia: Only Just Beginning. . ." *Washington Post*, September 11, 1995, p. A21. Kissinger echoes an argument made earlier—and more memorably—by Robert D. Kaplan: "The principal illness of the Balkans [is] conflicting dreams of lost imperial glory. Each nation demands that its borders revert to where they were at the exact time when its own empire had reached the zenith

of ancient medieval expansion." Robert D. Kaplan, *Balkan Ghosts: A Journey through History* (Vintage Books, 1993), p. 57.

12. Roger Cohen, "NATO and the UN Quarrel in Bosnia as Serbs Press On," *New York Times,* November 27, 1994, p. A1.

13. John F. Burns, "Conflict in the Balkans: Nationalist Says Serbs' Rejection of Pact Means the End of Bosnia," *New York Times,* May 17, 1993, p. A1.

14. Allegations were made that unusual numbers of troops on all sides of the Bosnian conflict—including UN peacekeepers—made heavy use of drugs. See John Veit, "Bosnia: A Real Drug War," *High Times,* vol. 247 (March 1996), found on Internet at www.hightimes.com/ht/mag/9603/bosnia.htm/.

15. For an entertaining introduction to the latest scientific and philosophical debates on the subject of irrationality, see John McCrone, *The Myth of Irrationality: The Science of the Mind from Plato to* Star Trek (New York: Carroll and Graf, 1993). For the perspective of psychologists, see Megan Rosenfeld, "A World Gone Mad? Mental Health Experts Say It's All Too True," *Washington Post,* May 27, 1995, pp. C1–C5.

During recent years a host of editorials have echoed the *Wall Street Journal,* whose judgment on events in Bosnia and Waco was: "The hard and discomfiting truth is that we seem to have stumbled into an age when reason is routinely humbled by the irrational—or at least by events for which traditional sources of authority fail to offer any adequate explanation." ("Weird in Waco," *Wall Street Journal,* April 20, 1993, p. A20).

My favorite judgment on the subject was an op-ed cartoon that showed two federal agents standing and watching the Branch Davidian compound at Waco explode in flames. The FBI agent says, "We could have picked Koresh up while he was jogging. We could have picked him up in town buying supplies. We could have waited him out. . . Why this?" The ATF agent replies, "He wasn't rational." (*Washington Post,* April 24, 1993, p. A27).

16. Yehezkel Dror, "High-Intensity Aggressive Ideologies as an International Threat," *Jerusalem Journal of International Relations,* vol. 9 (March 1987), pp. 153–72; and Yehezkel Dror, *Crazy States: A Counterconventional Strategic Problem* (Lexington, Mass.: Heath Lexington Books, 1971). Dror's ideas were taken over and popularized—if that is the right word—in the United States by the futurist Alvin Toffler. See Alvin Toffler, *Powershift: Knowledge, Wealth, and Violence at the Edge of the Twenty-First Century* (Bantam Books, 1990), p. 255.

17. Neil Jordan, *The Crying Game,* script; 1992. In earlier versions of this story, the punch line—the scorpion's explanation for its behavior—is: "After all, this is the Middle East" or "This is Yugoslavia" or wherever (see Leonard Mosely, *Power Play: Oil in the Middle East* (Random House, 1973)). But the differences in the punch line do not alter the basic moral of the story. The fable of the scorpion and the frog has a message: In the Middle East—or in similar anarchic environments—violence does not arise from rational causes. It is not triggered by struggles over land or water or power; instead, it is genetic, ingrained, and explosive. Scorpions and frogs fight because of "ancient tribal rivalries," "feuds that go back thousands of years," whose origins have long since been forgotten. This type of violence not only has irrational origins, but it also is not sub-

ject to restraint by rational self-interest. The scorpion's hatred of frogs is so powerful that it is ultimately self-defeating and suicidal. The narrator of the tale is
saying, in effect, "Don't ask me for explanations of the behavior of scorpions
and frogs (or Bosnians and Serbs). They are crazy, and you have to accept their
endless violence as a force of nature—something like bad weather in the
Antarctic."

18. Two books appeared in the early 1990s that helped to popularize the idea
that entire societies could go mad. Both were written as critiques of the multicul-
turalist trend in American education, and both helped to lay an intellectual foundation for chaos theory: Robert B. Edgerton, *Sick Societies: Challenging the Myth
of Primitive Harmony* (Free Press, 1992); and Howard K. Bloom, *The Lucifer
Principle: A Scientific Expedition into the Forces of History* (New York: Atlantic
Monthly Press, 1995). Unfortunately, the former work, written by a serious if
controversial anthropologist, attracted less attention than the latter, which is little more than a racist screed.

19. For an excellent translation of Emile Durkheim's remarks on anomie,
which are scattered throughout several of his major works, see Anthony Giddens,
ed., *Emile Durkheim: Selected Writings* (Cambridge, England: Cambridge University Press, 1972), especially pp. 173–79.

20. Emile Durkheim, *Suicide* (Paris: Alcan, 1897), pp. 280–81; translation
taken from Steven Lukes, *Emile Durkheim: His Life and Work* (Harper and Row,
1972), pp. 210–11.

21. "Social Structure and Anomie" in Robert K. Merton, *Social Theory and
Social Structure: Toward the Codification of Theory and Research* (Glencoe,
N.Y.: Free Press, 1949), pp. 125–49. On the popularity of this article, see Stephen
Cole, "The Growth of Scientific Knowledge: Theories of Deviance as a Case
Study," in Lewis A. Coser, ed., *The Idea of Social Structure: Papers in Honor of
Robert K. Merton* (Harcourt, Brace, Jovanovich, 1975), pp. 175–220. Merton's
work drew heavily on the pioneering sociology of Talcott Parson's, who intro-
duced Durkheim's ideas to Americans in *The Structure of Social Action: A Study
in Social Theory with Special Reference to a Group of Recent European Writers*
(McGraw-Hill, 1937). Samuel P. Huntington first made his mark on the discipline
of comparative politics by applying Parson's theories (particularly his ideas about
how institutionalization of values could curb the propensity toward violence) to
the developing countries. See Samuel P. Huntington, *Political Order in Changing
Societies* (Yale University Press, 1968).

22. For an introduction to the issues, see James Davison Hunter, *Culture Wars:
The Struggle to Define America* (Basic Books, 1991). For some fascinating epi-
sodes, see the series of articles, "Great Divides: Scenes from the Politics of Ameri-
can Culture," which begins with Dennis Farney, "For Peggy McIntosh, 'Excel-
lence' Can Be a Dangerous Concept," *Wall Street Journal*, June 14, 1994, p. A1.
Probably the best overview of the culture wars is Todd Gitlin, *The Twilight of
Common Dreams: Why America Is Wracked by Culture Wars* (New York:
Metropolitan Books, 1995).

23. In addition to Charles Murray's tour de force, *Losing Ground: American
Social Policy, 1950–80* (Basic Books, 1984), see James Q. Wilson and Richard

Herrnstein, *Crime and Human Nature* (Simon and Schuster, 1985); and Myron Magnet, *The Dream and the Nightmare: The Sixties' Legacy to the Underclass* (William Morrow, 1993).

24. In the 1996 presidential campaign, the one candidate who regularly invoked the concept of anomie was Pat Buchanan. See Lloyd Grove, "Populist Pat Shakes Hands While Potomac Pat Shakes His Rivals," *Washington Post,* March 1, 1996, pp. D1ff.

25. For a brilliant discussion (and critique) of this trend in conservative thought, see Albert O. Hirschman, *The Rhetoric of Reaction: Perversity, Futility, Jeopardy* (Belknap Press at Harvard University, 1991), especially chapter 2.

26. William J. Bennett, *The De-Valuing of America: The Fight for Our Culture and Our Children* (Simon and Schuster, 1992), p. 33.

27. William J. Bennett, *The Index of Leading Cultural Indicators: Facts and Figures on the State of American Society* (Washington: Empower America, Heritage Foundation, Free Congress Foundation, March 1993). The 1994 edition was printed as a mass edition paperback by Simon and Schuster.

28. The modern source of this claim is the highly influential text by James Q. Wilson and Richard Herrnstein, *Crime and Human Nature* (Simon and Schuster, 1985), p. 217. For a brilliant extension of its arguments, see James Q. Wilson, *The Moral Sense* (Free Press, 1993).

29. William J. Bennett, John J. DiIulio, Jr., and John P. Walters, *Body Count: Moral Poverty . . . and How to Win America's War against Crime and Drugs* (Simon and Schuster, 1996), p. 56.

30. The most detailed analysis of this famous incident is Michael Stone, "What Really Happened in Central Park," *New York,* August 14, 1989, pp. 30–43.

31. "So Young to Kill, So Young to Die," *Time,* September 19, 1994, pp. 54–59. At the age of twenty-two months, Sandifer had been admitted to a hospital after being abused by an adult; by the age of three, he was a ward of the court; at age nine, he was arrested for armed robbery. By the time he died, his police record included eight felony arrests.

32. Commenting on the tragedy of Susan Smith, House Speaker Newt Gingrich noted: "The mother killing her two children in South Carolina vividly reminds every American how sick the society is getting and how much we have to change." Gingrich, sincerely believing that Democratic social policy was to blame for most crime, argued that the way to prevent recurrences would be to vote Republican. See "The 1994 Campaign: Vice President Rebukes Gingrich for Citing Murder Case," *New York Times,* November 8, 1994, p. A21.

33. See "Reported Major Crimes Fell 3 Percent in 1994: Over Longer Term, Gun Homicides by Boys 14–17 Have Risen Sharply," *Washington Post,* May 22, 1995, p. A5. American concern rose rapidly in the early 1990s, fueled partly by misperception (see Michel McQueen, "Political Paradox: People with the Least to Fear from Crime Drive the Crime Issue," *Wall Street Journal,* August 12, 1993, p. A1). Many Americans thought that crime rates had increased dramatically in recent years, reaching unprecedented levels. In fact, crime rates moderated somewhat in the early 1990s. The best-documented crime rate—the number of homicides—had increased dramatically during the 1960s and then leveled off, plateauing at a level

comparable to the rate that had prevailed in the 1930s. (See "Measuring Crime: A Shadow on Society," *Economist*, October 15, 1994, pp. 21–23. This superb article should be required reading for anyone discussing the issue of crime in America.)

34. Kaplan, "The Coming Anarchy," p. 46.

35. Robert D. Kaplan, "Cities of Despair," *New York Times*, June 6, 1996, p. A29.

36. Moira Farrow, "Welfare Warlords," *New Republic*, November 22, 1993, p. 10.

Chapter Four

1. Francis Fukuyama, "The End of History," *National Interest* (Summer 1989), pp. 3–18.

2. The most influential statement of this thesis in recent years has been Michael Doyle, "Kant, Liberal Legacies, and Foreign Affairs," *Philosophy and Public Affairs*, vol. 12, no. 3 (Summer 1983), part 1, pp. 205–35 and vol. 12, no. 4 (Fall 1983), part 2, pp. 323–53.

3. One of the first and most articulate critiques of Francis Fukuyama's optimism came from Samuel P. Huntington, who later emerged as a leading luminary of global chaos theory. His fundamental criticism of Fukuyama's dream of an "end of history"—a doctrine that Huntington dubbed "endism"—was that it "tends to ignore the weakness and irrationality of human nature. Endist arguments often assume that because it would be rational for human beings to focus on their economic well-being, they will act in that way, and therefore they will not engage in wars that do not meet the test of cost-benefit analysis or in ideological conflicts that are much ado about nothing. Human beings are at times rational, generous, creative, and wise, but they are also often stupid, selfish, cruel, and sinful. The struggle that is history began with the eating of the forbidden fruit and is rooted in human nature. In history there may be total defeats, but there are no final solutions. So long as human beings exist, there is no exit from the traumas of history." Samuel P. Huntington, "No Exit: The Errors of Endism," *National Interest*, no. 17 (Fall 1989), p. 10.

4. Graham E. Fuller, *The Democracy Trap: The Perils of the Post–Cold War World* (New York: Dutton Books, 1991).

5. Fuller, *The Democracy Trap*, p. 2.

6. Fuller, *The Democracy Trap*, p. 29. See also p. 183.

7. Fuller, *The Democracy Trap*, pp. 64–76.

8. Fuller, *The Democracy Trap*, p. 90.

9. Fuller, *The Democracy Trap*, pp. 63–64.

10. Fuller, *The Democracy Trap*, p. 89.

11. Fuller, *The Democracy Trap*, p. 3.

12. Fuller, *The Democracy Trap*, p. 86.

13. Fuller, *The Democracy Trap*, p. 88.

14. Fuller elaborated on the idea that democracies could be warlike, and on the connections between democratization and hypernationalism, in several articles,

including Graham E. Fuller, "The Breaking of Nations—and the Threat to Ours," *National Interest,* no. 26 (Winter 1991–92), pp. 14–21.

15. Fuller, *The Democracy Trap,* p. 92.

16. Thomas L. Hughes, "Pluralism and the Politics of Peace," *Cosmos,* vol. 1, no. 1 (1991), pp. 4–7.

17. For another analysis that presents a more theoretically sophisticated version of a similar argument, see Timothy M. Frye, "Ethnicity, Sovereignty, and Transitions from Non–Democratic Rule," *Journal of International Affairs,* vol. 45, no. 2 (Winter 1992), pp. 599–623.

18. Stanley Kober, "Revolutions Gone Bad," *Foreign Policy,* no. 91 (Summer 1993), p. 64. The Kober article is also noteworthy for an attempt (not very sophisticated) to provide a tour de horizon of the ways in which irrationality can become the defining element of a country's foreign policy.

19. Kober, "Revolutions Gone Bad," pp. 63–64.

20. Kober, "Revolutions Gone Bad," pp. 82–83.

21. Benjamin R. Barber, "Jihad vs. McWorld," *Atlantic Monthly,* vol. 269, no. 3 (March 1992), p. 53. Barber later expanded his argument in a book length treatment, *Jihad vs. McWorld* (Random House, 1995). For a review of the latter, see Muhammad ʿAli Salih, " ʿandama Yatahawil Kull Man La Yashrub ʿal-Kukakula ila ʿAdu,' ["When Anyone Who Doesn't Drink Coca-Cola Is Transformed into an Enemy,"] *al-Majalla* (February 4–10, 1996), pp. 67–68.

22. Barber, "Jihad vs. McWorld," p. 61.

23. For a wonderful example of this, see Richard Morin, "Unconventional Wisdom," *Washington Post,* January 2, 1994, p. C2, about the growing audience for American wrestlers, such as "Macho Man" Randy Savage, in India. The expansion of the McDonald's hamburger chain in the country of sacred cows is described in John Ward Anderson, "The Lure of India's Big Market: Liberalized Economy Attracts Hundreds of U.S. Firms," *Washington Post,* December 31, 1993, p. A1.

24. Mark Schapiro, "Lust-Greed-Sex-Power: Translatable Anywhere," *New York Times,* June 2, 1991, p. B29.

25. Douglas Davis, "TV View: The Screen as a Tool of Revolution," *New York Times,* July 14, 1991, p. B25.

26. John Rockwell, "A Culture Strives to Root in Freedom's Stony Soil," *New York Times,* November 9, 1992, p. A1; see also Michael Dobbs, "Moscow Turns to Mexican Soap Opera: Switched Off by Politics, Ex-Soviets Embrace Saintly Heroine," *Washington Post,* September 11, 1992, p. A1.

27. Celestine Bohlen, "In a New Climate of Freedom, Few Russian Newspapers Thrive," *New York Times,* Jan. 26, 1993, p. A6.

28. Dmitry Shlapentokh, "Lovemaking in the Time of *Perestroika:* Sex in the Context of Political Culture," *Studies in Comparative Communism,* vol. 25 (June 1992), p. 154. This is an unusually provocative and original treatment of the evolution of sexual mores in contemporary Russia. For an equally fascinating study that reinforces many of Shlapentokh's conclusions, see Laura Engelstein, *The Keys to Happiness: Sex and the Search for Modernity in Fin-de-Siecle Russia* (Cornell University Press, 1992). For an amusing account of how the same trend

manifested itself in another society, see Molly Moore, "India's Lewd Awakening: MTV and the Film Industry Are Putting Sexy Lyrics on Everyone's Lips," *Washington Post,* August 2, 1994, p. F1.

29. Andrew Solomon, "Young Russia's Defiant Decade," *New York Times Magazine,* July 18, 1993, pp. 16ff.

30. William McNeill, one of America's leading historians, has helped to popularize this idea. See William McNeill, "Peasants, Politics, and Television," *Washington Post,* December 30, 1991, p. C1; and William McNeill, "Fundamentalism and the World of the 1990s," in Martin E. Marty and R. Scott Appleby, eds., *Fundamentalisms and Society: Reclaiming the Sciences, the Family, and Education* (University of Chicago, 1993), pp. 558–73.

31. Barber, "Jihad vs. McWorld," p. 60.

32. Barber, "Jihad vs. McWorld," p. 62.

33. Barber, "Jihad vs. McWorld," p. 61.

34. Charles Krauthammer, "The Tribalization of America," *Washington Post,* August 6, 1990, p. A11.

35. Krauthammer, "The Tribalization of America."

36. Zbigniew Brzezinski, *Out of Control: Global Turmoil on the Eve of the Twenty-First Century* (Charles Scribner's Sons, 1993), p. xii.

37. Jay Mathews, "First Poll of China Finds Materialism Alive," *Washington Post,* February 16, 1995, p. A13.

38. Kathy Chen, "Undoing Tradition: As Millions of Chinese Try to Get Rich Quick, Values Get Trampled," *Wall Street Journal,* May 2, 1995, p. A1. See also "China: A 'Soulless Society'—Rampant Materialism Has Unleashed a Crisis of Morality," *Asiaweek,* February 17, 1995, pp. 24–25.

39. Brzezinski, *Out of Control,* p. 54.

40. This argument that envy provokes violence is similar to, but fundamentally distinct from, the claim that economic inequality is an invitation to conflict. The former argument stresses the emotional and potentially irrational response to economic contrasts, while the latter claim usually focuses on the struggle over control of economic resources. For discussions of the latter thesis, see Ted Robert Gurr, "On the Political Consequences of Scarcity and Economic Decline," *International Studies Quarterly,* vol. 29, no. 1 (March 1985), pp. 51–75; and Mark Irving Lichbach, "An Evaluation of 'Does Economic Inequality Breed Political Conflict?' Studies," *World Politics,* vol. 41 (July 1989), pp. 431–70.

42. Gurr, "On the Political Consequences of Scarcity and Economic Decline," p. 52.

43. Brzezinski's use of envy makes the origins of anomie seem—at first—more concrete and tangible than the identity crisis described by Barber. But one of the most notable trends in modern anthropology sociology has been the growing appreciation that emotions such as envy are cultural constructs whose operation varies widely from one society to the next. For a study of this cultural variance focusing on an emotion that is closely related to envy, see Peter N. Stearns, *Jealousy: The Evolution of an Emotion in American History* (New York University Press, 1989). For an intimation of even more radical problems that may arise from projecting Western ideas about emotion and personality onto other

societies, see Daniel Goleman, "The Self: From Tokyo to Topeka, It Changes," *New York Times*, March 7, 1989, p. C1.

43. Robin Wright and Doyle McManus, *Flashpoints: Promise and Peril in a New World* (Alfred A. Knopf, 1991). For a surprisingly upbeat synopsis of their work, see Robin Wright and Doyle McManus, "History Tomorrow: Four Choices between Reason and Chaos," *Washington Post*, December 29, 1991, p. C3.

44. Richard L. Holman, "Global Tourism Grew in '94," *Wall Street Journal*, January 3, 1995, p. A10.

45. These figures are drawn from United Nations Population Fund, *The State of World Population 1993* (New York: United Nations Fund for Population Activities, 1993); and Eugene Robinson, "Worldwide Migration Nears Crisis: Politics, Economics Cited in UN Study," *Washington Post*, July 7, 1993, p. A1. See also "123 Million People on the Move: The Tides of Humanity," *World Press Review*, October 1994, pp. 8–12.

46. Wright and McManus, *Flashpoints*, p. 170.

47. Molly Moore, "New Delhi's Decay: A Tale of Too Much City," *Washington Post*, August 31, 1994, p. A27.

48. Wright and McManus, *Flashpoints*, 179.

49. Wright and McManus, *Flashpoints*, pp. 180–81.

50. Nicholas Lehman argues the opposite. See Nicholas Lehman, *The Promised Land: The Great Black Migration and How It Changed America* (Vintage Books, 1992). See also Jacqueline Jones, *Labor of Love, Labor of Sorrow: Black Women, Work, and the Family from Slavery to the Present* (Vintage Books, 1985).

51. Myron Weiner, *Sons of the Soil: Migration and Ethnic Conflict in India* (Princeton University Press, 1978). Weiner is the joint director, with Samuel P. Huntington, of the Harvard–Massachusetts Institute of Technology Joint Seminar on Political Development (JOSPOD), where Walker Connor, another chaos theorist, delivered his first paper on "ethnonationalism." See Walker Connor, *Ethnonationalism: The Quest for Understanding* (Princeton University Press, 1994), p. 67.

52. In this discussion, the issue of displaced persons and refugees—populations that have been forced to move because of war—is circumvented. Their exclusion is a matter of logic: Refugees are a symptom of war, not its cause. They may help to spread fear and pave the way for the sweep of war into new territories, but none of the chaos theorists has argued that this role is new or specific to ethnic conflicts.

53. United Nations Population Fund, *The State of World Population 1993*, pp. 5, 16–20. See also Robinson, "Worldwide Migration Crisis Nears," p. A1.

54. United Nations Population Fund, *The State of World Population 1993*, pp. 5, 16–20; and Robinson, "Worldwide Migration Crisis Nears," p. A1.

55. Aaron Segal, *An Atlas of International Migration* (London: Hans Zell, 1993), p. 111.

56. "Open to Us, Closed to Them," *Economist*, August 13, 1994, pp. 43–45.

57. Michael J. Mandel, "It's Really Two Immigrant Economies," *Business Week*, June 20, 1994, pp. 74–78. Some estimates suggest that illegal immigrants

provide a net benefit for the economy; see Julian L. Simon, *Immigration: The Demographic and Economic Facts* (Washington: Cato Institute, 1995), especially p. 42.

58. For a shocking exposé of how badly out of line public perceptions of immigration in the United States are with the realities, see Frederick Rose, "Muddled Masses: The Growing Backlash against Immigration Includes Many Myths," *Wall Street Journal,* April 26, 1995, p. A1.

59. For a great read on the history of this allegation, see Alan M. Kraut, *Silent Travelers: Germs, Genes, and the "Immigrant Menace"* (Basic Books, 1994). For an example of its resurrection in contemporary America, see Peter Brimelow, *Alien Nation: Common Sense about America's Immigration Disaster* (Random House, 1995), especially chapter 9.

60. William Drozdiak, "European Unity—For Organized Crime," *Washington Post,* August 2, 1994, p. A20.

61. For some of the major works, see Claire Sterling, *Thieve's World: The Threat of the New Global Network of Organized Crime* (Simon and Schuster, 1994); Arkady Vaksberg, *The Soviet Mafia* (St. Martin's Press, 1991); Lev Timofeyev, *Russia's Secret Rulers* (Alfred A. Knopf, 1992); and Stephen Handelman, *Comrade Criminal: Russia's New Mafiya* (Yale University Press, 1995). On the expansion of Russian mafias abroad, see Steve Coll, "Russian Crime Syndicates Moving West," *Washington Post,* April 2, 1994, p. A1; Seymour M. Hersh, "The Wild East," *Atlantic Monthly,* June 1994, pp. 61–86; Neela Banerjee, "Russian Organized Crime Goes Global: Gangs Use Skills Honed in Former Police State," *Wall Street Journal,* December 22, 1994, p. A10; and Patrice Claude, "Russian Mafia Finds Its Promised Land," *Guardian Weekly,* October 1, 1995, p. 16 (from *Le Monde,* September 15, 1995).

62. Richard Preston, *The Hot Zone* (Random House, 1994), pp. 11–12. See also " 'Emerging Viruses' in Films and Best-Sellers," *New York Times,* May 10, 1995, p. A14; and John Schwartz, "Media's Portrayal of Ebola Virus Sparks Outbreak of Wild Scenarios," *Washington Post,* May 14, 1995, p. A3. For a scientific overview of the threat of new diseases, see Laurie Garrett, *The Coming Plague: Newly Emerging Diseases in a World Out of Balance* (Farrar, Straus, and Giroux, 1995).

63. Dennis Pirages, "Microsecurity: Disease Organisms and Human Well-Being," *Washington Quarterly,* vol. 18, no. 4 (Autumn 1995), pp. 5–12.

64. Robert D. Kaplan, "The Coming Anarchy: How Security, Crime, Overpopulation, Tribalism, and Disease Are Rapidly Destroying the Social Fabric of Our Planet," *Atlantic Monthly,* February 1994; and Robert D. Kaplan, *The Ends of the Earth: A Journey at the Dawn of the Twenty-First Century* (Random House, 1996).

65. Michael Lind, "Liberals Duck Immigration Debate," *New York Times,* September 7, 1995, p. A27; and Joel Kotkin, "Nativists on the Left," *Wall Street Journal,* July 25, 1995, p. A12. For an early overview of Pat Buchanan's foreign policy views, see Patrick J. Buchanan, "Now That Red Is Dead, Come Home, America; The New World Order Is Bunk; It's Time to Look Out for No. 1," *Washington Post,* September 8, 1991, p. C1.

66. Joel Kotkin, "Is Fascism Back in Fashion? Yes, And Stopping It Will Require Candor about Immigration and Multiculturalism," *Washington Post,* January 2, 1994, p. C4. See also Joel Kotkin, "Can We Reheat the Melting Pot?" *Washington Post,* July 3, 1994, p. C2; Joel Kotkin, "Hotheads in California," *New York Times,* October 27, 1994, p. A29; and Joel Kotkin, "White Flight to the Fringes," *Washington Post,* March 10, 1996, pp. C1–C2.

67. Joel Kotkin, *Tribes: How Race, Religion, and Identity Determine Success in the New Global Economy* (Random House, 1993), pp. 4–5.

68. Kotkin, *Tribes,* p. 241.

69. Kotkin, *Tribes,* p. 3.

70. John Naisbitt, *Global Paradox: The Bigger the World Economy, the More Powerful Its Smallest Players* (William Morrow and Co., 1994), p. 13.

71. Naisbitt, *Global Paradox,* p. 23.

72. Naisbitt was not the only business pundit impressed by this trend. Kenichi Ohmae penned a dramatic account entitled *The End of the Nation State: The Rise of Regional Economics* (Free Press, 1995). See also William Drozdiak, "Regions on the Rise: As European Borders Become More Porous, Cities Replace Countries in Transnational Economic Alliances," *Washington Post,* October 22, 1995, p. A22; and Daniel Williams, "Driven by Small Firms, Italy's Economy Thrives: Northern Manufacturers Beat the Odds," *Washington Post,* October 17, 1995, p. A31.

73. Naisbitt, *Global Paradox,* p. 40.

74. Bob Davis, "Global Paradox: Growth of Trade Binds Nations, But It Also Can Spur Separatism," *Wall Street Journal,* June 20, 1994, p. A1.

75. Stephen P. Cohen, "U.S. Security in a Separatist Season," *Bulletin of the Atomic Scientists* (July/August 1992), pp. 28–32. See also Keith B. Richburg, "Fall of African Dictatorships Fuels Separatist Feeling," *Washington Post,* March 25, 1992, p. A1.

76. Wright and McManus, *Flashpoints,* pp. 20–21.

Chapter Five

1. "Isolationism is a multidimensional phenomenon, of which a number of different species may exist. Isolationists may have different geographical foci: one clearly definable group may reject all foreign involvements; another may oppose all activity outside the Western Hemisphere; and a third may wish to avoid contact with Europe, while participating actively in Asian affairs ('Asia-firsters')." Leroy N. Rieselbach, *The Roots of Isolationism* (Indianapolis, Ind.: Bob-Merrill Co., 1966), pp. 7–8.

2. For a description of the various intellectual and organizational linkages that bound its members together, see Gary Dorrien, *The Neoconservative Mind: Politics, Culture, and the War of Ideology* (Temple University Press, 1993).

3. Both of these television series also released "companion volumes," which distributed their ideas in written form. See Michael Ignatieff, *Blood and Belonging: Journeys into the New Nationalism* (Farrar, Straus, and Giroux, 1993); and Martin

E. Marty and R. Scott Appleby, *The Glory and the Power: The Fundamentalist Challenge to the Modern World* (Boston, Mass.: Beacon Press, 1992).

4. Mathew Horsman and Andrew Marshall, *After the Nation-State: Citizens, Tribalism, and the New World Disorder* (Glasgow: Harper Collins, 1994).

5. Carla Anne Robbins, "Some Foreign-Policy Conservatives Are Bolting Clinton Camp, Endorsing Dole's Campaign Bid," *Wall Street Journal*, June 21, 1996, p. A16.

6. Benjamin R. Barber, *Jihad vs. McWorld* (Ballantine Books, 1996), p. 299. Barker was responding to Philip Gourevitch, "Misfortune Tellers," *New Yorker*, April 8, 1996, pp. 96–100.

7. Summaries of their remarks are available in *Sources of Conflict: G. M. Tamás and Samuel Huntington on "Identity and Conflict" and Robert Kaplan and Jessica Tuchman Mathews on "The Coming Anarchy" and the Nation-State under Siege*, Peaceworks no. 4 (Washington: U.S. Institute of Peace, 1995). This conference launched a major research program by the institute, which concluded with the publication of a mammoth volume: Chester A. Crocker and Fen Osler Hampson with Pamela Aall, eds., *Managing Global Chaos: Sources of and Responses to International Conflict* (Washington: U.S. Institute of Peace, 1996).

8. Many social psychologists (beginning with Freud) thought that dense crowding produced the same kind of collapse of values and resultant irrational violence that Emile Durkheim had dubbed anomie. One of the best studies of this in recent years was Bill Buford, *Among the Thugs: The Experience, and the Seduction, of Crowd Violence* (London: Secker and Warburg, 1991), which recounted his travels with a band of British soccer hooligans.

9. Thomas F. Homer-Dixon, "On the Threshold: Environmental Changes as Causes of Acute Conflict," *International Security*, vol. 16 (Fall 1991), pp. 76–116. See also Thomas F. Homer-Dixon, "Environmental Scarcities and Violent Conflict," *International Security*, vol. 19 (Summer 1994), pp. 5–40. For an account of Homer-Dixon's growing following in Washington, see Ross Laver, "Looking for Trouble," *Maclean's* (September 5, 1994), pp. 18–21.

10. Norman Myers, "Environment and Security," *Foreign Policy*, no. 74 (Spring 1989), pp. 23–41; Norman Myers, *Ultimate Security: The Environmental Basis of Political Stability* (W. W. Norton, 1994); and George D. Moffett, *Critical Masses: The Global Population Challenge* (Viking Press, 1994). Interest in new killer diseases formed a special extension of this perspective. See Frank Ryan, *Virus X: Tracking the New Killer Plagues Out of the Present and into the Future* (Little, Brown, 1997).

11. Jessica Mathews, "The New Security Puzzles," *Washington Post*, July 24, 1994, p. C7. See also her major statement of her views: Jessica Tuchman Mathews, "Redefining Security," *Foreign Affairs*, vol. 68 (Spring 1989), pp. 162–77.

12. Robert D. Kaplan, *The Ends of the Earth: A Journey at the Dawn of the Twenty-First Century* (Random House, 1996), p. 300. Kaplan's account drew heavily on the work of Vaclav Smil, which had also triggered major discussions at the U.S. Central Intelligence Agency. See Vaclav Smil, *China's Environmental Crisis: An Inquiry into the Limits of National Development* (Armonk, N.Y.: M. E. Sharpe, 1993).

13. Kaplan, *The Ends of the Earth*, p. 292.

14. To mention only their two most important works: Donald Horowitz *Ethnic Groups in Conflict* (Berkeley, Calif.: University of California Press, 1985); and Ted Robert Gurr, *Minorities at Risk: A Global View of Ethnopolitical Conflicts* (Washington: U.S. Institute for Peace, 1993). In addition to these major scholars, hundreds of less prominent thinkers tried to grapple with the problem of ethnic conflict. For a good introduction to the type of work produced during this period, see Charles A. Kupchan, ed., *Nationalism and Nationalities in the New Europe* (Cornell University Press, 1995).

15. Conor Cruise O'Brien, *On the Eve of the Millennium: The Future of Democracy through an Age of Unreason* (Free Press, 1994). See also Conor Cruise O'Brien, "The Wrath of Ages: Nationalism's Primordial Roots," *Foreign Affairs*, vol. 72 (November/December 1993), pp. 142–49.

16. Mark Juergensmeyer, *The New Cold War?: Religious Nationalism Confronts the Secular State* (Berkeley, Calif.: University of California Press, 1993).

17. See Neil J. Kressel, *Mass Hate: The Global Rise of Genocide and Terror* (New York: Plenum Press, 1996).

18. This was quoted approvingly by Daniel Patrick Moynihan in *Pandaemonium: Ethnicity in International Politics* (Oxford, England: Oxford University Press, 1993), p. 16. He cites the December 21, 1991, issue of the *Economist*, p. 45.

19. For his major works on the subject, see Samuel P. Huntington, "The Renewal of Strategy," in Samuel P. Huntington, ed., *The Strategic Imperative: New Policies for American Security* (Cambridge, Mass.: Ballinger Publishing, 1982), pp. 1–52; Samuel P. Huntington, "Coping with the Lippmann Gap," *Foreign Affairs*, vol. 66 (America and the World 1987–88), pp. 453–77; Samuel P. Huntington, "The U.S.—Decline or Renewal?" *Foreign Affairs*, vol. 67 (Winter 1988–89), pp. 76–96; and Samuel P. Huntington, "America's Changing Strategic Interests," *Survival*, vol. 33 (January/February 1991), pp. 3–17.

20. In the 1980s grand strategy, in which policies toward every issue were derived from an overarching plan, again became vogue among foreign policy thinkers. For a sampling, see Paul Kennedy, ed., *Grand Strategies in War and Peace* (Yale University Press, 1991).

21. Huntington, "America's Changing Strategic Interests," p. 8.

22. Realism is, with Wilsonianism, one of the two great foreign policy traditions in the United States. It emphasizes the inevitability of international conflict and the importance of realpolitik. Realists have long argued that the only (sometimes) effective antidote to war is deterrence, particularly through maintenance of the balance of power. For an eloquent introduction to classical realist thought, written with American policy issues of the 1990s in mind, see Henry Kissinger, *Diplomacy* (Simon and Schuster, 1994).

Because of their interest in the balance of power, realists have always paid particular attention to the operation of alliances. By the 1970s the study of international relations in American universities was largely dominated by a group of scholars, self-dubbed "structural realists" or "neorealists," who claimed that all the important features of international affairs could be deduced from the international distribution of power and alliances. For the locus classicus of this school, see Kenneth N. Waltz, *Theory of International Politics* (McGraw Hill, 1979).

23. The definitive articulation of this vision by the dean of neorealism is Kenneth N. Waltz, "The Emerging Structure of International Politics," *International Security,* vol. 18 (Fall 1993), pp. 44–79. For a lucid introduction to the realist debate about whether the post–cold war world would be divided into competing political-economic blocs, see Aaron L. Friedberg, "Ripe for Rivalry: Prospects for Peace in a Multipolar Asia," *International Security,* vol. 18 (Winter 1993–94), pp. 5–33.

24. See Franz Schurmann, *The Logic of World Power: An Inquiry into the Origins, Currents, and Contradictions of World Politics* (Pantheon Books, 1974), chapter 2.

25. Samuel P. Huntington, "The Coming Clash of Civilizations: Or, the West against the Rest," *New York Times,* June 6, 1993, p. E19.

26. Samuel P. Huntington, "Why International Primacy Matters," *International Security,* vol. 17 (Spring 1993), p. 76.

27. Samuel P. Huntington, "The Clash of Civilizations?" *Foreign Affairs,* vol. 72, no. 3 (Summer 1993), p. 34.

28. Huntington, "The Clash of Civilizations?" p. 42.

29. Huntington, "The Clash of Civilizations?" p. 46.

30. The only attempt to take Huntington seriously and to extend his ideas about the Balkans that has come to my attention is in two works by a historian: Dennis P. Hupchick, *Culture and History in Eastern Europe* (St. Martin's Press, 1994); and Dennis P. Hupchick, *Conflict and Chaos in Eastern Europe* (St. Martin's Press, 1995).

31. William Pfaff, "Reflections: On Nationalism," *New Yorker,* May 25, 1987, p. 44.

32. William Pfaff, *Barbarian Sentiments: How the American Century Ends* (New York: Hill and Wang, 1989), p. 10.

33. William Pfaff, "Order, Chaos, and the National Interest," *New Yorker,* November 14, 1983, p. 111.

34. William Pfaff, "Islam and the West," *New Yorker,* January 28, 1991, p. 85. Not surprisingly, Pfaff's main source for insight into Islamic fundamentalism was Bernard Lewis.

35. Pfaff, "Islam and the West," p. 88.

36. Pfaff, "Reflections," pp. 44–55, quote on p. 47.

37. Pfaff, "Reflections," p. 50.

38. Pfaff, "Reflections," p. 54.

39. Pfaff, a man who is unusually respectful of non–Western cultures and sensitive to the dark side of the history of the West, employs the term "barbarism" in a distinctly ironic manner. The "barbarians" from whom his book *Barbarian Sentiments* takes its title are themselves Westerners. That book opens with the following quotation: "In order to handle barbarian affairs, you have to know barbarian sentiments: in order to know barbarian sentiments, you have to know barbarian conditions." These are the words of Wei Yuan, member of the

Manchu Court, introducing a collection of documents about European life published just before the Opium War. Pfaff, *Barbarian Sentiments*, p. 1.

40. William Pfaff, "The Absence of Empire," *New Yorker,* August 10, 1992, pp. 59–69.

41. Pfaff, "Islam and the West," p. 83.

42. Max Singer and Aaron Wildavsky, *The Real World Order: Zones of Peace/Zones of Turmoil* (Chatham, Mass.: Chatham House, 1993), p. 3.

43. Patrick E. Tyler, "U.S. Strategy Plan Calls for Insuring No Rivals Develop," *New York Times,* March 8, 1992, p. 1.

44. Robert D. Kaplan, "Into the Bloody New World: A Moral Pragmatism for America in an Age of Mini-Holocausts," *Washington Post,* April 17, 1994, p. C2.

45. Robert D. Kaplan, "The Coming Anarchy: How Security, Crime, Overpopulation, Tribalism, and Disease Are Rapidly Destroying the Social Fabric of Our Planet," *Atlantic Monthly,* February 1994, p. 60.

46. Kaplan, "The Coming Anarchy," p. 59.

47. William Pfaff, *The Wrath of Nations: Civilization and the Furies of Nationalism* (Simon and Schuster, 1993), pp. 213–14.

Chapter Six

1. Samuel P. Huntington, "The Clash of Civilizations?" *Foreign Affairs,* vol. 72, no. 3 (Summer 1993), pp. 22–49; Daniel Patrick Moynihan, *Pandaemonium: Ethnicity in International Politics* (Oxford, England: Oxford University Press, 1993); and William Pfaff, *The Wrath of Nations: Civilization and the Furies of Militant Nationalism* (Simon and Schuster, 1993).

2. Zbigniew Brzezinski, *Out of Control: Global Turmoil on the Eve of the Twenty-First Century* (Charles Scribner's Sons, 1993); and Paul Kennedy, *Preparing for the Twenty-First Century* (Random House, 1993).

3. Anthony Lake, "Lake Says U.S. Interests Compel Engagement Abroad," remarks at Johns Hopkins' SAIS, September 21, 1993, as reprinted at gopher://198.80.36.82:70/OR64739949-64781172-range/archives/1993/pdq.93.

4. For a study of how nationalism came to be discussed in terms of the metaphor of disease, see Paula Franklin Little, "U.S. Policy toward the Demise of Yugoslavia: The 'Virus of Nationalism,'" *East European Politics and Societies,* vol. 6, no. 3 (Fall 1992), pp. 303–18.

5. A major debate ensued over what forces drove the dominance of the soundbite (or even whether this was a new phenomenon at all). Robert McNeil, co-anchor of public television's popular *MacNeil-Lehrer Newshour,* argued that television was primarily responsible. See Robert MacNeil, "Is Television Shortening Our Attention Span?" *New York University Education Quarterly,* vol. 14, no. 2 (Winter 1983). James Fallows, one of America's leading print journalists, contended that the fault lay with broad changes in the press rather than in any one medium. See James Fallows, *Breaking the News: How the Media Undermine American Democracy* (Vintage Books, 1997).

6. The best detailed analysis of how soundbites work, written by America's foremost sociolinguist, is George Lakoff *Moral Politics: What Conservatives Know That Liberals Don't* (University of Chicago Press, 1996).

7. For the major study of this trend in the realm of presidential campaigns, see Thomas E. Patterson, *Out of Order* (A. Knopf, 1993), particularly the graph on p. 76.

8. Hans Magnus Enzensberger, "Balkan Tribalism, As Uganda Sees It," *New York Times,* September 16, 1992, p. A25; John Tagliabue, "The World: Old Tribal Rivalries in Eastern Europe Pose Threat of Infection," *New York Times,* October 13, 1991, p. D2; Will Huton, "Europe's New Tribalism Could Infect Us All," *Guardian Weekly,* February 7, 1993, p. 8; and Jacques Attali, "Europe's Descent into Tribalism," *NPQ* (Fall 1992), pp. 38–40.

9. Robert D. Kaplan, "After 'Balkan Ghosts,'" *Weekly Standard,* vol. 1, no. 14 (December 18, 1995), p. 23. For another example of Kaplan attempting to repudiate President Bill Clinton's reading of *Balkan Ghosts,* see his exchange of letters with Timothy Garton Ashe, "The Foul Balkan Sky?" in *New York Review of Books,* March 21, 1996, p. 53.

10. Kaplan, "After 'Balkan Ghosts.'" Kaplan's comments have not been wholly accurate. In his first policy piece about Bosnia, "Ground Zero," *New Republic,* August 2, 1993, pp. 15–16, he argued, "Rolling back the Serbs would require several hundred thousand troops and a stay of perhaps a decade in the Balkans. That is just not on." He thought that the Bosnian Muslims would have to accept partitioning of separated enclaves. However, he did argue that the West should defend the physical integrity of those enclaves—something akin to the "safe havens" strategy that the UN would eventually implement without success. Kaplan only grew more hawkish later.

11. Benjamin Schwarz, "The Diversity Myth: America's Leading Export," *Atlantic Monthly,* vol. 275, no. 5 (May 1995), p. 66.

12. Schwarz, "The Diversity Myth," p. 67.

13. Lt. Gen. Patrick M. Hughes, "Global Threats and Challenges to the United States and Its Interests Abroad." Statement for the Senate Select Committee on Intelligence, February 5, 1997, as found at http://www.fas.org/irp/congress/1997.hr/5970205d.htm.

14. Anthony Flint, "Marines Chief Foresees New Type of War," *Boston Globe,* April 10, 1996, p. 6.

15. Thomas E. Ricks, "Colin Powell's Doctrine on Use of Military Force Is Now Being Questioned by Senior U.S. Officers," *Wall Street Journal,* August 30, 1995, p. A12.

16. Ralph Peters, "The New Warrior Class," *Parameters: U.S. Army War College Quarterly,* vol. 24, no. 1 (Summer 1994), p. 16.

17. Peters, "The New Warrier Class," p. 24.

18. For the invocation of these threats, see Office of the Secretary of Defense, *Proliferation: Threat and Response* (Government Printing Office, April 1996), especially pp. 43ff; and Patrick Pexton, "Future Seizes Operations Other Than War," *Army Times,* November 25, 1996, p. 8.

19. Steve Ginsburg, ed., transcript supplied by News Transcripts, of Senate Intelligence Committee hearing on the nomination of R. James Woolsey to be director of central intelligence, held February 2, 1993, p. 2.

20. "Statement of the Honorable R. James Woolsey, Director of Central Intelligence, on International Organized Crime and Nuclear Security," *Congressional Record*, daily ed., June 27, 1994, p. E1335.

21. John Lancaster and Barton Gellman, "National Security Strategy Paper Arouses Pentagon, State Department Debate," *Washington Post*, March 3, 1994, p. A14.

22. Steven Greenhouse, "The Greening of U.S. Diplomacy: Focus on Ecology," *New York Times*, October 9, 1995, p. A6.

23. Thomas W. Lippman, "Christopher Puts Environment High on Diplomatic Agenda: Abuse of Natural Resources Imperils U.S. Interests, Secretary of State Says," *Washington Post*, April 15, 1996, p. A10.

24. "Atwood Assesses Africa's Strengths and Weaknesses," gopher://198.80.36.82:70/OR259981-275764-range/archives/1994/pdq.94 File ID: AEF104, June 27, 1994; and J. Brian Atwood, "Suddenly, Chaos," *Washington Post*, June 31, 1994, p. C9.

25. Personal correspondence, September 8, 1995.

26. Paul Kennedy, "Doomsterism," *New York Review of Books*, September 19, 1996, p. 20.

27. In a June 29, 1994, speech to the National Academy of Sciences in which he laid out his plans for the upcoming G-7 summit in Naples, Clinton said: "But when you look at the long-run trends that are going on around the world—when you read articles like Robert Kaplan's article in *The Atlantic* a couple of months ago that some say its too dour—still, if you really look at what is going on, you could visualize a world in which a few million of us live in such opulence we could all be starring on nighttime soaps and the rest of us look like we're in one of those Mel Gibson 'Road Warrior' movies." "Clinton Urges Broad, Simultaneous Attack on Global Problems," gopher://198.80.36.82:70/OR259981-275764-range/archives/ 1994/pdq.94 File ID: EPF414.

28. Ann Devroy, "President Cautions Congress on 'Simplistic Ideas' in Foreign Policy," *Washington Post*, May 26, 1994, p. A31.

29. Maureen Dowd, "Clinton Warns of Violent Nationalism," *New York Times*, June 8, 1994, p. A16.

30. Benjamin R. Barber, *Jihad vs. McWorld* (Times Books, 1995).

31. Blaine Harden, "Ego and Ambition Scarcely Hidden in Gingrich's Writings," *Washington Post*, January 22, 1997, pp. A1, A4; see also, "Word for Word: The Gingrich Report," *New York Times*, January 26, 1997, p. E7.

32. Paul Lewis, "Stoked by Ethnic Conflict, Refugee Numbers Swell," *New York Times*, November 10, 1993, p. A6.

33. See Mahathir Mohammed and Shintaro Ishihara, *The Voice of Asia: Two Leaders Discuss the Coming Century* (Tokyo: Kodansha International, 1995). For other Japanese reactions to Huntington, see Paul Blustein, " 'Just Say No' to Those Western Allies: A Strident Malaysian Nationalist Urges Japan to Tilt

toward Asia," *Washington Post,* December 11, 1994, p. C2; Tetsuya Kataoka, *The Truth about the Japanese "Threat": Misperceptions of the Samuel Hunting-ton Thesis* (Stanford, Calif.: Hoover Institution, 1995); and Masakazu Yamazaki, "Asia, A Civilization in the Making," *Foreign Affairs* (July/August 1996), pp. 106–18. For Malay perspectives, see Anwar Ibrahim, "Gearing Up ASEAN for the New Century," *Business Times,* September 15, 1993; and Chandra Muzaffar, "The West's Hidden Agenda," *World Press Review* (February 1994), pp. 25–26. A sampling of Chinese responses includes Wang Jisi, "An Academic Analysis of the Theory of the Clash of Civilizations," *Chinese Social Sciences Quarterly* (Spring 1994), pp. 16–31; and Li Xiaobing, "Civilization Strategy after the Cold War—Reviewing Huntington's 'Theory of Civilization Conflict,'" *People's Daily,* June 29, 1994, p. 5.

34. Peter Rutland, "Russia Sizes Up the 'Threat from the South,' Part 1: Clash of Civilizations on Russia's Southern Frontier," *OMRI Analytical Brief* (1996). For some Arab reactions, see Mohamed Sid-Ahmed, "Huntington Put to the Test," *al-Ahram Weekly* (February 15-21, 1996), p. 8; and Abd al-Malik Salman, "Beware the Zionist-Catholic Alliance," *Akhbar al- Khalij,* translated in *Mideast Mirror* (February 10, 1994), pp. 17–19.

35. "Eastern Approaches: Germany and Islam," *Economist,* April 19, 1997, pp. 50–51.

36. For a history of the development of this consensus, see Walter LaFeber, *The American Age: O.S. Foreign Policy at Home and Abroad, 1750 to the Present,* 2d ed. (W. W. Norton, 1994); and Richard J. Barnet, *Roots of War: The Men and Institutions behind U.S. Foreign Policy* (New York: Penguin Books, 1973).

37. Noam Chomsky, *American Power and the New Mandarins* (Pantheon Books, 1969).

Chapter Seven

1. Unlike the term "Bosnian," which refers to any citizen of Bosnia irrespective of his or her religion or nationality, the term "Bosniak" is sometimes used to refer specifically to the Muslim population of Bosnia.

2. Samuel P. Huntington called this the "kin-country syndrome," citing a series of newspaper articles about ethnic conflict by H. D. S. Greenway, particularly "Adversaries Create Devils of Each Other," *Boston Globe,* December 15, 1992, p. 1.

3. Samuel P. Huntington, "Religion and the Third Wave," *National Interest,* no. 24 (Summer 1991), p. 40.

4. Huntington acknowledges having gleaned the phrase "clash of civilizations" from Bernard Lewis, "The Roots of Muslim Rage," *Atlantic Monthly,* September 1990, p. 60, in a passage that read: "It should by now be clear that we are facing a mood and a movement far transcending the level of issues and policies and the governments that pursue them. This is no less than a clash of civilizations—the perhaps irrational but surely historic reaction of an ancient rival against our Judeo-Christian heritage, our secular present, and the worldwide expansion of

both." The metaphor quickly became a stock phrase in Orientalist writings. See, for example, the jacket liner of Daniel Pipes, *The Rushdie Affair: The Novel, the Ayatollah and the West* (New York: Carol Publishing Group, 1990), which listed some of the results of the publication of Salmon Rushdie's novel *The Satanic Verses* (New York: Viking Penguin, 1989): "an edict by a head of state calling for the assassination of a foreign author; riots, bombings, and assassinations resulting in the deaths of over twenty people; a threat of censorship hitting at the heart of the West's belief in freedom of expression; even a clash of civilizations—that of the fundamentalist Muslim versus the free-thinking Westerner."

5. Bernard Lewis, "The Map of the Middle East: A Guide for the Perplexed," *American Scholar,* vol. 58 (Winter 1989), pp. 19–38; quote on p. 37. The idea that the current problems of the Middle East arise from the attempt to impose modern concepts of nationality over traditional Islamic ones is also evident in David Fromkin, *A Peace to End All Peace: The Fall of the Ottoman Empire and the Creation of the Modern Middle East* (New York: Avon Books, 1989). Fromkin appears to have derived this perspective from another Orientalist, Elie Kedourie.

6. Bernard Lewis explains this task in *The Middle East and the West* (New York: Harper and Row, 1964), pp. 25–26. For an elegant example of its application, see Bernard Lewis, *The Political Language of Islam* (University of Chicago Press, 1988).

7. Bernard Lewis, *Islam in History: Ideas, Men, and Events in the Middle East* (Chicago: Open Court, 1993), p. 21.

8. For Lewis's history of this process, see Bernard Lewis, *The Muslim Discovery of Europe* (W. W. Norton, 1982).

9. Lewis, "The Roots of Muslim Rage"; also reprinted in *Current,* no. 329 (January 1991).

10. John L. Esposito, *The Islamic Threat: Myth or Reality?* (New York: Oxford University Press, 1992), p. 173.

11. Lewis, "The Roots of Muslim Rage," p. 49.

12. Lewis, "The Roots of Muslim Rage," pp. 59–60.

13. In addition to the authors, such as Lewis, that he cited in "The Clash of Civilizations?" *Foreign Affairs,* vol. 72, no. 3 (Summer 1993), pp. 22–49, Samuel P. Huntington credited a long train of scholars with having influenced his work, including Max Weber, Emile Durkheim, Oswald Spengler, Arnold Toynbee, A. L. Kroeber, Philip Bagby, Carroll Quigley, S. N. Eisenstadt, Christopher Dawson, Fernand Braudel, Adda B. Bozeman, and Immanuel Wallerstein. (See Samuel P. Huntington, letter to the editor, *Economist,* September 3, 1994, p. 8.) Of all the names on this list, one has not received adequate acknowledgment. Adda B. Bozeman's article "War and the Clash of Ideas," *Orbis* (Spring 1976), pp. 61–102, anticipates virtually all of the themes that Huntington would resurrect in "The Clash of Civilizations?": the division of the globe into civilizational value systems, the special nature of conflicts between civilizations, the obstacle such conflicts pose to Wilsonian dreams of international cooperation, and so on. Bozeman's ideas were still popular in certain military circles in the early 1990s, which may help to explain their later receptivity

to Huntington. See Political-Military Affairs Division, Airpower Research Institute, with the participation of Adda B. Bozeman, *The International Dimension of Culture and Conflict: Proceedings of the Symposium,* symposium of the International Dimension of Culture and Conflict (Maxwell Air Force Base, Ala.: Air University Press, 1991).

14. Huntington, "The Clash of Civilizations?" pp. 31–32. His use of Islam as an icon for the West's clash with other civilizations also attracted immediate media attention. The *Economist* devoted an entire issue to the subject ("The Fundamental Fear," August 6, 1994).

15. The most famous attack on Orientalism was that launched by Edward W. Said in his tour de force, *Orientalism* (Random House, 1978). This elicited a defense by Bernard Lewis, and a long and bitter debate between the two followed. See Bernard Lewis, "The Question of Orientalism," *New York Review of Books,* June 24, 1982, pp. 49–56. Many of the key criticisms that Said laid at Orientalism's door—particularly the charge that it was "essentialist," that is, that it constructed an ahistorical ideal vision of Islam against which reality was compared unfavorably—had already been made in the 1960s. See, particularly, Anouar Abdel-Malek, "Orientalism in Crisis," *Diogenes,* no. 44 (Winter 1963), pp. 103–43.

16. Clifford Geertz, *Islam Observed: Religious Development in Morocco and Indonesia* (Yale University Press, 1968), p. v.

17. Geertz, *Islam Observed,* p. 16.

18. Geertz, *Islam Observed,* pp. 13–14.

19. The idea of "Islamic civilization" did not die overnight. For two impressive attempts to liberate the concept from the hypostasis imposed on it by Orientalists, see Marshall G. S. Hodgson, *The Venture of Islam,* 3 vols. (University of Chicago Press, 1974), especially vol. 1, pp. 22–99; and Ernest Gellner, *Muslim Society* (Cambridge, England: Cambridge University Press, 1981). For the most recent, and probably the most persuasive, account of how many of the supposedly "universal" features of Islamic societies developed and spread, see Richard Bulliet, *Islam: A View from the Edge* (Columbia University Press, 1994).

20. Ronald Inglehart and Marita Carballo, "Does Latin America Exist? (And Is There a Confucian Culture?): A Global Analysis of Cross-Cultural Differences," *Political Science and Politics,* vol. 30 (March 1997), pp. 34–46.

21. Fouad Ajami, "The Summoning," *Foreign Affairs,* vol. 72, no. 4 (September/October 1993), p. 3. Ajami elaborated further on his critique via television; see Ben Wattenberg's *Think Tank,* October 20, 1995, episode: "Islam and the West: Is There a Clash of Cultures?" with Fouad Ajami, Milton Viorst, and John Esposito.

22. Ajami, "The Summoning," p. 5.

23. Ajami, "The Summoning," p. 7. The quotation is from Michael Ignatieff, "The Balkan Tragedy," *New York Review of Books,* May 13, 1993.

24. Ljubo Sirc, "The National Question in Yugoslavia," *South Slav Journal,* vol. 9 (1986), pp. 80–93. For an authoritative discussion, see Ivo Banac, *The National Question in Yugoslavia: Origins, History, Politics* (Cornell University Press, 1984), pp. 47–50.

25. Denis P. Hupchick, *Conflict and Chaos in Eastern Europe* (St. Martin's Press, 1995), p. 227.

26. "The names Serb and Croat, though occasionally appearing in peripheral areas, were not used in Bosnia proper. Bosnians then belonged to one of three Christian denominations: Orthodox, Catholic or a local institution, the Bosnian Church; but religious affiliation was not strong and was easily shed. The Bosnians did not fight one another for religious or for ethnic reasons. When they fought—and they fought a lot—it was over territory or for regional hegemony." John Fine, "What Is a Bosnian?" *London Review of Books,* April 28, 1994, pp. 9–10.

27. The Croats were slightly more religious, with 77.4 percent calling themselves believers of some sort. See Steven L. Burg, "The Political Integration of Yugoslavia's Muslims: Determinants of Success and Failure," *Carl Beck Papers in Russian and East European Studies,* no. 203 (University of Pittsburgh, 1983), p. 30.

28. Blaine Harden, "Bosnia's Muslims Say Stereotypes Are Costing Lives," *Washington Post,* December 16, 1992, p. A1.

29. Ed Vulliamy, *Seasons in Hell: Understanding Bosnia's War* (St. Martin's Press, 1994), p. 63.

30. Cornelia Sorabji, *Bosnia's Muslims: Challenging Past and Present Misconceptions* (London: 1992), pp. 5–6, quoted in Noel Malcolm, *Bosnia: A Short History* (New York University Press, 1994), p. 222.

31. Srdan Bogosavljeviacc, "Bosnia and Herzegovina in the Mirror of Statistics," in Josep Palav and Radha Kumar, eds., *Ex-Yugoslavia: From War to Peace* (Valencia, Spain: Citizen's Conference for the Peaceful and Democratic Integration of the Balkans into Europe, September 4–6, 1992), p. 209.

32. Remy Ourdan, "The Bosnian Dream of a Multiethnic Future Is Dying," *Guardian Weekly,* October 19, 1994, p. 19.

33. For a good discussion of the convergence of values in Bosnia, see Dusan Janjic, "State-Political Identity of a Multiethnic and Multiconfessional Community: Outstanding Issues," in Josep Palau and Radha Kumar, eds., *Ex-Yugoslavia from War to Peace* (Madrid: Helsinki Citizen's Assembly, 1993), pp. 191–207.

34. For analyses of Serb hatred of the Bosnian Muslims, see Anna Husarska, "Letter from Bosnia: Unsafe Zone," *New Yorker,* July 12, 1993, pp. 29–37; and Peter Maass, "Bosnian Serbs Say They're Fighting against Islamic Fundamentalism," *Washington Post,* August 11, 1992, p. A13. Although the Serbian media works hard to exacerbate and manipulate this Islamophobia (see Mark Thompson, *Forging War: The Media in Serbia, Croatia, and Bosnia-Herzegovina* (London: Article 19, May 1994)), most observers believe such fears are sincere, albeit preposterous. However, Ed Vulliamy, one of the keenest observers of the conflict, offers a chilling dissent. He notes: "The Croats drive a mixture of fear, hatred and respect into the Serbs. Serbian fighters speak about bloody vengeance for Jasenovac, but in two years I never heard a single derogatory remark from a Serb about the Croats as a people. Hatred, yes; contempt, never. But the Muslims are another matter, they are 'gypsies', 'filth', 'bitches', 'animals'. The Bosnian pro-

ject did not entail seeing the Muslims as an enemy—the threat of the Jihad was all hot air—so much as sub-humans." Ed Vulliamy, *Seasons in Hell: Understanding Bosnia's War* (St. Martin's Press, 1994), p. 46.

35. Yahya Sadowski, "Bosnia's Muslims: A Fundamentalist Threat?" *Brookings Review,* vol. 13, no. 1 (Winter 1995).

36. "In a discussion with senior Burundi officials, the question as to whether they could always tell a Tutsi from a Hutu received the ambiguous response of 'Yes, but with a margin of error of 35 percent.'" Francis M. Deng and others, *Sovereignty as Responsibility: Conflict Management in Africa* (Brookings, 1996), p. 234, note 7.

37. H. D. Lasswell, *Politics* (McGraw Hill, 1933).

38. Roy Licklider, "How Civil Wars End: Questions and Methods," in Roy Licklider, ed., *Stopping the Killing: How Civil Wars End* (New York University Press, 1993), pp. 3–19.

39. Benzion Netanyahu makes the controversial claim that this idea can already be found fully developed in fifteenth century Spain; see Benzion Netanyahu, *Origins of the Inquisition in Fifteenth Century Spain* (Random House, 1995). The more widely accepted position is that, although the Christian West was unusual in seeking to purge non-Christian elements, it still tolerated enormous linguistic and tribal diversity. See R. I. Moore, *The Formation of a Persecuting Society: Power and Deviance in Western Europe* (Oxford, England: Blackwell, 1991).

40. Robert Jay Lifton, *The Protean Self: Human Resilience in an Age of Fragmentation* (Basic Books, 1993), pp. 26–27, 206.

41. Lewis F. Richardson, *Statistics of Deadly Quarrels* (Pittsburgh, Pa.: Boxwood Press, 1960), p. 173.

42. The classic statement of the contemporary (or structuralist) realist position is Kenneth N. Waltz, *Theory of International Relations* (McGraw Hill, 1979).

43. John Mueller, *Retreat from Doomsday: The Obsolescence of Major War* (Basic Books, 1989); and Edward N. Luttwak, "Where Are the Great Powers?" *Foreign Affairs,* vol. 73 (July/August 1994), pp. 23–28.

44. Christer Ahlstrom, *Casualties of Conflict: Report for the World Campaign for the Protection of Victims of War* (Uppsala University, Department of Peace and Conflict Research, 1991), p. 5.

45. Stockholm International Peace Research Institute, *SIPRI Yearbook 1996: Armaments, Disarmament, and International Security* (Oxford, England: Oxford University Press, 1996), p. 15.

46. James Shreeve, "Terms of Estrangement," *Discover,* vol. 15, no. 11 (November 1994), pp. 56–63; and Jared Diamond, "Race without Color," *Discover,* vol. 15, no. 11 (November 1994), pp. 82–91.

47. For a concise and inoffensive discussion of the concept, see H. L. Morris, "Ethnic Groups," in David L. Sills, ed., *International Encyclopedia of the Social Sciences* (Macmillan, 1968), pp. 167–72. For a more detailed history, see Marvin Harris, *The Rise of Anthropological Theory: A History of Theories of Culture* (New York: Crowell, Kegan Paul, 1968).

48. Sometimes it was deliberately used as a polite synonym for race.

49. The term "ethnic cleansing" is a translation of the Serbo-Croat term "etnicko ciscenje." It appears to have first entered English in 1990, when it was used in communiqués from the Croatian government alleging that the Serbs intended to create a Greater Serbia by "ethnic cleansing" of contested areas such as Slavonia. (Rudolf Arapovic, "In Defense of Croatia," *Washington Post,* November 28, 1990, p. A22; and Blaine Harden, "Croatian Militia Falling Back as Conflict with Serbs Intensifies," *Washington Post,* August 2, 1991, p. A19.) The term began to appear regularly in American newspapers in spring 1992, as the Serb separatists began to evict and sometimes massacre the non–Serb population as they occupied new districts of Bosnia. (Chuck Sudetic, "Breaking Cease-Fire, Serbs Launch Attacks into Bosnia," *New York Times,* April 15, 1992, p. A6; and Chuck Sudetic, "Fear of Serb Onslaught Increases as Europe's Monitors Quit Bosnia," *New York Times,* May 13, 1992, p. A1.)

50. David Binder with Barbara Crossette, "As Ethnic Wars Multiply, U.S. Strives for a Policy," *New York Times,* February 7, 1993, p. A1.

51. For an excellent review of this problem, see John R. Bowen, "The Myth of Global Ethnic Conflict," *Journal of Democracy,* vol. 7 (1996), pp. 3–14.

Chapter Eight

1. Samuel P. Huntington is a noteworthy exception to this trend. His book-length elaboration of the "clash of civilizations" thesis is crammed full of charts and maps. Samuel P. Huntington, *The Clash of Civilizations: The Debate* (New York: Council on Foreign Affairs, 1993).

2. Paul Kennedy, "Doomsterism," *New York Review of Books,* September 19, 1996, p. 22.

3. Richard L. Holman, "Global Tourism Grew in '94," *Wall Street Journal,* January 3, 1995, p. 10. However, the great majority of tourists (315 million) visited European sights instead of the more exotic attractions of the non–Western world.

4. For a collection of detailed studies of how the tourist industry becomes a major force of Westernization, see "Tourism and the Business of Pleasure" issue of *Middle East Report,* no. 196 (September/October 1995).

5. As spelled out in the appendix, the technical term "culture clash" or "culture conflict" is used to describe all those violent episodes that global chaos theorists point to as evidence for their theory. This large category, in turn, is divided into two subgroups: culture wars and culture strife. Wars involve organized units of troops and lead to correspondingly higher casualty tolls; culture strife can range from bloody rioting to sporadic immigrant bashing. The Pentagon considered calling culture conflicts "ENS violence," for "ethnic, national, separatist violence." See Benjamin Schwartz, "The Diversity Myth: America's Leading Export," *Atlantic Monthly,* vol. 275 (May 1995), p. 57. See, for example, "Feeding Fundamentalism," *Economist,* August 21, 1993, p. 36.

6. This point was stressed in a recent series of articles about "hypernationalism" in Eastern Europe. See Jack Snyder, "Averting Anarchy in the New Europe,"

International Security, vol. 14 (Spring 1990), pp. 5–41; John J. Mearsheimer, "Why We Will Soon Miss the Cold War," *Atlantic Monthly,* August 1990, pp. 35–50; Barry R. Posen, "Nationalism, the Mass Army, and Military Power," *International Security,* vol. 18 (Fall 1993), pp. 80–124; and Barry R. Posen, "The Security Dilemma and Ethnic Conflict," *Survival,* vol. 35 (Spring 1993), pp. 27–47.

7. The phrase "high tech and low culture" seems to have originated with the brilliant African political scientist and specialist on cultural engineering Ali Mazrui.

8. For a useful introduction to these debates, see Carol Wekesser, ed., *Violence in the Media* (San Diego, Calif.: Greenhaven Press, 1995).

9. "Videodrome," *Economist,* August 13, 1994, p. 73. Anyone with even a passing interest in the debate over television violence will profit from reading this excellent two-page essay.

10. Thomas B. Edsall, "TV Tattered Nation's Social Fabric, Political Scientist Contends," *Washington Post,* Sept. 3, 1995, p. A5. Some of Robert Putnam's findings are laid out in his "Tuning In, Tuning Out: The Strange Disappearance of Social Capital in America," *PS: Political Science and Politics,* vol. 28 (December 1995), pp. 664–83.

11. For this phrase, and an excellent analysis of the forces inhibiting the television component of the global communications revolution, see Richard Parker, "The Future of Global Television News," Research Paper R-13, Harvard University, John F. Kennedy School of Government, Joan Shorenstein Center for Press, Politics, and Public Policy, September 1995, p. 15.

12. "And Nation Shall Speak Guff Unto Nation," *Economist,* May 2, 1992, pp. 21–24.

13. Perhaps the closest any radio program comes to being an international hit is news broadcasts of the BBC World Service. Even these are not global, but carefully tailored to specific regions. For a discussion of their success, see Donald Wilhelm, *Global Communications and Political Power* (New Brunswick, N.J.: Transaction Books, 1990).

14. John Pomfret, "Islam Takes Message to Turkish Television: Fundamentalists Benefit from Eased Controls," *Washington Post,* April 19, 1995, p. A25.

15. Peter Waldman, "Iran Fights New Foe: Western Television," *Wall Street Journal,* August 8, 1994, p. A10; and Geraldine Brooks, "Teen-age Infidels Hanging Out," *New York Times Magazine,* April 30, 1995, pp. 44–49.

16. For a collection of sophisticated essays that document this point, see Lawrence A. Babb and Susan S. Wadley, eds., *Media and the Transformation of Religion in South Asia* (University of Pennsylvania Press, 1995).

17. John Huey, "What Pop Culture Is Telling Us," *Fortune,* June 17, 1991, pp. 89–92.

18. Bill Berkeley, "Sounds of Violence," *New Republic,* August 22 and 29, 1994, pp. 18–19.

19. Democracy is a classic example of an "essentially contested concept," an idea whose core is so intensely politicized that members of different societies or

234 / *Notes to Pages 106–18*

adherents of distinct ideologies are unlikely to ever agree upon a common definition. This inability to agree upon the meaning of, much less to operationalize, key
terms is likely to always prevent the study of society from becoming a science. For
a survey of the divergent ways in which different people have tried to define
democracy, see C. B. MacPherson, *Real Worlds of Democracy* (New York:
Oxford University Press, 1972). For the idea of essentially contested concepts,
and their implications for the social "sciences," see William E. Connolly, *The
Terms of Political Discourse* (Lexington, Mass.: Heath, 1974).

20. The Freedom House data are not consistent over time, because a major
change in the method of assessing freedom was made in 1989.

21. Renee de Nevers, "Democratization and Ethnic Conflict," *Survival,* vol. 35
(Summer 1993), pp. 31–48.

22. Samuel P. Huntington, *The Third Wave: Democratization in the Late
Twentieth Century* (University of Oklahoma Press, 1991).

23. Samuel P. Huntington, "Religion and the Third Wave," *National Interest,*
(Summer 1991), pp. 29–42.

24. Central Intelligence Agency, *The World Factbook 1992* (Government
Printing Office, 1992), p. 144.

25. Hanna Batatu, *The Old Social Classes and the Revolutionary Movements
of Iraq* (Princeton University Press, 1978), p. 166. This is by far the best single
work ever written about modern Arab politics.

26. The source for these figures is International Monetary Fund, *Direction of
Trade Statistics Yearbook 1994* (Washington: International Monetary Fund, 1994).

27. World Bank, *World Development Report 1993: Investing in Health* (New
York: Oxford University Press, 1993), tables 1, 13, 14.

28. Spreadsheet FDI94C, taken from United Nations Conference on Trade and
Development, *World Investment Report 1994* (New York: United Nations,
1994), pp. 409–12.

29. Keith Bradsher, "U.S. Is Attracting New Money Pool," *New York Times,*
July 31, 1994, p. A1.

30. Another recent study examining similar variables reached different conclusions. It suggested that, in the early stages of economic development, countries
did better if the state was more interventionist. But this advantage wore away
over time, and countries well on the road to development did better when state
intervention was curbed. See Vinod Thomas and Yan Wang, "Distortions,
Interventions, and Productivity Growth: Is East Asia Different?" *Economic
Development and Cultural Change,* vol. 44 (January 1996), pp. 265–88. For a
discussion of the debate, focused on the Heritage Foundation report , see "Of
Liberty, and Prosperity," *Economist,* January 13, 1996, pp. 21–23.

31. G. E. M. de Ste. Croix, *The Class Struggle in the Ancient Greek World,
From the Archaic Age to the Arab Conquests* (Cornell University Press, 1981),
pp. 285–89.

32. The effects of unsatisfied needs forms the foundation of most modern psy-
chologies. For one summary of how these effects lead to violence, see Anthony
Storr, *Human Destructiveness* (Ballantine, 1991), especially chapter 1.

33. One of the best students of this particularly painful road to collective violence is Peter Gay. See Peter Gay, *Weimar Culture: The Outsider as Insider* (Harper and Row, 1968); but also see his wider work on the violent tendencies in early twentieth century European culture, *The Cultivation of Hatred,* vol. 3, *The Bourgeois Experience: Victoria to Freud* (W. W. Norton, 1994).

34. Struggles over distribution are the centerpieces of even the most civic politics. That is why Harold Lasswell entitled his great introduction to the subject *Politics: Who Gets What, When, How* (New York: P. Smith, 1950).

35. Among modern American sociologists, Charles Tilly has presented the strongest and most nuanced arguments that economic factors, not anomie, forms the taproot of collective violence. See his "Does Modernization Breed Revolution?" *Comparative Politics,* vol. 5 (April 1973), pp. 425–47; "Revolutions and Collective Violence," in Fred I. Greenstein and Nelson W. Polsby, eds., *Macropolitical Theory* (Reading, Mass.: Addison-Wesley, 1975), pp. 483–555; and "Collective Violence in European Perspective," in Hugh Davis Graham and Ted Robert Gurr, eds., *Violence in America: Historical and Comparative Perspectives* (Beverly Hills, Calif.: Sage, 1979), pp. 83–118.

36. For a survey, see D. L. Blackwood and R. G. Lynch, "The Measurement of Inequality and Poverty: A Policy Maker's Guide to the Literature," *World Development,* vol. 22 (April 1994), pp. 567–78.

37. For surveys of the problem, see Clifford Cobb, Ted Halstead, and Jonathan Rowe, "If the GDP Is Up, Why Is America Down?" *Atlantic Monthly,* October 1995, pp. 59–78; and Robert D. Hershey, Jr., "Statistic That Gets No Respect," *New York Times,* December 19, 1995, pp. D1, D17. For some experimental alternatives, see "Grossly Distorted Picture," *Economist,* February 5, 1994, p. 71; and Michael Prowse, "Better Ways to Measure Progress," *Financial Times,* October 2, 1995, p. 21.

38. John Schwartz, "World Bank Retools Economic Yardstick to Find Hidden Value," *Washington Post,* September 18, 1995, p. A3.

39. For a technical discussion of the human development index (HDI), outlining its strengths and weaknesses, see Irmgard Nübler, "The Human Development Index Revisited," *Intereconomics* (July/August 1995), pp. 171–76.

Chapter Nine

1. William J. Bennett, *The Index of Leading Cultural Indicators: Facts and Figures on the State of American Society* (Simon and Schuster, 1994).

2. For a surprisingly useful introduction to the problems attending the interpretation of crime statistics, see Charles Murray, *Losing Ground: American Social Policy, 1950–1980* (Basic Books, 1984), pp. 113–23.

3. See "Battle against Domestic Violence Hampered by Flawed Data," *Washington Post,* January 1, 1996, p. A7.

4. All figures are based on Interpol, *International Crime Statistics for 1989 and 1990* (Saint-Cloud, France: International Criminal Police Organization, 1990).

5. Gene Stephens, "The Global Crime Wave and What We Can Do about It," *Futurist* (July/August 1994), pp. 22–28. For a similar argument, see also Richard Eckersley, "The West's Deepening Cultural Crisis," *Futurist* (November/December 1993), pp. 8–12.

6. For an excellent collection of data, see Richard Lotspeich, "Crime in the Transition Economies," *Europe-Asia Studies*, vol. 47 (June 1995), pp. 555–89.

7. "Crime Decline Is Biggest for Forty Years," *Financial Times*, September 28, 1995, p. 11.

8. "Reported Major Crimes Fell 3 Percent in 1994," *Washington Post*, May 22, 1995, p. A5.

9. Pierre Thomas, "Violent Crime Rate Drops 7 Percent Nationwide," *Washington Post*, June 2, 1997, p. A1; Clifford Kraus, "Now, How Low Can Crime Go?" *New York Times*, January 28, 1996, p. D5. See also Clifford Kraus, "New York Crime Rate Plummets to Levels Not Seen in Thirty Years," *New York Times*, December 20, 1996, p. A1; and Fox Butterfield, "'95 Data Show Sharp Drop in Reported Rapes," *New York Times*, February 3, 1997, p. A1. Clear evidence of declining crime rates has not reassured Americans much. Despite the decrease in crime overall, Americans find other things to be alarmed by: the growing incidence of juvenile crime or the increased likelihood that the perpetrator of a homicide will be a stranger instead of a relative of the victim. See Adam Walinsky, "The Crisis of Public Order," *Atlantic Monthly*, July 1995, pp. 39–54.

10. Dane Archer and Rosemary Gartner, *Violence and Crime in Cross-National Perspective* (Yale University Press, 1984), chapter 4.

11. Douglas Farah, "Killing in El Salvadoran Crime Wave Outpaces Deaths during Civil War," *Washington Post*, March 16, 1996, p. A23.

12. Julia Preston, "Born Out of War, Nicaragua's Police Keep the Peace," *New York Times*, Feburary 22, 1996, p. A4.

13. In many societies, ethnic loyalties provide a valuable basis for criminal organization. See Charles W. Hall, "Area's Ethnic Drug Rings Proving Tougher to Crack," *Washington Post*, October 2, 1995, p. A1.

14. For the concept of social banditry, see Eric Hobsbawm, *Primitive Rebels: Studies in Archaic Forms of Social Movement in the Nineteenth and Twentieth Centuries* (Manchester University Press, 1959). For the Chechen case, see Yo'av Karny, "The Three Hundred Years' War," *Washington Post*, December 18, 1994, p. C3; and N. A. Kellett, *The Situation in Chechnia*, Directorate of Strategic Analysis Research Note 94/18 (Ottawa: Department of National Defense, Operational Research and Analysis, November 1994).

15. "Take Out Insurance before You Enter," *Economist*, March 8, 1997, p. 44.

16. See Elisabeth Bumiller, *May You Be the Mother of a Hundred Sons: A Journey among the Women of India* (New York: Fawcett Columbine, 1990), particularly chapter 3, pp. 44–74.

17. David Lester, "National Suicide and Homicide Rates: Correlates versus Predictors," *Social Science and Medicine*, vol. 29 (1989), pp. 1249–52.

18. Mary Jordan, "In Japan, Reading, 'Riting, Bullying: Student Suicides Follow Harassment for Being Different," *Washington Post*, January 15, 1996, p. A1.

19. For details, see Lee A. Headley, ed., *Suicide in Asia and the Near East* (Berkeley, Calif.: University of California Press, 1983).

20. Christopher Zinn, "Samoans Face Up to Despair," *Guardian Weekly,* October 1, 1995, p. 7.

21. Donald Morris, *The Washing of the Spears: A History of the Rise of the Zulu Nation under Shaka and Its Fall in the Zulu War of 1879* (Simon and Schuster, 1965); Noel Mostert, *Frontiers: The Epic of South Africa's Creation and the Tragedy of the Xhosa People* (Alfred Knopf, 1992); and Jeffrey Brian Peires, *The Dead Will Arise: Nongqawuse and the Great Xhosa Cattle-Killing Movement of 1956–57* (Indiana University Press, 1989).

22. See the diverse entries for these variables in Glen Evans and Norman L. Farberow, *The Encyclopedia of Suicide* (New York: Facts on File, 1988).

23. Robert D. Kaplan pointed out, citing the research of another chaos theorist, the historian John Lukacs, that Transylvania had always been part of "the West"—unlike Hungary itself, which had been occupied by the Ottomans for a couple of centuries. See Robert D. Kaplan, *Balkan Ghosts: A Journey through History* (St. Martin's Press, 1993), p. 149.

24. For a detailed culturalist analysis that deals with Japanese attitudes toward suicide and death in combat, see Ivan Morris, *The Nobility of Failure: Tragic Heroes in the History of Japan* (New York: Holt, Rinehart, and Winston, 1975), particularly chapter 10.

25. John W. Dower, *War without Mercy: Race and Power in the Pacific War* (Pantheon Books, 1986), p. 52. Forty years have not changed these attitudes much; see Ken Ringle, "The Unending Battle of Okinawa," *Washington Post,* April 1, 1995, p. C1.

26. Paul Carell, *Hitler Moves East: 1941–1943* [original title: *Unternehmen Barbarossa*] (Bantam Books, 1966), p. 451.

27. David Hoffman, "The Making of a 'Martyr': Vision of Paradise Propels Islamic Bombers," *Washington Post,* March 12, 1996, pp. A1, A9.

28. Two-thirds of the suicide bombers in Lebanon were not Shiʿa; see "Israeli Expert Presents Profile of 'Suicide Terrorist,'" in Joint Publications Research Service, *Foreign Broadcast Information Service Daily Report: Near East and South Asia* (U.S. Government, March 1996), p. 36.

29. Robert Block, "UN Left 8,000 to Die in Bosnia," *Independent,* October 31, 1995, p. 1. See also David Rohde, *Endgame: The Betrayal and Fall of Srebrenica, Europe's Worst Massacre since World War II* (Farrar, Straus, and Giroux, 1997).

30. Rick Atkinson, "Air Assault Set Stage for Broader Role," *Washington Post,* November 11, 1995, pp. A1–A21; and Rick Atkinson, "In Almost Losing Its Resolve, NATO Alliance Found Itself," *Washington Post,* November 16, 1995, pp. A1, A32.

31. Laura Silber, *Yugoslavia: The Death of a Nation,* part IV, "No Escape," (BBC, 1995).

32. For an early assessment of Serb military capacities that subsequently appeared to be accurate, see J. P. Mackley, "The Balkan Quagmire Myth: Taking On the Serbs Would Be More Grenada than Vietnam," *Washington Post,* March 7, 1993, p. C3.

33. Peter Reuter and others, *Money from Crime: A Study of the Economics of Drug Dealing in Washington, D.C.* (Santa Monica, Calif.: Rand Corporation, 1990); and "Crime in U.S. Pays Better Than Entry-Level Jobs, Says Economist," *Financial Times,* February 22, 1996, p. 5.

34. For an excellent review of the literature on this point, see Mary Elaine Hegland, "Religious Resurgence in Today's World—Refuge from Dislocation and Anomie or Enablement for Change?" in Richard T. Antoun and Mary Elaine Hegland, eds., *Religious Resurgence: Contemporary Cases in Islam, Christianity, and Judaism* (Syracuse University Press, 1987), pp. 233–56.

35. See the brilliant and moving study of Gerard Prunier, *The Rwanda Crisis: History of a Genocide* (Columbia University Press, 1995), especially pp. 229–68.

36. Barbara Harff defines genocide in a way that includes cases in which only a small number of victims are killed but excludes instances in which the killing is precipitate instead of protracted. For example, the massacre of Palestinians at Sabra and Shatila in 1982 is excluded.

37. Donald McFarlan, ed., *The Guiness Book of Records 1991* (New York: Facts on File, 1990), p. 261. For detailed revisions to the figures on those killed by the Maoist regime in China—suggesting the total between 1950 and 1976 may have reached eighty million—see Daniel Southerland, "Uncounted Millions: Mass Death in Mao's China; Repression's Higher Toll," *Washington Post,* July 17, 1994, p. A1; and Daniel Southerland, "Uncounted Millions: Mass Death in Mao's China; Cultural Revolution," *Washington Post,* July 18, 1994, p. A1.

38. For an argument that the nineteenth century genocides by Europeans in Africa provided the blueprint for Hitler's plan to use genocide as a means to create Lebensraum in Eastern Europe, see Sven Lindqvist, *"Exterminate All the Brutes!"* (New York: New Press, 1996).

39. Mahfoud Bennoune, *The Making of Contemporary Algeria, 1830–1987* (New York: Cambridge University Press, 1988), p. 42.

40. Nelson Reed, *The Caste War of the Yucatan* (Stanford University Press, 1964), p. 127.

41. Ritchie Calder, *Agony of the Congo* (London: Victor Gollancz Ltd., 1961), p. 15.

42. Basil Davidson, *Africa in History: Themes and Outlines* (New York: Collier Books, 1974), pp. 253–54.

43. For an attempt to describe the psychological foundations of genocide in terms other than anomie or Erik Erickson's pseudospeciation, see Elisabeth Young-Bruehl, *The Anatomy of Prejudices* (Harvard University Press, 1996). Young-Bruehl claims that many of the different prejudices that have been implicated in efforts to justify genocide—racism, sexism, anti-Semitism, and so on—spring from distinct and diverse psychological foundations.

44. For details, see the horrifying accounts of the detailed techniques used to inure "good Germans" into the casual exercise of genocide; recent studies are particularly revealing: Wolfgang Sofsky, *The Order of Terror: The Concentration Camp* (Princeton University Press, 1997); and Robert Jan van Pelt and Deborah Dwork, *Auschwitz: 1270 to the Present* (Norton, 1996).

45. This was precisely the central insight of the work of Hanna Arendt, not only in her *Eichmann in Jerusalem: A Report on the Banality of Evil* (London: Penguin, 1977) but also in her less known *Origins of Totalitarianism* (Harcourt, Brace, Jovanovich, 1973). It has been developed further in one of the best—as well as one of the more provocative—histories of the holocaust: Arno J. Mayer, *Why Did the Heavens Not Darken?: The "Final Solution" in History* (Pantheon Books, 1988).

46. A fascinating history of these techniques—which advanced enormously between World War II and the Vietnam War—can be found in Lt. Col. Dave Grossman, *On Killing: The Psychological Cost of Learning to Kill in War and Society* (Little, Brown, 1995).

47. For a major summary of such research, see Daniel Jonah Goldhagen, *Hitler's Willing Executioners: Ordinary Germans and the Holocaust* (Alfred A. Knopf, 1996).

48. Alexander Werth, *Russia at War, 1941–45* (New York: Discus Books, 1964), p. 198.

49. See Anthony DePalma, "Canada Ponders Its Peacekeeper Role: Warriors or Watchdogs?" *New York Times,* April 13, 1997, p. 16. Even normally amiable Italian troops were implicated in similar atrocities; see John Tagliabue, "Photos of Troops Abusing Somalis in '93 Shock Italians," *New York Times,* June 14, 1997, p. 4.

50. Jonathan S. Landay, "New Star of the Serbian Right," *Christian Science Monitor,* December 3, 1993, p. 8; and Laura Silber, "The Folk Star and the Tiger," *Financial Times,* February 18, 1995, p. 2.

51. David Rieff suggests that their common bond as professional officers made many United Nations Protection Force (UNPROFOR) officers, including their British commander (Lt. Gen. Sir Michael Rose, commander of UN troops in Bosnia from January 1994 to January 1995), unwilling to cross their Serb counterparts. See David Rieff, *Slaughterhouse: Bosnia and the Failure of the West* (Simon and Schuster, 1995), pp. 29–30. Rieff's analysis of why the UN bureaucracy, military and civilian, accorded greater respect to the Serbs than to the Bosnian government may be the most valuable part of his book.

52. For a discussion of the legal definition of genocide, see Helen Fein, *Genocide: A Sociological Perspective* (London: Sage Publications, 1993), pp. 8–32.

53. Noel Malcolm, *Bosnia: A Short History* (New York University Press, 1994), pp. 192–93; and Robert J. Donia and John V. A. Fine, Jr., *Bosnia and Hercegovina: A Tradition Betrayed* (Columbia University Press, 1994), pp. 139–41.

54. One of the few works to hint at the full significance of the war is Bradely F. Smith, *The War's Long Shadow: The Second World War and Its Aftermath—China, Russia, Britain, America* (Simon and Schuster, 1986).

55. The legitimation of strategic bombing during World War II has made prosecuting officers for war crimes more difficult than it had been a generation earlier. Serb separatist officers being tried for their role in the systematic shelling of noncombatants in Sarajevo by the International Criminal Tribunal for the former

240 / Notes to Pages 133-42

Yugoslavia are likely to invoke the legitimacy of strategic bombing in their defense. See Edward Cody, "Is It a War Crime, Or Just War?" *Washington Post*, April 7, 1996, p. C5; and the reply by Kemal Kurspahic, "Sarajevo Siege: Crime Not War," *Washington Post*, April 17, 1996, p. A23.

56. George Lichtheim, *The Concept of Ideology and Other Essays* (Random House, 1967), pp. 225-37.

57. Christer Ahlstrom, *Casualties of Conflict: Report for the World Campaign for the Protection of Victims of War* (Uppsala, Sweden: Department of Peace Conflict Research, 1991), pp. 8, 19.

58. Barbara Crossette, "UNICEF Report Calls Children Major Victims of Recent Wars," *New York Times*, December 11, 1995, p. A11.

59. Michael Farr, "Soviet War Dead May Top 40m," *Guardian Weekly*, May 8, 1994, p. 7.

60. Gerhard L. Weinberg, *A World at Arms: A Global History of World War II* (Cambridge, England: Cambridge University Press, 1994), p. 894. I have raised Weinberg's estimate by fifteen million to correct for the newly released figures about Soviet war dead.

61. UNICEF, *The State of the World's Children 1996* (New York: United Nations, 1996), p. 13.

62. John G. Heidenrich, "The Gulf War: How Many Iraqis Dead?" *Foreign Policy*, vol. 90 (Spring 1993), pp. 108-25.

63. Barbara Crossette, "Iraq Sanctions Kill Children, UN Reports," *New York Times*, December 1, 1995, p. A9.

64. Martin van Creveld, the military analyst whose work inspired Kaplan, defines "low-intensity conflicts" (LICs) this way: "First, they tend to unfold in 'less developed' parts of the world; the small-scale armed conflicts which do take place in 'developed' countries are usually known under a variety of other names, such as 'terrorism,' 'police work,' or—in the case of Northern Ireland—'troubles.' Second, very rarely do they involve regular armies on both sides, though often it is a question of regulars on one side fighting guerrillas, terrorists, and even civilians, including women and children, on the other. Third, most LICs do not rely primarily on the high-technology collective weapons that are the pride and joy of any modern armed force." Martin van Creveld, *The Transformation of War* (Free Press, 1991), p. 20. Van Creveld makes no distinction between ethnic and nonethnic LICs.

65. UNICEF, *The State of the World's Children 1996*, p. 33.

66. For example, this argument is made with elaborate supporting arguments in Anthony D. Smith, *The Ethnic Revival in the Modern World* (Cambridge, England: Cambridge University Press, 1981). See also the authorities surveyed in Thomas W. Lippman, "Is the World More Violent, or Does It Just Seem that Way?" *Washington Post*, July 1, 1993, pp. A14, A18.

67. Electronic search of *Washington Post* on CD-ROM. The process of tallying conflicts, ethnic or otherwise, is intrinsically political. The press during the early 1990s often quoted conflict tallies supplied by the National Defense Council Foundation, an organization which favored larger defense budgets. In 1996 the council claimed that there were sixty-four conflicts in the world (down from a record seventy-one in 1995). In 1996 the Center for Defense Information, an

institution established to combat militarization, listed only twenty-seven active conflicts and another ten that had turned largely nonviolent. See David Briscoe, "Wars, Or Rumors of Wars? Wonks Differ," *Washington Times,* December 30, 1996, p. 13.

Chapter Ten

1. Daniel Patrick Moynihan has been considered a leading U.S. expert on ethnicity since 1963, when he coauthored *Beyond the Melting Pot,* a book that claimed immigrant and ethnic groups were not assimilating into mainstream American culture as had been hoped. (Nathan Glazer and Daniel Patrick Moynihan, *Beyond the Melting Pot: The Negroes, Puerto Ricans, Jews, Italians, and Irish of New York City* (M.I.T. Press, 1963). For two excellent critiques of this argument, which remain relevant to global discussions of ethnic conflict, see Orlando Patterson, *Ethnic Chauvinism: The Reactionary Impulse* (New York: Stein and Day, 1977); and Stephen Steinberg, *The Ethnic Myth: Race, Ethnicity, and Class in America* (New York: Atheneum, 1981).)

2. Daniel Patrick Moynihan, *Pandaemonium: Ethnicity in International Politics* (Oxford, England: Oxford University Press, 1993), p. 40–41. Recent research does not support Moynihan's claim that the emigration drive formed a "mass movement" among Soviet Jews; see Yaacov Ro'i, ed., *Jews and Jewish Life in Russia and the Soviet Union* (London: Frank Cass and Co., 1995); and Piet Buwalda and Petrus Bulwalda, *They Did Not Dwell Alone: Jewish Emigration from the Soviet Union, 1967–1990* (Washington: Woodrow Wilson Center Press, 1997).

3. Daniel Patrick Moynihan, "Will Russia Blow Up?" *Newsweek,* November 19, 1979, p. 145.

4. Moynihan, *Pandaemonium,* pp. 41–51.

5. Moynihan, "Will Russia Blow Up?" p. 145.

6. Hélène Carrère d'Encausse, *The End of the Soviet Empire: The Triumph of Nations* (Basic Books, 1993), p. 31.

7. Carrère d'Encausse, *The End of the Soviet Empire,* p. 231.

8. The idea was also put forward by many other scholars, including David Fromkin. For an example of how the idea was conveyed into policymaking circles, see the article by the director of the Institute for National Strategic Studies, Alvin H. Bernstein, "Ethnicity and Imperial Break-Up: Ancient and Modern," *SAIS Review,* vol. 13, no. 1 (Winter/Spring 1993), pp. 121–32.

9. For a collection of essays that reflect a similar perspective, see Crawford Young, ed., *The Rising Tide of Cultural Pluralism: The Nation-State at Bay?* (University of Wisconsin Press, 1993).

10. Moynihan's own research has not always been rigidly primordialist. For an example of unadulterated primordialism, see the work of his friend Harold Robert Isaacs, *Idols of the Tribe: Group Identity and Political Change* (Harper and Row, 1975). Many primordialists trace the origins of their school back to the work of the anthropologist Clifford Geertz, "The Integrative Revolution, Primordial

Sentiments, and Civil Politics in the New States," in Clifford Geertz, ed., *Old Societies and New States: The Quest for Modernity in Asia and Africa* (New York: Free Press of Glencoe, 1963). For a collection of essays presenting the primordialist position and some dissents, see John F. Stack, Jr., ed. *The Primordial Challenge: Ethnicity in the Contemporary World* (New York: Greenwood Press, 1986).

11. Clifford Geertz, *The Interpretation of Cultures: Selected Essays* (Basic Books, 1973), p. 259; originally published as "The Integrative Revolution: Primordial Sentiments, and Civil Politics in the New States," in Clifford Geertz, ed., *Old Societies and New States* (New York: Free Press of Glencoe, 1963).

12. Daniel Bell, "Ethnicity and Social Change," in Nathan Glazer and Daniel Patrick Moynihan, eds., *Ethnicity: Theory and Experience* (Harvard University Press, 1975), p. 174; quoted approvingly in Daniel Patrick Moynihan, *Pandaemonium: Ethnicity in International Politics* (Oxford, England: Oxford University Press, 1993), p. 61. The term "primordialism" was coined by Glazer and Moynihan in the same volume (p. 19).

13. Walker Connor, *Ethnonationalism: The Quest for Understanding* (Princeton University Press, 1994), p. 195.

14. In addition to the work of Moynihan and Glazer, Michael Novak's *The Rise of the Unmeltable Ethnics: Politics and Culture in the 1970s* (Macmillan, 1972) played a major role in purveying this idea.

15. Harold Isaacs, "Basic Group Identity: The Idols of the Tribe," in Nathan Glazer and Daniel P. Moynihan, eds., *Ethnicity: Theory and Experience* (Harvard University Press, 1975), p. 30.

16. The locus classicus is Pierre van den Berghe, *The Ethnic Phenomenon* (Praeger Publishers, 1987).

17. For an enjoyable and thought-provoking introductions to these dangerous ideas, see Robert Wright (a senior editor at the *New Republic*), *The Moral Animal: Evolutionary Psychology and Everyday Life* (Pantheon Books, 1994); and Matt Ridley, *The Red Queen: Sex and the Evolution of Human Nature* (Macmillan, 1993). For a revolting example of how the new Darwinism can be blended with primordialism to produce old-fashioned racism, see Howard Bloom, *The Lucifer Principle: A Scientific Expedition into the Forces of History* (New York: Atlantic Monthly Press, 1995). For a fine history of these debates, see Pat Shipman, *The Evolution of Racism: Human Differences and the Use and Abuse of Science* (Simon and Schuster, 1994).

18. The description of the consensus of the experts draws heavily on the work of Donald L. Horowitz, who is perhaps the "dean" of the study of ethnic conflict. See his magnum opus, *Ethnic Groups in Conflict* (Berkeley, Calif.: University of California Press, 1985).

19. Instrumentalism was pioneered by marxist scholars but later found favor among rational choice theorists. For classic instrumentalist texts, see Michael Hechter, *Internal Colonialism: The Celtic Fringe in British National Development, 1536–1966* (Berkeley, Calif.: University of California Press, 1975); and Edward A. Tiryakian and Ronald Rogowski, eds., *New Nationalisms of the Developed West: Toward Explanation* (Boston, Mass.: G. Allen and Unwin, 1985), pp. 128–46.

20. Anthropologists were the first to reject the idea that ethnic urges were primordial. In *The Political System of Highland Burma: A Study of Kachin Social Structure* (Atlantic Highlands, N.J.: Athlone Press, 1986), Edmund Leach criticized Clifford Geertz's notion of primordiality, noting that the boundaries among ethnic groups and the strength of ethnic attachments were far more fluid and variable than the primordial image allowed. (For a good collection of critiques of primordiality by anthropologists, see Fredrik Barth, *Ethnic Groups and Boundaries: The Social Organization of Culture Difference* (Little, Brown, 1969).) Among historians, the idea of primordiality was shaken by the publication of Eugene Joseph Weber, *Peasants into Frenchmen: The Modernization of Rural France, 1870–1914* (Stanford University Press, 1976), which showed that French national identity did not spread into rural France until late in the nineteenth century.

21. For a deconstruction of some of the myths surrounding the battle by a Serbophile, see Thomas A. Emmert *Serbian Golgotha: Kosovo, 1389* (Columbia University Press, 1990); for the composition of forces, see pp. 55–56. For a Turkish perspective, see Kemal H. Karpat, "Review of *Kosovo: Legacy of Medieval Battle*," in Wayne S. Vucinich and Thomas A. Emmert, eds., *A Modern Greek Studies Yearbook Supplement* (University of Minnesota Press, 1991). *Slavic Review,* vol. 52, no. 2 (Summer 1993), pp. 383–84. Recently, some of the other key myths of Serb nationalism have also been refuted by historians. For example, it now seems that the "Great Migration" of 1689 in which Serbs supposedly abandoned the Ottoman Expire to seek freedom in Habsburg territory never occurred. See Noel Malcolm, *Kosovo: A Short History* (New York University Press, 1998).

22. The best introduction to the early period of Serb nationalism is still Leften Stavros Stavrianos, *The Balkans since 1453* (New York: Rinehart and Co., 1958). For an illuminating background study, see Miroslav Hroch, *Social Preconditions of National Revival in Europe: A Comparative Analysis of the Composition of Patriotic Groups among the Smaller European Nations* (Cambridge, England: Cambridge University Press, 1985).

23. For an especially nuanced account of the rise and fall of competing ideologies of identity in the states of the former Yugoslavia, see Ivo Banac, *The National Question in Yugoslavia: Origins, History, Politics* (Cornell University Press, 1984).

24. Sabrina P. Ramet, "Serbia's Slobodan Milošević: A Profile," *Orbis,* vol. 35, no. 1 (Winter 1991): pp. 94–95.

25. Banac, *The National Question in Yugoslavia,* p. 46.

26. For a description of Slobodan Milošević's alliance with Kosovo Serb activists, based upon detailed interviews with the latter, see Laura Silber and Allan Little, *Yugoslavia: Death of a Nation* (New York: TV Books, 1996), especially chapter 2, pp. 37–47.

27. For one case study, see Davor Glavas, "The Roots of Croatian Extremism," *Mediterranean Quarterly,* vol. 5 (Spring 1994), pp. 37–50.

28. For an excellent survey of the ways in which ethnonational conflicts can be aggravated or even created by self-serving politicians, see Human Rights Watch,

Slaughter among Neighbors: The Political Origins of Communal Violence (Yale University Press, 1995).

29. As part of the complex process of maintaining the balance of Yugoslav federalism, Muslims had been declared one of the country's official constituent nationalities in 1968. This category, however, was only a fuzzy unit for use in affirmative action programs instead of an acknowledgment of growing nationalist sentiment. It included Muslims outside of Bosnia, such as those in the Sandzak and Macedonia (where some were ethnic Turks)—although it did not include Albanians, who were also overwhelmingly Muslim but did not speak a Slavic language. For a description of the complex politics of Muslim identity in Yugoslav federalism, see Dennison I. Rusinow, "Yugoslavia's Muslim Nation," *UFSI Reports* 1982/No. 8 Europe; Steven L. Burg, "The Political Integration of Yugoslavia's Muslims: Determinants of Success and Failure," *Carl Beck Papers in Russian and East European Studies,* no. 203 (University of Pittsburgh, 1983); and Sabrina Petra Ramet, "Primordial Ethnicity or Modern Nationalism: The Case of Yugoslavia's Muslims, Reconsidered," in Andreas Kappeler, Gerhard Simon, and Georg Brunner, eds., *Muslim Communities Reemerge: Historical Perspectives on Nationality, Politics, and Opposition in the Former Soviet Union and Yugoslavia* (Duke University Press, 1994), pp. 111–40.

30. The absence of a common nationalist tradition among the Muslims of Bosnia was noted (and misunderstood) by their neighbors a long time ago. Both Serbs and Croats claimed the Muslims for their own, insisting that they were Catholics or Orthodox who had been forcibly converted to Islam by the Ottomans. However, most conversions were voluntary, and the converts were drawn not only from both Catholics and Orthodox, but also from the indigenous and independent Church of Bosnia. See Robert J. Donia and John V. A. Fine, Jr., *Bosnia and Herzegovina: A Tradition Betrayed* (Columbia University Press, 1994), pp. 35–36.

31. Susan Woodward, *Balkan Tragedy: Chaos and Dissolution after the Cold War* (Brookings, 1995), p. 33.

32. Adil Zulfikarpašić was one of the original founders of the Party of Democratic Action, but, believing it had become dominated by religious revivalists, he split to form his own organization. For his views, see Adil Zulfikarpašić "The Moslems in Bosnia," *South Slav Journal,* vol. 20 (March 1984), pp. 2–20. Izetbegovć was imprisoned in the 1980s for writing "The Islamic Declaration," a document that the Yugoslav government (and, later, Serb nationalists) claimed was the blueprint for an Islamic state in Bosnia. But Izetbegović made clear in the declaration that an Islamic state could only be created in societies where Muslims constituted a majority—explicitly excluding Bosnia. For the text of the declaration, see "Documents: The Trial of Moslem Intellectuals in Sarajevo," *South Slav Journal,* vol. 6, no. 1 (Spring 1993), pp. 55–89. For an analysis, see Noel Malcolm, *Bosnia: A Short History* (New York University Press, 1994), pp. 219–21.

33. The decision to declare Bosnia independent was a controversial and painful one for President Alia Izetbegović. He has said that having to choose between following the lead of Croatia's President Franjo Tudjman and seceding or

remaining within a Yugoslavia dominated by Serbian President Milošević was like "having to choose between leukemia and a brain tumor." Malcolm, *Bosnia* (1994), p. 228.

34. Ivo Banac, "Bosnia Muslims: From Religious Community to Socialist Nationhood and Post–Communist Statehood, 1918–1992," in Mark Pinson, ed., *The Muslims of Bosnia-Herzegovina: Their Historic Development from the Middle Ages to the Dissolution of Yugoslavia* (Harvard University Press, 1994), p. 147.

35. Milan Andrejevich, "The Presidency of Bosnia and Herzegovina: A Profile," *R.F.E./RL Research Report,* vol. 2, no. 32, August 13, 1992, p. 21. For *Oslobodenjenje* and other symbols of Bosnia's multicultural ambitions, see Tom Gjelten, *Sarajevo Daily: A City and Its Newspaper under Siege* (Harper Collins, 1995).

36. The conflict in Bosnia was not just a civil war; it was also a war of aggression by neighboring Serbia, and later Croatia, who were attempting to seize territory and assets at the expense of the nascent Bosnian state. But even in its earliest phases, the war had a heavily civil character that loomed larger as it dragged on.

37. "Sarajlije" was the traditional term for the inhabitants of Sarajevo, irrespective of their religion or nationality. In Sarajevo and throughout urban Bosnia, secularism and multiculturalism were the norm. Since World War II, 30 to 40 percent of urban marriages in Bosnia were between members of different faiths (Donia and Fine, *Bosnia and Herzegovina,* p. 9). The Serbs of Sarajevo were far less likely to endorse separatism or Serb nationalism than their rural cousins; see Chuck Sudetic, "Serbs of Sarajevo Stay Loyal to Bosnia," *New York Times,* August 26, 1994, p. A6.

38. David Rieff, *Slaughterhouse: Bosnia and the Failure of the West* (Simon and Schuster, 1995), p. 110.

39. A joke popular all over the former Yugoslavia captured the logic behind this trend: "Why should I be a minority in your country, when you can be a minority in my country?" Rieff, *Slaugherhouse,* p. 65.

40. Chuck Sudetic, "Bosnia's Elite Force: Fed, Fit, Muslim," *New York Times,* June 16, 1995, p. A12; and Ed Vulliamy, *Seasons in Hell: Understanding Bosnia's War* (St. Martin's, 1994), p. 291.

41. John Pomfret, "Muslims Using Nationalism as Force in Bosnia: Assembly on Peace Plan Shows Group's Fervor," *Washington Post,* October 10, 1993, p. A33.

42. Remy Ourdan, "The Bosnian Dream of a Multi-Ethnic Future Is Dying," *Le Monde,* September 28, 1994, translated in *Guardian Weekly,* October 19, 1994, p. 19.

43. Kurt Schork, "Premier Quits Amid Bosnian Party Feud," *Washington Post,* January 22, 1996, p. A15; and John Pomfret, "Sarajevo Acts to Boost Party, Silence Dissent; Some Government Plans Violate Dayton Accords," *Washington Post,* February 1, 1996, p. A18.

44. See Yahya Sadowski, "Bosnia's Muslims: A Fundamentalist Threat?" *Brookings Review* (Winter 1995), pp. 10–15.

45. "'First, I was a Yugoslav,' a friend in Sarajevo said to me once. 'Then, I was a Bosnian. Now I'm becoming a Muslim. It's not my choice. I don't even believe in God. But after two hundred thousand dead, what do you want me to do? Everybody has to have a country to which he can belong.'" Rieff, *Slaughterhouse*, p. 12, note 39.

46. If Americans understood their own history better, they would have an easier time comprehending what has happened in Bosnia. The idea of "being an American"—like "being a Bosnian"—was something that emerged suddenly in the midst of a violent struggle. One of the greatest students of the American revolution of 1776 noted: "Nationalism has been the great begetter of revolutions. In Europe, in Asia, in Africa, we have seen it stir one people after another: they grow proud of their traditions, of their language, of their identity, and they strike for independence. In our case it was the other way round: we struck for independence and were thereby stirred into nationality; our nation was the child, not the father, of our revolution." Edmund S. Morgan, *The Birth of the Republic, 1763–89* (University of Chicago Press, 1992), p. 101. Morgan was wrong—as American historians so often are—in thinking that the way the revolution preceded the discovery of nationality made America "exceptional."

47. Deborah Christie, producer, *Disappearing World: War Trilogy*, "We Are All Neighbors," for Granada Television (Chicago, Ill.: Public Media/Film Inc. Video, 1993).

48. On these issues, two outstanding works should be required reading for anyone interested in ethnic conflict: Eric Hobsbawm and Terence Ranger, eds., *The Invention of Tradition* (Cambridge, England: Cambridge University Press, 1983); and Suzanne Hoeber Rudolph and Lloyd I. Rudolph, "Modern Hate: How Ancient Animosities Get Invented," *New Republic*, March 22, 1993, pp. 24–29. The latter draws upon a literature about ethnicity, religion, and nationalism in India that is unusually rich—far superior to most treatments of these subjects in the Balkans or the Middle East. For an introduction to this literature, the following pieces are useful: Romila Tharpar, "Imagined Religious Communities? Ancient History and the Modern Search for a Hindu Identity," *Modern Asian Studies*, vol. 23 (1989), pp. 209–31; C. A. Bayly, "The Pre-History of 'Communalism'? Religious Conflict in India, 1700–1860," *Modern Asian Studies*, vol. 19 (1985), pp. 177–203; Gunther D. Sontheimer and Hermann Kulke, eds., *Hinduism Reconsidered* (New Delhi, India: Manohar, 1989); and Partha Chatterjee, "History and the Nationalization of Hinduism," *Social Research*, vol. 59 (Spring 1992), pp. 111–49. For an exceptionally subtle study of ethnic relations in Eastern Europe, see Katherine Verdery, *Transylvanian Villagers: Three Centuries of Political, Economic, and Ethnic Change* (Berkeley, Calif.: University of California Press, 1983).

49. Barrington Moore, Jr., *The Social Origins of Dictatorship and Democracy: Lord and Peasant in the Making of the Modern World* (Boston, Mass.: Beacon Press, 1966), p. 486.

50. Flush with the discovery that ethnic identities are inventions, some scholars have been guilty of excessive optimism. They present ethnic conflicts as a horrible misunderstanding, something that can be cleared up by a good historical

exposé that would show how artificial such differences are. (The U.S. Institute for Peace has published a series of exuberant monographs on this theme.) That is not what is being suggested here. Just because ethnic identities are invented, sometimes recently invented, does not mean they are inauthentic or not deeply felt. Ethnic hostilities are usually intertwined with material disputes over access to land, water, money, and power. Any policy program for dealing with ethnic conflict must not only help people to reconstruct their identities in a more benign fashion, but it also must (perhaps even more importantly) help them to deal with the attendant material conflicts.

51. An argument that reinforces the one presented here can be found in Sumantra Bose, "State Crises and Nationalities Conflict in Sri Lanka and Yugoslavia," *Comparative Political Studies,* vol. 28 (April 1995), pp. 87–116.

52. For an excellent account of the early years of Serb nationalism, one that understands their wider, Ottoman context, see Stavrianos, *The Balkans since 1453.*

53. For a wider background on this conflict, see Malcolm, *Kosovo* (1998).

54. The same pattern seems to apply in Somalia. The original opposition to the Barre regime was not organized along clan lines; groups made a concerted effort to recruit members from multiple clans. But as the state collapsed, such coalitions proved difficult to sustain. Once the civil war was in full swing and central authority disappeared, clans proved the most effective means for mobilizing people in local politics.

55. This point is admirably made in Stephen Holmes, "What Russia Teaches Us Now: How Weak States Threaten Freedom," *American Prospect,* no. 33 (July/August 1997), pp. 30–39.

56. Robert D. Kaplan, "After 'Balkan Ghosts,'" *Weekly Standard,* December 18, 1995, pp. 22–23.

57. This paragraph attempts to summarize the much richer and more subtle argument of Susan L. Woodward, *Balkan Tragedy: Chaos and Dissolution after the Cold War* (Brookings, 1995), chapter 3. See also Steven L. Burg, "Elite Conflict in Post–Tito Yugoslavia," *Soviet Studies,* vol. 38 (April 1986), pp. 170–93; and Dragomir Vojnic, "Disparity and Disintegration: The Economic Dimension of Yugoslavia's Demise," in Payam Akhavan, ed., *Yugoslavia the Former and Future: Reflections by Scholars from the Region* (Geneva, Switzerland: United Nations Research Institute for Social Development, 1995), pp. 75–111.

58. Keith Griffin, "Toward a Cooperative Settlement of the Debt Problem," *Finance and Development,* vol. 25 (June 1988), pp. 12–14.

59. Lenard J. Cohen, *Broken Bonds: Yugoslavia's Disintegration and Balkan Politics in Transition,* 2d ed. (Boulder, Colo.: Westview Press, 1995), pp. 45–66.

60. Woodward, *Balkan Tragedy,* p. 51.

61. Woodward claims that the Slovenes initiated the problem. But the Slovene campaign against the military never garnered the attention (much less emulation) from other republics that Milošević's power plays in Kosovo did. The scale of the Milošević power play had much deeper repercussions within Serbian society than any of the Slovene movements.

62. For a nuanced account of these developments, see V. P. Gagnon, Jr., "Ethnic Nationalism and International Conflict: The Case of Serbia," *International Security,* vol. 19 (1994–95), pp. 130–66; and Sabrina P. Ramet, "Serbia's Slobodan Milošević: A Profile," *Orbis,* vol. 35 (1991), pp. 93–105. The film coverage in the BBC series *The Death of Yugoslavia* is particularly chilling; see the companion volume by Laura Silber and Alan Little, *Yugoslavia: Death of a Nation* (U.S.A.: T.V. Books, 1995).

63. For an excellent discussion of this trend, with good insights into how it played out in Leninist regimes other than Yugoslavia, see Susan L. Woodward, "Soviet Rehearsal in Yugoslavia? Contradictions of the Socialist Liberal Strategy," in Ralph Miliband and Leo Panitch, eds., *Communist Regimes: The Aftermath; Socialist Register 1991* (London: Merlin Press, 1991), pp. 322–47.

64. The best general history of nationalisms in Yugoslavia is still Ivo Banac's masterful *The National Question in Yugoslavia: Origins, History, Politics* (Cornell University Press, 1984). However, his work should be read in combination with studies that give a more global perspective on how nationalism can be manipulated, suppressed, or aggravate, such as Eric Hobsbawm, *Nations and Nationalism since 1780: Programme, Myth, Reality* (Cambridge, England: Cambridge University Press, 1990). For updates on the national question in the 1980s, see Burg, "Elite Conflict in Post–Tito Yugoslavia"; and Ivo Banac, "The Fearful Asymmetry of War: The Causes and Consequences of Yugoslavia's Demise," *Daedalus* (September 1992), pp. 141–74.

65. One Croatian economist noted that after independence the economic policy of President Tudjman seemed to consist largely of "maintaining the privileges of those members of the communist nomenclature who had declared themselves in favor of his party," even though this contradicted his outspoken commitment to economic liberalization. See Misha Glenny, *The Fall of Yugoslavia: The Third Balkan War* (New York: Penguin, 1992), p. 63. For a case study, see Milan Andrejevich, "Elections in Slovenia Maintain Status Quo," *RFE/RL Research Report,* vol. 1, no. 50 (December 18, 1992), pp. 28–31. For comparisons with the "nationalization" of the nomenklatura in other formerly Leninist states, see the provocative essay by Ernest Gellner, "Nationalism and Politics in Eastern Europe," *New Left Review,* no. 189 (September/October 1991), pp. 127–34.

66. "The ex-colonial states have been internationally enfranchised and possess the same external rights and responsibilities as all other sovereign states: juridical statehood. At the same time, however . . . their populations do not enjoy many of the advantages traditionally associated with independent statehood. Their governments are often deficient in the political will, institutional authority, and organized power to protect human rights or provide socioeconomic welfare. The concrete benefits which have historically justified the undeniable burdens of sovereign statehood are often limited to fairly narrow elites and not yet extended to the citizenry at large whose lives may be scarcely improved by independence or even adversely affected by it. These states are primarily juridical. . . I therefore refer to them as 'quasi-states.'" Robert H. Jackson, *Quasi-States: Sovereignty, Interna-*

tional Relations, and the Third World (New York: Cambridge University Press, 1990), p. 21.

67. Misha Glenny, "The Age of the Parastate," *New Yorker,* May 8, 1995, p. 45.

68. Branka Magas, *The Destruction of Yugoslavia: Tracking the Break-Up 1980–92* (London: Verso, 1993), pp. 111–12; and Woodward, *Balkan Tragedy,* p. 87.

69. Cohen, *Broken Bonds,* p. 182; Milan Vego, "The Muslim Defense Industry in Bosnia and Herzegovina," *Jane's Intelligence Review,* vol. 6 (May 1994), pp. 213–14; and Mark Almond, *Europe's Backyard War: The War in the Balkans* (London: Heinemann, 1994), pp. 265–66.

70. Glenny, *The Fall of Yugoslavia,* p. 153. For an inventory of the resources the different parties scrambled to control, see Steve Coll, "Balkans Face New Test: Splitting Spoils of War: Oil Fields, Arms Plants at Stake in Talk," *Washington Post,* March 7, 1993, p. A1. For a detailed account of how most of the Yugoslav federal army in Bosnia evolved first into an arm of the government of Serbia and then was seconded to the control of Gen. Ratko Mladić and his allies in the Serb Democratic Party (SDS) of Bosnian Serb separatists, see James Gow, "One Year of War in Bosnia and Herzegovina," *RFE/RL Research Report,* vol. 2, no. 23 (June 1993), pp. 1–13. Gow provides strong evidence that President Slobodan Milošević, working through semi-autonomous agents, orchestrated the Serb secession in Bosnia.

71. For the early history of these parties, see Cohen, *Broken Bonds,* pp. 94–102, 128, 141, 161.

72. For the early history of the Party of Democratic Action (SDA), see Mark Thompson, *A Paper House: The Ending of Yugoslavia* (Pantheon Books, 1992), pp. 98–99; and Milan Andrejevich, "The Presidency of Bosnia and Herzegovina: A Profile," *RFE/RL Research Report,* vol. 2, no. 32 (August 13, 1992), p. 21.

73. For Maglaj, see John Pomfret, "A Cry from Maglaj: 'We Want to Live,'" *Washington Post,* March 10, 1994, pp. A1, A36; for Zenica, see Ed Vulliamy, *Seasons in Hell: Understanding Bosnia's War* (St. Martin's, 1994), p. 293.

74. For a good case study on another example, see Michael Palairet, "Ramiz Sadiku: A Case Study in the Industrialization of Kosovo," *Soviet Studies,* vol. 44 (1992), pp. 897–912. For a historical account of how Soviet industrial firms wound up developing power networks that made them dominant in local politics and a major force in national affairs, see Gregory Grossman, "The Party as Manager and Entrepreneur," in Gregory Guroff and Fred V. Carstensen, eds., *Entrepreneurship in Imperial Russia and the Soviet Union* (Princeton University Press, 1983), pp. 284–305. For a comparison with the "company towns" that characterized early industrial development in England and the United States, see Margaret Crawford, *Building the Workingman's Paradise: The Design of American Company Towns* (London: Verso, 1995).

75. Ironically, the shady finances of Agrokomerc were at the center of the 1987 corruption scandal that wrought such havoc among the Bosnian political elite. The firm, which had employed thirteen thousand people, had lost many of its

productive assets. But its director, Fikret Abdić, survived the purges with much of his local political influence intact.

76. See Hrvoje Šošić, *Treće pokriće "Agrokomerca"* (Zagreb: 1989); and "Agrokomerc: The Decline of a Model Enterprise," *Radio Free Europe Situation Report* (November 19, 1987).

77. Glenny, *The Fall of Yugoslavia,* pp. 151–53; and Misha Glenny, "The Godfather of Bihać," *New York Review of Books,* August 12, 1993, pp. 18–19.

78. Roger Cohen, "Fratricide in Bosnia: Muslim vs. Muslim," *New York Times,* June 22, 1994, p. A3; and Roger Cohen, "A Muslim's Quandry: Peace or Betrayal," *New York Times,* June 27, 1994, p. A6.

79. Roger Cohen, "Besieged Bosnian Pocket Fights Sense of Betrayal," *New York Times,* June 26, 1994, p. A3; Charles Lane, "Picked Pocket: The Real Story of Bihać," *New Republic,* December 19, 1994, pp. 12–14; and Raymond Bonner, "Bosnian Splinter Group Is Exiled and Unwanted," *New York Times,* August 22, 1995, p. A7.

80. James Rupert, "Siege of Its Yuppie Suburb Sours Sarajevo's Mixing Bowl Image," *Washington Post,* July 21, 1993, p. A13; and Tom Gjelten, *Sarajevo Daily: A City and Its Newspaper under Siege* (Harper Collins, 1995), pp. 103–106.

81. John F. Burns, "For Sarajevo's Fearful Serbs, Misery Cushioned by Mercy," *New York Times,* July 29, 1993, p. A1; Chuck Sudetic, "Serbs of Sarajevo Stay Loyal to Bosnia," *New York Times,* August 26, 1994, p. A6; and Roger Cohen, "Sarajevo Girl Killed, Yet Serbs Suffer," *New York Times,* April 26, 1995, p. A8. The Croats of Sarajevo maintained their own militia, which operated as part of government forces until 1993; see Chuck Sudetic, "Bosnians Disband Sarajevo Croats," *New York Times,* November 7, 1993, p. A7.

82. For a detailed order of battle, counting both regular and irregular forces, see Milan Vego, "The Army of Bosnia and Herzegovina," *Jane's Intelligence Review,* vol. 5, no. 2 (February 1993), pp. 63–67.

83. While the participation of criminals in the process of state formation might seem surprising to those who were raised on fairy stories about how governments are formed by conclaves of thoughtful, bewigged "founding fathers," it is commonplace. The institutions that the modern state developed out of in Western Europe were a type of criminal enterprise, and in much of the world modern police forces emerged from a process of negotiation and cooptation of social bandits. See Frederic C. Lane, "Economic Consequences of Organized Violence," in Frederic C. Lane, ed., *Venice and History: The Collected Papers of Frederic C. Lane* (Johns Hopkins University Press, 1966), pp. 412–30; Charles Tilly, "War Making and State Making as Organized Crime," in Peter B. Evans, Dietrich Rueschemeyer, and Theda Skocpol, eds., *Bringing the State Back In* (Cambridge, England: Cambridge University Press, 1985), pp. 169–91; and Paul J. Vanderwood, *Disorder and Progress: Bandits, Police, and Mexican Development* (University of Nebraska Press, 1981).

84. John Pomfret, "Murders or War Heroes? Legal Cases Divide Sarajevo," *Washington Post,* May 14, 1993, p. A34; and John F. Burns, "Gangs in Sarajevo Worry Diplomats," *Washington Post,* November 4, 1993, p. A3.

85. John Pomfret, "Weapons, Cash and Chaos Lend Clout to Srebrenica's Tough Guy," *Washington Post,* February 16, 1994, p. A14.

86. John Pomfret, "Gang Violence Imperiling Bosnia's Fragile Muslim-Croat Federation," *Washington Post,* May 14, 1995, p. A21.

87. "Serbia: Profits and Losses under Sanctions," *Economist,* vol. 326, no. 7803 (March 20, 1993), pp. 55–58; John Kifner, "An Outlaw in the Balkans Is Basking in the Spotlight," *New York Times,* November 23, 1993, p. A1; and Chris Hedges, "Top Leader of Bosnian Serbs Now under Attack From Within," *New York Times,* January 4, 1996, p. A1.

88. For details on the international effort to support and rebuild Bosnia, see David Segal, "Now for the Gold Rush," *Washington Post,* January 25, 1996, p. D10.

89. For an empirical critique of primordialist interpretations of ethnicity in Russia, see Daniel S. Treisman, "Russia's Ethnic Revival: The Separatist Activism of Regional Leaders in a Postcommunist Order," *World Politics,* vol. 49 (January 1997), pp. 212–49.

90. Ken Jowitt coined the evocative phrase "Leninist extinction" in *New World Disorder: The Leninist Extinction* (Berkeley, Calif.: University of California Press, 1992).

91. John Clark and Aaron Wildavsky, *The Moral Collapse of Communism: Poland as a Cautionary Tale* (San Francisco: Institute for Contemporary Studies, 1990); Abbott Gleason, *Totalitarianism: The Inner History of the Cold War* (New York: Oxford University Press, 1995); Martin E. Malia, *The Soviet Tragedy: A History of Socialism in Russia, 1917–91* (Free Press, 1994); Nancy Bernkopf Tucker, "China as a Factor in the Collapse of the Soviet Empire," *Political Science Quarterly,* vol. 110 (1995–96), pp. 501–18; Henry S. Rowan and Charles Wolf, Jr., eds., *The Impoverished Superpower: Perestroika and the Soviet Military Burden* (San Francisco: ICS Press, 1990); and Peter Schweitzer, *Victory: The Reagan Administration's Secret Strategy that Caused the Collapse of the Soviet Union* (New York: Atlantic Monthly Press, 1994).

92. Alec Nove, *Glasnost in Action: Cultural Renaissance in Russia* (Boston, Mass.: Unwin Hyman, 1989), p. 125. For a wider background, see Farhang Mehr, "Ethnic Situations in the USSR," in Bernard Rubin and Ladislav Bittman, eds., *Shock Waves: Consequences of Glasnost and Perestroika,* Boston University College of Communication, Program for the Study of Disinformation Papers, vol. 2, no. 6 (Fall 1989), pp. 89–111; Valery Tishkov, "'Don't Kill Me, I'm a Kyrgyz!': An Anthropological Analysis of Violence in the Osh Ethnic Conflict," *Journal of Peace Research,* vol. 32 (1995), pp. 133–49; and Muriel Atkin, "The Islamic Revolution That Overthrew the Soviet State," *Contention,* vol. 2 (Winter 1993), pp. 296–313. For an opposing viewpoint, see James Critchlow, "'Corruption', Nationalism, and the Native Elites in Soviet Central Asia," *Journal of Communist Studies,* vol. 4 (1988), pp. 142–61.

93. Gerald B. Helman and Steven R. Ratner, "Saving Failed States," *Foreign Policy,* no. 89 (Winter 1992–93), pp. 3–21.

94. "Failed States and Their Reconstruction," *MIT Center for International Studies Precis* (Spring 1994), pp. 1–9.

95. Charles H. Fairbanks, Jr., "The Withering of the State," *Uncaptive Minds,* vol. 8, no. 2 (Summer 1995), p. 19.

96. This account is based on Terence Lyons and Ahmed I. Samatar, *Somalia: State Collapse, Multilateral Intervention, and Strategies for Political Reconstruction* (Brookings, 1995), chapter 2. See also Alex de Waal, "The Shadow Economy," *Africa Report* (March/April 1993), pp. 24–29.

97. World Bank, *World Debt Tables, 1994–95,* vol. 2 (Washington: World Bank, 1994), p. 430. For a critique of International Monetary Fund (IMF) operations in Somalia, see Fayza Rady, "Visions of the Impossible," *al-Ahram Weekly* (August 18-24, 1994), p. 5.

98. Mohamed Sahnoun, *Somalia: The Missed Opportunities* (Washington: U.S. Institute of Peace, 1994), pp. 5–6.

99. For a lively, if highly partisan, account of these developments, see Jama Mohamed Ghalib, *The Cost of Dictatorship: The Somali Experience* (New York: Lilian Barber Press, 1995).

100. The history of the Somali National Movement (SNM) is recounted in Ioan M. Lewis, *Blood and Bone: The Call of Kinship in Somali Society* (Lawrenceville, N.J.: Red Sea Press, 1994), pp. 177–219.

101. For detailed accounts of developments in Somaliland, see Rakiya Omaar, "The Best Chance for Peace," *Africa Report* (May/June 1993), pp. 44–48; and Rakiya Omaar, "Somaliland: One Thorn Brush at a Time," *Current History,* vol. 93 (May 1994), pp. 232–36.

102. Kenneth B. Noble, "Islamic Militants, Pushed Aside, Express Anger in Somali Port," *New York Times,* January 15, 1993, p. A9. For a survey of the other Islamic movements in Somalia, see Yusuf Khazim, Ahmad Hassan Dahali, and Russel Warren Howie, "al-Islamiyyun Yunazilun Amrika min al-Sumal," *al-Wasat* (September 27, 1993), pp. 12–19. The same movements that operate in Somalia have begun to extend their operations to Eritrea and Ethiopia, where state authority is also weak; see Jennifer Parmelee, "Radicals Gain Strength in Horn of Africa," *Washington Post,* January 5, 1994, p. A26.

103. A major debate is going on among experts on Somalia, and every other country, about the effectiveness and character of "primordial loyalties" to clans and similar associations. Lewis in *Blood and Bone* claims that clan loyalties are the determining force in Somali politics and explains its current fratricide as well as the collapse of the state in 1990–91. Abdi Ismail Samatar, "Destruction of State and Society in Somalia: Beyond the Tribal Convention," *Journal of Modern African Studies,* vol. 30 (1992), pp. 625–41, however, argues that Lewis and others have exaggerated and misunderstood the importance of clan. In recent years, the latter view has certainly been more accurate: "In Somalia, the clan identifications are a pretext for a more sinister form of control. 'It's the tough and the vicious vs. the peaceful and the weak,' says Ibrahim Bursalid, a young Somali who founded Soma Action, a homegrown relief organization, two years ago when the civil war broke out." "The Clans are just a means to rally young, impressionable Somalis around a cause," which supports nothing more than each leader's own ambition. Alexander Tuttle, "Somalia and the Spoils of Power," *Wall Street*

Journal, January 5, 1993, p. A14. In any case, no militia in Somalia is un-ambiguously identified with a single lineage. The Hawiye clan alone is subdivided into forty-eight distinct factions, many with their own militias.

104. Some of the best accounting of the operations of Somali militias after the civil war were supplied by Michael Maren, a former U.S. aid worker. See his "Cleaning Up from the Cold War in Somalia," *Somalia News Update,* vol. 2, no. 25 (September 20, 1993); "The Somalia Experiment," *Village Voice,* September 28, 1993, pp. 33–39; and "Aidid's Endgame," *Village Voice,* November 30, 1993, p. 22.

105. This point is excellently made in Umar al-Ansari, "al-Sumal: Awwal Dawlat Qita^c Khass fil-^cAlim" [Somalia: The First Private Sector State in the World] *al-Majalla* (October 21, 1995), pp. 28–30.

106. This should not surprise anyone. Two of the most horrifying but least appreciated facts about the world are that (1) in modern times famines are almost always caused by economic or political forces rather than failures of climate or environment and that (2) wars have always killed more people by means of the famines and epidemics they trigger rather than through direct military action. On these issues, see Amartya Sen, *Poverty and Famines: An Essay on Entitlement and Deprivation* (Oxford, England: Oxford University Press, 1984); and William A. Dando, *The Geography of Famine* (Silver Spring, Md.: V. H. Winston, 1980).

107. For mortality figures, see Jonathan Stevenson, "Hope Restored in Somalia?" *Foreign Policy,* no. 91 (Summer 1993), pp. 138–54. For a skeptical view of the statistics on famine deaths, see Alexander Cockburn, "A Cold Look at Operation Restore Hope," *Wall Street Journal,* December 24, 1992, p. A5.

108. Stephen Buckley, "Somalis Are Not Starving, Nor Are They Coalescing," *Washington Post,* October 21, 1995, p. A18.

109. George Kenney, undersecretary of state in charge of the Yugoslav desk, resigned from the State Department for the lack of U.S. action in Bosnia. He cited the number of dead from twenty-five thousand to sixty thousand. See *U.S. News and World Report,* April 10, 1995, p. 53.

110. Donatella Lorch, "Despite Chaos in Mogadishu, UN Hopes New Talks Will Bring Peace," *New York Times,* September 22, 1994, p. A10; and Keith B. Richburg, "Somalis Slips Back to Bloodshed," *Washington Post,* September 4, 1994, pp. A1–A43.

111. The three key institutions that characterize the modern state are a large standing army; a centralized, professionally trained bureaucracy; and a national fiscal apparatus that organizes not only taxation but also public borrowing. The specific character of these institutions distinguishes the modern state from earlier systems of power: city-states, agrarian empires, tribes, and so on.

112. Alexis de Tocqueville, *L'Ancien Regime* (Oxford, England: Clarendon Press, 1969).

113. Herbert Franz Schurmann, *The Logic of World Power: An Inquiry into the Origins, Currents, and Contradictions of World Politics* (Pantheon Books, 1974), p. xxiii.

Chapter Eleven

1. This meaning of "civilization" is found, not in the work of Samuel P. Huntington, but in the studies of Norbert Elias. See Norbert Elias, *The Civilizing Process*, Edmund Jephcott, trans. (New York: Urizen Books, 1978). Not surprisingly, Elias was one of the first modern scholars to appreciate the contribution of the state to maintaining civic order.

2. John Mueller, *Retreat from Doomsday: The Obsolescence of Major War* (Basic Books, 1988); and Ronald Inglehart, *Culture Shift in Advanced Industrial Society* (Princeton University Press, 1990).

3. For this reason, the United States may develop (perhaps as a result of domestic lobbying) a national interest in a particular case of ethnic or cultural strife—say the problem of Cyprus or the Tibetans in China. But its allies and the wider international community cannot be expected to automatically share that interest.

4. This has been clear in the recent downturn of ethnic violence in Bulgaria, Northern Ireland, and Quebec. See Christophe Chatelot, "Bulgaria Learns to Live with Its Turks," *Guardian Weekly*, May 11, 1997, p. 17; Christopher Chipello, "Economy Saps Quebec's Separatist Ardor," *New York Times*, October 31, 1997, p. A18; and Nuala O'Faolain, "Good Fortune in Belfast," *New York Times*, April 12, 1998, p. A13.

5. Kevin M. Cahill, ed., *Preventive Diplomacy: Stopping Wars before They Start* (Basic Books, 1996); Michael S. Lund, *Preventing Violent Conflicts: A Strategy for Preventive Diplomacy* (Washington: U.S. Institute of Peace, 1996); and United Nations, *Agenda for Peace: Preventive Diplomacy, Peacemaking, and Peace Keeping* (New York: United Nations, June 1992).

6. Misha Glenny, *The Fall of Yugoslavia: The Third Balkan War* (New York: Penguin, 1992).

7. For a concrete proposal to construct similar systems, for monitoring the likelihood of ethnic conflict, see Ted Robert Gurr, "Early-Warning Systems: From Surveillance to Assessment to Action," in Kevin M. Cahill, ed., *Preventive Diplomacy: Stopping Wars Before They Start* (Basic Books, 1996), pp. 123–43; and David Carment, "The Ethnic Dimension in World Politics: Theory, Policy, and Early Warning," *Third World Quarterly*, vol. 15, no. 4 (1994), pp. 551–82.

8. Regarding the problems that afflict this group, see Robert H. Jackson, *Quasi-States: Sovereignty, International Relations, and the Third World* (Cambridge, England: Cambridge University Press, 1990).

9. A growing body of data rank countries according to their level of political corruption. A 1995 study suggested that, in a sample of forty-one countries, Indonesia (no. 41) was the most corrupt and New Zealand the least (no. 1). The United States ranked in the middle—no. 15. See Barbara Crossette, "A Global Gauge of Greased Palms," *New York Times*, August 20, 1995, p. D3. Transparency International, a nongovernmental organization dedicated to exposing government corruption, maintains a list of rankings on the internet at http://www.gwdg.de/~uwvw/icr.htm.

10. For a readable introduction to the general problems of assessing country risk, see John Calverly, *Country Risk Analysis,* 2d ed. (London: Butterworths, 1990).

11. Although the *Economist* never repeated this experiment, its sister organization, the Economist Intelligence Unit, began to do its own country risk analyses that included, inter alia, political risk. For a survey of their results, see "Risk ratings," *Economist,* August 21, 1993, p. 84; "Risk ratings," *Economist,* February 19, 1994, p. 124; and "Country Risk," *Economist,* January 6, 1996, p. 90.

12. For a detailed discussion of *Euromoney's* decision to pay closer attention to political variables, and some indication of which criteria they employ, see "How to Rate a State," *Euromoney* (September 1992), pp. 61–64. For a discussion of how some other organizations study country risk, see Jeanne B. Pinder, "Salomon's Guru on the Third World," *New York Times,* March 21, 1993, p. C6.

13. In more recent years (since the death of Kim Il Sung), some evidence exists that the North Korean state may be in decay. See Elaine Sciolino, "An Economic Basket Case: In North Korea the Threat Is Total Collapse," *New York Times,* February 18, 1996, p. D5.

14. Samuel P. Huntington, *Political Order in Changing Societies* (Yale University Press, 1968), p. 1.

15. The idea that inequality promotes violence can be traced back (through Rousseau) to Aristotle's writings about stasis; see Moses Finley, *Politics in the Ancient World* (Cambridge, England: Cambridge University Press, 1983), pp. 105–11. For more recent studies, see John Hagan and Ruth D. Peterson, eds., *Crime and Inequality* (Stanford University Press, 1995).

16. Martin Walker, *The Cold War: A History* (Henry Holt and Co., 1993), pp. xiv–xv.

17. United Nations Development Program, *Human Development Report 1994* (New York: Oxford University Press, 1994), p. 2.

18. United Nations Development Program, *Human Development Report 1996* (New York: Oxford University Press, 1996), p. 3.

19. The term "Washington consensus" was coined by John Williamson; see his "In Search of a Manual for Technopols," in John Williamson, ed., *The Political Economy of Policy Reform* (Washington: Institute for International Economics, 1994), pp. 26–28.

20. For a sampling of such studies, see Tony Killick and others, *The IMF and Stabilisation: Developing Country Experiences* (London: Overseas Development Institute, 1984); Manuel Pastor, "The Effects of IMF Programs in the Third World: Debate and Evidence from Latin America," *World Development,* vol. 15, no. 2 (February 1987), pp. 249–62; Jane Harrigan and Paul Mosley, "Evaluating the Impact of World Bank Structural Adjustment Lending: 1980–87," *Journal of Development Studies,* vol. 27, no. 3 (April 1991), pp. 63–94; Herman Schwartz, "Can Orthodox Stabilization and Adjustment Work? Lessons from New Zealand, 1984–90," *International Organization,* vol. 45 (Spring 1991), pp. 221–56; G. K. Helleiner, "The IMF, the World Bank, and Africa's Adjustment and External Debt Problems: An Unofficial View," *World Development,* vol. 20 (1992), pp. 779–92;

and Carl Jayarajah and William Branson, *Structural and Sectoral Adjustment: The World Bank Experience, 1980–92* (Washington: World Bank, 1995).

21. Paul Krugman, "Dutch Tulips and Emerging Markets," *Foreign Affairs*, vol. 74, no. 4 (July/August 1995), p. 30. One of the first economists to begin to spell out the implications of this understanding was Dani Rodrik; see his "Liberalization, Sustainability, and the Design of Structural Adjustment Programs," *Discussion Paper Series 177D* (Harvard University, John F. Kennedy School of Government, March 1989).

22. Faiza Rady, "Arrested Development," *al-Ahram Weekly* (November 3–9, 1994), p. 5.

23. Thomas J. Biersteker, "Reducing the Role of the State in the Economy: A Conceptual Exploration of IMF and World Bank Prescriptions," *International Studies Quarterly*, vol. 34 (1990), pp. 477–92.

24. "Biting the Hand That Squeezed Them," *Economist*, October 21–27, 1995, p. 48; and "Affray: The IMF in Africa," *Economist*, vol. 337, no. 7938 (October 28–November 3, 1995), p. 46.

25. For a long time, such "income policies" were the hallmark of so-called heterodox adjustment programs; see Miles Kahler, "Othodoxy and Its Alternatives: Explaining Approaches to Stabilization and Adjustment," in Joan M. Nelson, ed., *Economic Crisis and Policy Choice: The Politics of Adjustment in the Third World* (Princeton University Press, 1990), pp. 33–62. See also Giovanni Andrea Cornia, Richard Jolly, and Frances Stewart, *Adjustment with a Human Face* (New York: Oxford University Press, 1988).

26. The most outspoken proponent of this idea has been Jeffrey Sachs, who argues that the adjustment efforts in Russia have been grotesquely underfunded. See Jeffrey Sachs, "From Rubles to Reform: Western Dollars Can Keep the Soviets on the Road to Democracy," *Washington Post*, May 12, 1991, p. C3; Jeffrey Sachs, "Helping Russia: Goodwill Is Not Enough," *Economist*, December 21, 1991–January 3, 1992, pp. 101–104; and Jeffrey Sachs, "Betrayal: How Clinton Failed Russia," *New Republic*, January 31, 1994, pp. 14–18.

27. For a critique of shock therapy, see Peter Murrell, "What Is Shock Therapy? What Did It Do in Poland and Russia?" *Post–Soviet Affairs*, vol. 9 (1993), pp. 111–40. The importance of sequencing was first made forcefully in Ronald I. McKinnon, "The Order of Economic Liberalization: Lessons from Chile and Argentina," *Carnegie Rochester Conference Series on Public Policy*, vol. 17 (1982), pp. 159–86. See also Sebastian Edwards, *The Order of Liberalization of the External Sector in Developing Countries*, Essays in International Finance, no. 156 (Princeton University, Department of Economics, December 1984); and Alison Harwood and Bruce L. R. Smiths, eds., *Sequencing?: Financial Strategies for Developing Countries* (Brookings, 1997).

28. George Graham, "Dogma on Multilateral Debt Questioned," *Financial Times*, April 26, 1995, p. 4; Michael Holman, "Poor Countries 'Need Fresh Debt Initiatives,'" *Financial Times*, October 9, 1995, p. 4; and Michael Holman and Patti Waldmeir, "Poor Nations' Debt Burden Lies Heavily on World Bank Minds: A Dilemma for Lenders," *Financial Times*, March 14, 1996, p. 6. The International Monetary Fund (IMF) opposed and helped to undermine this initiative;

see Robert Chote, "Reluctance by Creditors Endangers Debt Relief: IMF–World Bank Effort for Poorest Nations Hits Trouble," *Financial Times,* April 10, 1996, p. 3.

29. Albert Hirschman seems to be one of the few policy intellectuals to have appreciated this.

30. See Paul Krugman, "Cycles of Conventional Wisdom on Economic Development," *International Affairs,* vol. 71 (October 1995), pp. 717–32; and Peter Evans and John D. Stephens, "Studying Development since the Sixties," *Theory and Society,* vol. 17 (1988), pp. 713–45.

31. The study of this subject began with Charles Tilly, ed., *The Formation of National States in Western Europe* (Princeton University Press, 1975). For a volume that cites the developments in the field since then, see Charles Tilly, *Coercion, Capital, and European States,* (Cambridge, Mass.: Blackwell, 1990).

32. John Burdon Sanderson Haldane, *On Being the Right Size and Other Essays* (Oxford, England: Oxford University Press, 1985).

33. Abbott Gleason, *Totalitarianism: The Inner History of the Cold War,* (Oxford: Oxford University Press, 1995).

34. A large literature critiques these flaws in Washington's cold war policies toward the developing countries. For good overviews, see Melvin Gurtov, *The United States against the Third World: Antinationalism and Intervention* (Praeger, 1974); and Jonathan Kwitny, *Endless Enemies: The Making of an Unfriendly World* (Viking Press, 1986). These problems were raised early in William J. Lederer and Eugene Burdick, *The Ugly American* (New York: Norton, 1958). The problem itself antedates the cold war. See Lloyd C. Gardner, *Safe for Democracy: The Anglo-American Response to Revolution, 1913–1923* (Oxford, England: Oxford University Press, 1987).

35. When Americans were asked "Do you happen to know the name of the ethnic group that has conquered much of Bosnia and surrounded Sarajevo," 60 percent responded with "don't know" or a wrong answer. See Anne Cronin, "America's Grade on Twentieth Century European Wars: F," *New York Times,* December 3, 1995, p. D5.

36. Signe, *Philadelphia Daily News,* 1994.

37. Other efforts have been made in this direction. In "The North-South Balance of Power," *International Affairs,* vol. 66 (October 1990), pp. 731–48, John Ravenhill proposed that the countries previously lumped together as the third world should be disaggregated into five groups:

1. High-income oil exporters (most OPEC members, excluding Nigeria and Indonesia);

2. Industrializing economies with strong states and low debt levels (primarily the East Asian Tigers);

3. Industrializing economies with weak states or debt problems (much of Latin America and Central Europe);

4. Potential newly industrializing countries (Malaysia, Thailand, and so on); and

5. Primary commodity producers (most of sub–Saharan Africa, Central America, and South Asia).

While this was a noble effort, it raised several problems. Since the slump in oil prices began 1985, many OPEC members turned out to be just another type of primary commodity producer. Many of the "potential newly industrializing countries" are growing so fast they have become barely distinguishable from the East Asian Tigers. This leaves three categories intact, which is more or less the same conclusion reached infra.

38. Ronald Reagan's "misery index," touted during his 1980 presidential campaign against Jimmy Carter, combined the percentage figures for the rate of inflation and the rate of unemployment. See Samuel Brittan, "Of Happiness and GDP," *Financial Times*, August 29, 1996, p. 16.

39. Zbigniew Brzezinski, *Out of Control: Global Turmoil on the Eve of the Twenty-First Century* (Charles Scribner's Sons, 1993), pp. 163–64. Part of me suspects Brzezinski coined this term in humorous self-parody.

40. Jeffrey E. Garten, *The Big Ten: The Big Emerging Markets* (Basic Books, 1997).

41. Robert D. Kaplan, "The Clairvoyance of Rebecca West," *National Interest* (Winter 1991–92), p. 70.

Chapter Twelve

1. Robert D. Kaplan, *Balkan Ghosts* (St. Martin's Press, 1993), p. 253.

2. Nikos Kazantzakis, *Zorba the Greek*, Carl Wildman, trans. (Simon and Schuster, 1981), pp. 225–26.

3. Donald Goleman, *Emotional Intelligence* (Bantam Books, 1995).

Index